Change Is Inevitable,
Happiness and Success Are Your Choice

Taming the Dragons of Change

10 Tips for Achieving Happiness and Success When Everything Around You Is Changing

by

Dick Stieglitz, Ph.D.

PublishAmerica
Baltimore

© 2006 by Dick Stieglitz, Ph.D.
All rights reserved. No part of this book may be reproduced, stored in a retrieval system or transmitted in any form or by any means without the prior written permission of the publishers, except by a reviewer who may quote brief passages in a review to be printed in a newspaper, magazine or journal.

First printing

ISBN: 1-4241-2222-8
PUBLISHED BY PUBLISHAMERICA, LLLP
www.publishamerica.com
Baltimore

Printed in the United States of America

To my wife Mary Ellen
and my daughters April and Tracy.
Thank you for standing by me
long enough to see me change
and enjoy it!

Taming the Dragons of Change

Table of Contents

Foreword..........7

Recognizing Your Dragons..........9

Part I Thoughts - *New Ways To See Change*..........15
Tip #1 Be Happy Today - *Don't Wait Until Tomorrow*..........27
Tip #2 Live in Abundance - *There's Plenty For Everyone*..........50
Tip #3 Stretch for Tomorrow - *Reach Beyond Your Grasp.*..........71

Part II Relationships - *Why Do It Alone?*..........95
Tip #4 Give Love Freely - *Love Spoils If We Keep It*..........110
Tip #5 Be Open and Honest - *Throw Away the Secrets*..........131
Tip #6 Just Say YES - *It's More Fun For Everyone*..........154

Part III Actions - *Path to Happiness and Success*..........177
Tip #7 Exercise Personal Responsibility - *Design Tomorrow*..........192
Tip #8 Make Clear Choices - *Pick From the Smorgasbord*..........214
Tip #9 Dare to Dream - *Imagine Your Future*..........240
Tip #10 Share Your Dreams- *Engage the Power of the Universe*..264

More Dragons Ahead..........289

Foreword

We all remember how the world changed on September 11, 2001. But it also changed on September 10th and September 12th of the same year. It changed again today. And it will change again tomorrow, next week and next year. Change is inevitable. However, it is our reactions to change that determine our happiness and success, not the changes themselves. When we consciously or subconsciously resist change, emotional habits emerge that become dragons in our lives. Like the mythical dragons in the Harry Potter novels, our emotional dragons are not real either. But they feel so real that we may become frustrated, afraid, overwhelmed, or angry at change. Even though the dragons are in our imagination, they can rob us of our happiness and success.

We face a barrage of changes every day. In addition to natural changes related to birth, growth, decline and death, the world around us is changing rapidly. Our jobs are changing. Our families and friends are changing. Change itself is changing faster than ever before. Even those of us who are feeling successful and happy today wonder what will happen tomorrow. It is unrealistic to expect that change will end. It is much more likely to accelerate. Since change is never-ending, we cannot slay the emotional dragons of change. At best we can be aware of them, embrace them, and tame them.

Accepting that *life is change* is the first step in taming the dragons. That small shift in thinking alters our habitual reaction to the unplanned events in our lives. Modifying our reactions alters the way we treat others as they experience change and react to our changes. Effective relationships with family, friends and co-workers increase our success and happiness by expanding the choices we can make and the actions we can take. This book offers ten tips that will increase your awareness of change, and help you tame your personal dragons. The tips are new ways to think about change, to improve relationships, and to take action each day as we face another set of changes.

This book was written by developing an outline and writing each section in order. Order is often an obsession with me. However, there is no reason why you must read the book from beginning to end. Have fun with it. Read first the changes you think may be controversial or interesting. Skip the boring ones and ones you already know. Read some today and others next year. Read one and discuss it with other people. Or read them all before you go to sleep tonight. Your choice.

But please do not believe anything in this book without testing it first. The vignettes are merely nostalgic recollections of my past life and current beliefs. All I did was retrieve them from my mental attic, dust them off, probably embellished them a little, and recited them for you to enjoy. I would be doing you a disservice if I either pushed my ideas on you, or hid them so you would be forced to discover them all by yourself. I cannot guarantee that this book has any answers that will work for you. Your best answers are inside you. This book will be worthwhile if it serves as a mirror that helps you find those answers, the ones that will work best in your unique life.

There are no "right" answers, certainly none that work for everyone every time. Truth is like clothes. Advertisements claiming one-size-fits-all cannot be true because some people are midgets less than four feet tall, and others are basketball players over seven feet. Similarly, any so-called "truth" probably will not fit in everyone's life.

The twenty-first century offers bountiful opportunities for those who are willing to consider new possibilities. This is a *what-if* book about possibilities, not a *how-to* book. Far from being overwhelmed or disappointed because there is no cookbook answers for life, I am intrigued and excited by the freedom to try any philosophy I want. I might think thoughts no man or woman in history has ever thought before. Some of those thoughts might be in this book. These vignettes are practical ideas intended to balance our lives and awaken our collective consciousness. My hope is the vignettes in this book will encourage you to examine your perspectives, replacing the ones that are not working for you and amplifying the ones that are.

Recognizing Your Dragons...

"I know that birds fly, fishes swim and animals run. What runs can be trapped, what swims can be caught in nets, and what flies can be shot with arrows. But what to do with my dragons I know not, for they rise on clouds and soar into the wind."
— Confucius

Imagine a three-year-old boy being driven to an orphanage on a rainy spring night. The silence is deafening as his eight-year-old brother sits quietly beside him and his father drives the car. The boy misses his mom and wonders what it means when they say: "She died and is gone forever." Died? Forever? What do those words mean? As the car arrives at the orphanage, nuns help the boys from the car. They take his brother away and his dad drives off without a word. Walking to the nursery, the nuns laugh at the youngster when he wets his pants. They strip his clothes, wash him in a big metal sink, and send him to bed in a long dark room. He feels abandoned by his mother, his father and his brother, and vows never to depend on anyone. The fear of rejection, a debilitating emotional *dragon*, creeps into his beliefs.

Fast-forward twenty-five years to a young Navy lieutenant in the engine room of a nuclear submarine. He is in charge of sailors and civilians who repair the ship. Machinery is torn apart everywhere, and the smell of oil permeates the air. But he knows how it will all fit together. The lieutenant snaps to attention as the admiral and captain enter the engine room. After an inspection tour and brief conversations with the workers, the admiral says: "You've got things under control. Keep it that way." Smiling from ear to ear, the lieutenant responds: "Yes sir!" The compulsion for perfection and control, another *dragon*, clouds his perspectives. He believes that change can be conquered through hard work, and he vows to always control every detail.

Later that day, the lieutenant arrives home and is greeted by his pretty wife and daughters. His wife is cooking dinner. He tells her to cut the bread with the knife pointing away from her body. He says it is for safety, but she resents being controlled. They discuss the budget, but he makes all the decisions. The girls, in the first and second grades, are proud of their near straight-A report cards, but he tells them they can do better. After dinner, he invents homework to help them stay ahead of the other kids. Average is unacceptable. They are quiet. Their poise shaken. Deaf to their pleas for autonomy, the *dragon* of blind self-confidence entices him into thinking that with enough control and discipline he can mold his daughters into what he wants them to be.

Turn the clock ahead eleven years, the lieutenant has left the Navy, climbed the business ladder, and started his own consulting company. He hires only top-notch employees, but tells them what to do and how to do it. Even though clients compliment their ability to "solve the really hard problems," the company grows slowly. He wonders why as he works twelve-hour days and weekends. The *dragon* of pride prevents him from seeing that there might be a better way. Meanwhile his lonely wife becomes a successful businesswoman in her own right, and his daughters go off to college. On the outside, the family appears to have everything. Inside, however, things are not as they seem.

Two years later, the phone rings and the Chicago police report that they arrested his youngest daughter for grand theft auto. She stole her mother's car. He and his wife, recently reunited after a year's separation, fly to Chicago. As he waits in the courtroom for his daughter to be arraigned, a drug addict, a drunk-driving manslaughter case, and a street bum charged with assault appear before the judge. Later that afternoon he calls his oldest daughter to tell her the news. She yells: "It's all your fault, Dad." The *dragons* of anger and shame scream at him: *You gave them everything. This shouldn't be happening!* The change hurts.

Leap ahead through much *dragon*-taming to a Caribbean cruise. Thirtieth wedding anniversary vows are exchanged in the ship's lounge. Family and friends witness the ceremony. The groom's handsome three-year old grandson tugs at his bow tie, this being the first time he has worn a dress suit. The groom's adult daughters are beautiful in their cocktail dresses. Everyone blows bubbles as his stunning wife walks down the aisle. Tears of joy trickle down his cheeks as the master of ceremonies says that thirty years of marriage teach the full meaning of "for better and for worse." The groom thinks to himself: "I am blessed to be enjoying this celebration of love." Dragons can be tamed after all!

Each of us has seen many changes and encountered many dragons in our lives. I just shared several of mine in the hope that seeing my dragons will help you recognize your unique set of personal dragons. The vignettes are not just celebrations of joyous moments or memoirs of past mistakes. Rather, they illustrate the major changes that shape our lives and our emotional response to those changes. Even amid fabulous new technologies, bountiful conveniences, and unparalleled abundance, it is easy to feel scorched by the frustration, confusion and stress of change. But change is not the dragon. The real dragon is the intense kaleidoscope of emotions that bubble up inside us in response to change.

When we react to changes with a fixed set of responses, our responses can become fire-breathing dragons.

Among the most ferocious dragons are: (1) lingering anger about yesterday's changes, (2) stubborn resistance to today's new changes, or (3) a crippling fear of the changes that might happen tomorrow. One strategy is to slay the dragons by trying to prevent change. Another is to seek safety by hiding from change. Neither of those strategies works. I know because I have tried them both. The emotional dragons that surround change are immortal. Even as we tame one dragon, two or three others take its place. We cannot hide from omnipresent emotional dragons in our homes, at work, and in our relationships. Even when we are alone, the dragons are with us. For most of my life, I fought the dragons with valiant determination and courage. I thought that I did not need change. But even when I felt I was winning the battle, I did not have the happiness and peace I expected. And fighting the dragons was exhausting work. Fortunately, a third strategy emerged in my thinking: *tame the dragons* by transforming them into helpful companions on the journey toward lasting happiness and new successes.

Today's tempo of social, political and technological change is as ominous as any fire-breathing dragon. You change, I change, and our families change every day. Our jobs, schools and churches change. Our friends and recreation change. Technology changes faster than we can learn to use it. As we begin the twenty-first century, rapid change releases a horde of emotional dragons that attack our need for consistency and stability. The natural tendency is to resist change. To hope it will go away so the old "normal" can return. But change is not going away. The world continues to change no matter what we do. Taming the dragons means discovering that the only changes we can control are the changes inside ourselves. Taming the dragons is not a quick fix that will be finished tonight, tomorrow, or next year. Rather, it is a new way of living each day.

==========================

Taming the dragons of change is not a quick fix. Rather it is a new way of living each day.

==========================

As we walk along our individual paths of change, each new step challenges our cherished beliefs about how things should be. Those beliefs have been around a long time. It is shocking when prized beliefs do not work anymore. Maybe they never worked, and we refused to see it. Maybe we searched for new answers to our questions, when we should have questioned the answers we already had. Answers that were right five or ten years ago may not work today. Questioning our answers stimulates creativity, while thinking that we have the final answer stifles growth. Rigid thoughts, static relationships, and habitual responses cannot work forever in a changing world. What we believe about ourselves, our family, our careers and our world determines: (1) what we see as possible, (2) what we see as impossible, and (3) what we do not see at all. When we become aware of how old beliefs control us, new possibilities that were unimaginable suddenly become real. Ultimately, our beliefs determine the happiness and peace we have in our lives, and the success and fulfillment we experience in our careers.

=======================

When we ignore indications of change, our past successes can become the barriers to greater success in the future.

=======================

By material measures, my life was good before I became aware that *life is change* and began to tame my dragons. I succeeded at almost everything I did. Small omens of change entered my life, but I ignored them until they screamed loudly that what I was doing was not working. Similar omens such as divorce, sickness, estranged relationships with children, getting fired, bankruptcy or getting arrested may be appearing today in your life. As founder of a small company, I enjoyed the ego satisfaction and financial rewards of a thriving career. I thought the few times that I did not succeed were because someone else did not do what they should. But I was forceful and intimidating in dealing with such situations. It seemed to work. Whenever I was more aggressive and stronger than everyone else, I got what I wanted. But the price was very high. My wife was not happy with me, but that was because she could not see things my way. My daughters were not what I wanted them to be, but that was because they did not listen to me. My company did not grow as fast as it should, but that was because the employees did not do what I told them to do. After decades of fighting dragons and an epiphany in a Chicago courtroom, *I changed.* I found that changing *me*, rather than everyone else around me, was an easier and much more effective way to tame my dragons. The ten simple tips described in this book were the keys that unlocked the door to greater happiness and success for me. The challenge is practicing them each day in our thoughts, relationships and actions.

==============================

It is not the strongest or the most intelligent that survive, rather those who respond effectively to change.
- Charles Darwin

==============================

Our *T*houghts, *R*elationships and *A*ctions (*TRA*) can be a *TRA*jectory toward increasing success and happiness, or make *TRA*sh of our lives. Since the dragons are born in our thoughts, the first three tips explore how we think about change. Dragons also show themselves in how we treat the people involved in our changes. So the next three tips address our relationships. Eventually, how we think and treat people produces action. Therefore, the book closes with four tips about the criteria we use to make choices and the actions we choose in a changing world. Thoughts, relationships and actions inherently are neither good nor bad. The salient question is: *Do they produce what we want in our lives?* Unfortunately, the courtroom demonstrated clearly that my thoughts, relationships and actions were not working very well. After several years of dragon taming, the cruise confirmed that my personal transformation had started to deliver more of what I wanted in my life. The good news is that all of us have the ability to change our thoughts, relationships and actions at any time. Even today.

Every so often in my fifty-plus years on this earth, an event occurred that instantly increased my awareness. I responded by saying: "*Ah-Ha*, I understand!" Most of the events I experienced myself, but some of my *Ah-Ha*'s came from watching the experiences of others. In this book I share my biggest *Ah-Ha*'s in the form of ten tips. Some of them you may reject, and others you will doubt. But challenging your cherished beliefs may be a magic key that unlocks the door to the happiness and success you have been seeking. Just one new belief, one small tip, might produce a huge improvement in the quality of your life.

========================

Any man who views the world the same at 50 as he did at 20, probably has wasted 30 years
- Mohammad Ali

========================

Enjoy reading the tips in this book. Consider each one carefully, neither unquestioningly accepting nor thoughtlessly rejecting it. A tip may be valuable even if you do not agree with it. The further it is from your current beliefs, the more useful it could be. Use the tips any way you like. Ignore those that appear as if they will not work for you. Blended with the panoramic view of your own experience, however, the tips may create possibilities for change that you did not imagine before today. One caveat. Even if all ten of the tips in this book were perfect on the day they were written, the world has changed since then and they may not be perfect when you read them. More valuable than the tips themselves is the ability you will acquire to adapt to the inevitable onslaught of changes by continuously discovering new tips for joyous and successful living on your own.

===============================

Don't replace your beliefs with the tips in this book. To do so would be to swap one imperfect set of dogma for another.

===============================

Part I

Thoughts
New Ways to See Change

"The dogmas of the quiet past are inadequate in the stormy present. The occasion is piled high with difficulty. As our case is new, we must think anew."
— Abraham Lincoln

Fish Food

The easiest way to change someone or something is to change the way you see them. The new perspective always creates new possibilities.

During a vacation in St. Thomas, my wife paid $2.95 for a four-ounce plastic bag of fish food for a snorkeling trip. She looked into the bag and exclaimed: "This is dog food like I have at home!" The man behind the water sports counter smiled and said: "The fish don't know that. It's only dog food when you feed it to dogs. It's fish food when fish eat it." Similarly, the way you and I think about change is shaped by our beliefs and past experiences. Wherever they came from, our thoughts rather than reality are the filter through which we see the changes in our lives, our families and our careers. That filter provokes the dragons of change, or tames them.

If the world did not change, we would not need to change. But it is rapidly changing. Taming our dragons begins by changing the way we think about people and events. We each were born a perfect diamond, a clear crystal with no judgements, expectations, habits or fears. What led us to think we excel at some things, and are weak at others? When did we become reluctant to share feelings, even with family? Why are we afraid to fail, so afraid that sometimes we do not even try? Who taught us to judge people and events as *good* or *bad*?

Such thoughts are just beliefs about how the world is. Some work well and others cause problems. Such problems cannot be solved with the same beliefs, the same thinking, that created them in the first place. Changing our thoughts and beliefs does not change the world. Rather it changes our perception of the world, which amounts to essentially the same thing. Hopefully, the following vignettes will help you become aware of and tame the dragons of fixed patterns of thinking.

Rent-a-Life

Anything can happen in life, and often does. But it is how we react to what happens that determines our happiness.

I often rent a car during personal and business travel. The car almost always works perfectly for the full rental period. Sometimes though, I am annoyed by minor things like a trunk that sticks, or electric windows that do not open and close. On one business trip the rental car just quit running. The engine would not start and the car had to be towed back to the airport. The rental agency apologized profusely and gave me an upgraded car for the remainder of the week. But they could not replace the hours I lost, or eliminate the aggravation that I felt for the inconvenience.

Similarly when I "rented" my life almost sixty years ago, the rental agreement contained no guarantee as to what would happen during the rental period. You cannot know what will happen during the term of your agreement either. So far, I have traveled through adolescence, education, parenthood, and three careers. In the future, I see mentoring young professionals, being a grandfather, retirement, and the exciting experience of death where the mysteries of life (*Is there a heaven and a hell? And who is God?*) will become clear for me. My family has known health and sickness. I have experienced thrilling triumphs and heart-breaking defeats, exquisite joy and intense sadness, peace and conflict, and financial mountaintops and valleys. You probably have encountered a similar range of up-and-down events during your rent-a-life agreement too, even though your peaks may have been higher or your valleys lower than mine.

We usually think of health, joy, peace, triumphs and financial peaks as *good*; and sickness, sadness, conflict, defeats and financial valleys as *bad.* But we can tame the dragons that judge events as *good* or *bad* by accepting that such events are a normal part of our rental agreements. Our valleys make peaks look higher. Conflict makes peace seem more comfortable. And pain helps us to appreciate good health when we have it. My valley in a Chicago courtroom was a first step toward the mountaintop I enjoy today. There probably is a valley (or valleys) ahead that I do not see, and I certainly do not want. *WOW*, what an exciting journey! While we have our rental agreements, we have a choice to:

- Stick with one way of thinking no matter what, or
- Try new ways of thinking to find ones that work better.

Some new ideas will work, and others will fail miserably. But we can be grateful even for the lessons provided by events we call "failures." We may be happy today with the *way of thinking* we have, and the results that those thoughts have produced. But they cannot remain perfect as our lives change and the world around us changes. We can either voluntarily tame the dragons of change today with new ways of thinking, or wait until tomorrow when unavoidable changes will force us to think differently.

Eventually, every rental agreement ends. Statistically speaking, it will last about seventy-eight years for me and eighty-one years for my wife. We are taking excellent care of ourselves in the hope that it will last longer and the last few decades will be enjoyable. But no one knows exactly when this fantastic rental agreement called life will end. For some, it will be today. Perhaps that possibility is a message telling us to give and receive the most joy and happiness we possibly can during every day of the agreement.

Grandma's Pot Roast

Old assumptions may be invalid in today's new world. Maybe we should consider changing them.

Among my grandmother's wonderful recipes, pot roast was my favorite. One afternoon while I watched her slice carrots and potatoes for a pot roast dinner, she told me the story of a mother who taught her daughter to cook. The menu was pot roast with all the trimmings. The mother bought a roast at the meat market that weighed six pounds and was fourteen inches long. She cut an inch-thick piece from each end, and put them in the pan beside the roast. The little girl asked: "Mommy, why did you cut off the ends?" Her mother answered: "Because that's how Grandma taught me to cook pot roast. I think it makes better gravy, but go ask her." So the girl ran to ask Grandma why. Grandma answered: "Because that's how my mother did it. Ask her why." Fortunately, the little girl was lucky enough to have a living great-grandmother, so she went to the sun porch where Great-grandma was rocking to ask her why. Great-grandma answered: "Because I had a twelve-inch pan and the pot roast wouldn't fit unless I trimmed the ends." For a long time, I thought my grandmother had told me a story from her childhood. Since then, I have heard the pot roast story in several different forums, always to illustrate the trap of habitual thought patterns.

My grandmother counseled me that cutting the ends off a pot roast was harmless. But she cautioned me not to mimic the things I saw her do without asking: *Why should I do that?* As the world changes, the basic questions of life remain the same. But the answers change. Our tendency is to teach our children the same answers that worked for us twenty years ago. The beliefs our children learn from us have a lasting and powerful influence in their lives.

Prejudices, fears, angers and behaviors can be perpetuated from generation to generation in a way that makes emotional dragons seem like family heirlooms. Just because a family has done something a certain way for generations does not mean it must continue to be done that way forever. At a minimum, we can re-validate axioms of the past in the shining light of an ever-changing world.

Playing in the Rain

Recognizing small events in the past that influence our attitudes helps us to understand how and why we treat others like we do.

I have always loved baseball. I have been a New York Yankees fan since Whitey Ford and Mickey Mantle were rookies in 1951. One summer day when I was ten, the neighborhood kids and I were playing baseball as it began to rain. We finished the game ignoring the warm raindrops. My clothes were soaked from head to toe when I got home. I remember vividly the sight of my adopted mother standing on the upstairs landing of our house as I bounced up the stairs smiling. I was blown away when she screamed at me: "*You're so stupid you don't even know enough to come in from the rain.*" My smile disappeared, and I was puzzled: *I don't feel stupid. Was it stupid to play in the rain?* I did not know. But I did know that being called stupid felt very bad. In that instant, with echoes of my mother's scream ringing in my ears, I vowed that no one would ever call me stupid again. A deep obsession with intellectual achievement was born in my beliefs that day.

That obsession has been a dragon that shapes how I react to change. It motivated me to get a PhD in nuclear engineering, an irrefutable symbol that I was not stupid. On the negative side, the dragon triggers a defensive response whenever someone disagrees with me, and it leads me to judge people by their intellectual achievements. As I look back on that rainy day, I am part angry about being called stupid and part thankful for the motivation those words provided.

I never discussed the incident with my mom, and I thought I had forgotten the anger I felt for being called stupid. But decades later, well after she had died, I confronted my dragon and realized how that brief incident influences how I react to people who oppose my views. You also may have seemingly small childhood experiences that have had an extraordinarily large influence on the way you think and the choices you make. Are you aware of them? Have you kept the ones that help you grow and prosper, and discarded those that limit your success and happiness?

The Yellow Hippo

Becoming aware of our sensitivities prevents them from awakening fierce dragons that cause anger and pain.

If I called you a yellow hippopotamus, you probably would laugh because you do not think of yourself anything like a yellow hippo. But if you were a lot overweight, the yellow hippo remark might strike a sensitive nerve. Why? Because in your beliefs, the remark triggers a voice that says: "*He thinks I'm fat.*" The remark hatches the dragons of self-consciousness and self-doubt. It is not truth, just a meaningless remark. It is possible that you are underweight, even while your beliefs tell you that you are overweight.

As Elisa Doolittle demonstrated in *My Fair Lady*, thoughts lead us to be what we are expected to be. The messages we collect from the world around us trigger such interpretations. In our minds, we compare what is happening to beliefs about our weaknesses. We are naturally sensitive about our weaknesses, and try to hide them. When people talk about something close to one of our perceived weaknesses, we react defensively. Our perceived weaknesses may not be real, but that does not make them any less frightening.

For me, two frightening areas are dancing and singing. I avoid dancing because I believe I have no rhythm. I am afraid people will laugh at me. I also believe I cannot sing. In church, I sing as softly as possible because I do not want people to laugh at me. Sometimes I lip-synch the words to look like I am singing, but no song comes out. I pretend to sing because if I did not, I would be judged badly for not participating. My yellow-hippo fears are very intense even though, in all my memory, I have never been laughed at for dancing or singing.

Yellow-hippo fears keep us in a small box because they stop us from trying new things and seeing new possibilities. By the way, as I write this vignette, I am taking two-step, waltz and west coast swing lessons with my wife. So, if you ever see a yellow hippo waddling around the dance floor at the local country-western bar, it could be me dancing with the dragons of self-consciousness and self-doubt! Please laugh with me.

Zero Gravity

The way we see or do not see a problem is the real problem.

When the American space program first sent astronauts into space, they learned that ballpoint pens do not write in the absence of gravity. Since astronauts need a reliable writing device to record mission notes, we began a high-priority research program to develop an instrument that would write upside down in zero gravity on any surface, even if the temperature was below freezing or above 100 degrees Fahrenheit. Three years and about ten million dollars later, they perfected such a writing instrument. The Russian astronauts use pencils in their space program.

The brain has difficulty separating what *is real* from what it *thinks is real* based on past experience. The patterns of our past experience become dragons that block our ability to adapt to new situations and recognize new possibilities. The scientists were so accustomed to solving spaceflight problems through exotic, expensive research programs that they naturally started another one to develop a space pen, rather than to first consider the possibility of a simple solution.

We assume that *the way we see things* is how they really are, and make choices and take action based on that assumption. Since our perceptions and experience often do not accurately reflect reality, the choices we make are based on what we think is true rather than what is really true. When we think we see a problem, that thought creates a problem. If we do not see a problem, we assume none exists. And that can be a problem too Once we see a problem (or fail to see a problem), we gather facts to support our belief and ignore facts that point to other possibilities.

The danger is our beliefs become magnets that attract supporting evidence. Our beliefs begin to have a life of their own, and we see only what we expect to see. Even though they may be causing significant problems, old beliefs and habits may control our perceptions and our actions. Taming the dragons of past experience is a challenging process that requires us to ask: *What new way can I see this situation that I have never before seriously considered?* Meeting that challenge is a prerequisite to achieving happiness and success in a changing world.

Five Dollars

We can change our thought patterns when we want new results, or when we are forced to change them. Either way, change cannot be avoided forever.

To learn how thoughts influence actions, a counselor suggested that I try to give a five-dollar bill to several strangers. Accepting the dare, I approached four strangers at random on the street, held out a five-dollar bill in my hand, and said: "Here, I'd like you to have this." The first gentleman glared at me as if he did not trust me, and walked away. Another man looked at me with disgust and said: "I don't need that." A woman was insulted and threatened to call the police. The fourth was a beggar who grabbed the money and ran. It probably was the best thing that had happened to him that day.

The strangers' reactions had nothing to do with me or the five-dollar bill. Instead their reactions were a reflection of how they thought about themselves in relation to five dollars. And such thoughts can change in an instant. For example, I started smoking a pipe when I was eighteen years old and smoked for thirty years. I thought of the pipe as relaxing and sophisticated. I tried unsuccessfully to quit many times. One day at a business meeting, I looked down and saw holes in my necktie and shirt from pipe ashes. In that instant, my thoughts about pipe smoking changed. I thought of it as a messy habit and have not smoked since.

Changing our lives is a painful and difficult process when we focus on changing *what we do,* rather than *how we think*. Fundamental changes in our thought patterns usually occur only if we begin a new role like spouse, parent or manager; or face a life-threatening crisis. A new role or crisis compels us to look at new possibilities and to set new priorities. A heart attack may cause an instant change in unhealthy exercise and eating habits that had persisted through decades of good health. A painful divorce may force changes in relationship attitudes that were ineffective for years.

What stops us from changing how we think *before* the dragons of our old habits breath their fire? It is within our ability to change our thought patterns before tragedy strikes. We could even do it today.

Masters of the Game

To master the game of life, we must design our future in our daily thoughts.

Some people visualize the possibility of grand success, while others seem to focus only on the possibility of failure and pain. Maybe that is the difference between:

• ***Masters of the Game*** who lead wonderful lives they change at will. Who gracefully transform ugly defeat into sweet victory. Who seem to have an advantage in everything they do.

• ***Victims of the Game*** who are trapped in situations they do not ask for and do not want. Whose lives seem hopelessly mired in poverty, disappointment, sickness and weak relationships.

Could it be that victims think they are helpless, while masters help themselves despite setbacks and adverse circumstances?

For me, Christopher Reeves was a Master of the Game. He was more inspiring to me as a quadriplegic than as Superman! Numerous people rise to extraordinary success despite debilitating handicaps, unhealthy childhoods, traumatic events, and multiple failures. It should be easy for those of us who enjoy complete freedom, good health, and above average intelligence to be Masters of the Game.

The game of life takes a long time to play, about eighty years on average. We all were born Masters, but sometimes during the game we forget to help ourselves when inevitable setbacks occur. Whether we use our power or throw it away, the significant events and directions in our lives are first created in our thoughts. Our lives can be the creation of our minds' ingenious design. Or they can be the reaction to someone else's actions, the battered result of unfortunate events, or a sad product of mindless habits or an unwillingness to change. Masters of the Game design their lives in their *thoughts*. Each of us has the power to create our thoughts and direct our future as a Master of the Game. We help ourselves and others when we use that power.

Three Essential Tips on Thoughts

Nothing is more dangerous to our future success and happiness than the thoughts we are unwilling to change.

How we think about people and things ultimately determines the joy and success in our lives. Thoughts determine the possibilities we see, options we consider, and choices we make. Victims get stuck in thoughts rooted in the past. Such thoughts grow from a sordid family history, traumatic events, past failures, and the like. By changing our thoughts, we can produce happiness today and leave the past behind.

Our minds have enormous capacity to store and process data. But too much capacity can be spent storing beliefs and memories that are irrelevant today. Create capacity for new ideas by picking beliefs from the past that work and throw away the rest. Consider the following tips for achieving success and happiness by changing the way you think:

• ***Be Happy Today.*** We actually think ourselves happy or sad, glad or mad, excited or depressed each day. Therefore, if we change our thoughts, we can experience happiness today, the only day that really exists. The vignettes in this chapter will show you how to tame the dragons no matter what happens around you, no matter what other people do.

• ***Live in Abundance.*** Do you see a kind and gentle world with giving, cooperative people? Or a heartless, competitive world where *they* will take everything you have? The vignettes in this chapter will reveal the secret of enjoying and sharing the bountiful treasures of our world.

• ***Stretch for Tomorrow.*** Thoughts about the future affect how we live today. Are you afraid of the future because of the past? Or do you believe today's challenges will help produce tomorrow's success? The vignettes in this chapter will show you that stretching today, and enjoying it, will bring happiness and success into your life and career.

These tips are essential in taming the dragons of unhappiness, scarcity, and fear. Hopefully, the tips will lead you to uplifting thoughts that are more effective today and tomorrow in achieving the results you want.

---Essential Tip #1---

BE HAPPY TODAY

~ Don't Wait Until Tomorrow

For myself I am an optimist. It does not seem to be much use being anything else.
—Sir Winston Churchill

Ruptured

Our minds have a picture of perfect. If we are unhappy when people orevents don't match the picture, it may be easier to change the picture.

Workers installing new phone lines in our neighborhood ruptured a thirty-inch water main that served 300 homes. It was a mess. No water, a muddy road, loud jackhammers at night, and cars parked a mile away because the entrance to the neighborhood was closed. The neighbors who gathered around the gushing hole in the road had varied reactions. Some saw the event as humorous, and joked with the workers and each other. Others were fascinated by the equipment used to locate and replace the broken pipe. A few whined about having no water at home. And a group of angry people considered suing the phone company. We all suffered exactly the same inconvenience and disruption. How could we have such a wide spectrum of reactions? The answer is that we each had a choice to be jovial, curious, complaining or angry about the broken pipe, and we made different choices. None of our reactions helped fix the water main, but the reaction we chose determined our happiness for the forty-eight hours it took to complete the repairs.

Is it possible to be happy about every change? If we were happy all the time, could we understand happiness? The concept of happiness requires that we simultaneously understand events and people that we associate with unhappiness. That understanding makes it easy to regain happiness if we are unhappy. Just embrace the dragons of regret, disappointment, worry, frustration, fear, anger, depression and other emotions that we label as "unhappy." Whenever we are unhappy about a change, enjoy the feeling, get whatever benefit there may be in the unhappiness, and switch to happy quickly. Get over it! The alternative is to feel bad about the change, and hope that feeling bad will produce happiness. Some people make that choice often, and are consistently unhappy as time after time they resist the dragons of desperation, disappointment and frustration. Fighting the dragons must help them feel better. If you do not enjoy being unhappy, choose to be happy today no matter what changes may seem to get in the way of your picture of happiness.

Since the words *happiness* and *success* are used frequently in this book, it is important for us to define those words and their opposites, *unhappiness* and *failure*. For purposes of our discussions:

> ***Success*** is achieving or obtaining what we want, while
> ***failure*** is wanting something and not achieving it.
>
> ***Happiness*** is wanting what we have, while
> ***unhappiness*** is wanting something other than what we have.

Under these definitions, it is possible to be successful and unhappy at the same time. Even though we achieve the things we want (*success*), they may not be what we thought they would be, or they may not be enough and we want more (*unhappiness*). On the other hand, if we are happy, by definition we also must be successful because we have what we want. The conclusion is that happiness always precedes success, which is diametrically opposite to the widely held belief that happiness will follow success. Therefore, this chapter focuses on being happy first and successful second. It offers tips on:

- Regaining happiness even when changes are not what we want
- Eliminating attitudes and beliefs that sabotage our happiness
- Being happy despite failure, or the fear of failure, and
- Achieving happiness by discarding judgements of good and bad.

With any luck, this tip will lead you to happiness. Success will surely follow. My wish is that you are happy as you begin to read the following vignettes. In any case, whether you are happy or unhappy, it is a self-inflicted condition.

Feelings Are Real

Feelings are not good, bad, right, wrong, real or imagined. They just are. Embrace them!

When my wife told me she was pregnant with our first daughter, my feelings were spontaneous and joyful. I took her into my arms, whirled her around, and said: *"I love you so much!"* A normal reaction. The problem was we were not married. Our wedding was six months away and, as a Navy midshipmen, I was not allowed to be married. Our families were embarrassed by the unwanted pregnancy. It was hard for us to be happy amid the blame, anger and disappointment. Because of the embarrassment, we celebrated a make-believe wedding anniversary date for twenty years. I look at that moment on the porch of my wife's house as among the happiest in my life. Our daughter is a gift from God. His plan was not to wait until the wedding to give us the gift.

My wife being pregnant before our wedding was not a change that I wanted. My reactions to the event easily could have become a dragon. I could have been angry about it then. I could still be angry today. I could blame myself, my wife, or something else for the pregnancy. But after being married over thirty-five years and seeing our daughter become a kind, beautiful and brilliant woman, wife and mother, I am happy today for what happened then. I also was happy on that day too for no other reason than I chose to be. Certainly, other choices were available.

Life is an erratic sequence of changes. Each day brings changes we like and others we do not like. But I define *like* and *don't like* for me, and you do for you. The changes themselves are neither good nor bad. What matters is our reaction to them. Happiness is wanting what we have, and accepting what is. From there we pick a new direction, and experience the next adventure in our lives. The option is to be angry, sad, hurt, or some other form of unhappy. If we are unhappy because someone or something put us where we are, we cannot be optimistic about the future because we do not control it. Hogwash! You can be happy reading this book. No matter how you feel about what happened today or last year, or how worried you may be about tomorrow, you can be happy right now.

This IS Normal!

Anything unexpected, different or new does not feel "normal." As we struggle to "get back to normal," we need to understand and accept that change is normal.

Sometimes there are so many concurrent changes that I feel like a salmon struggling to swim upstream with bears on one river bank trying to eat me, fishermen ready to hook me from the other bank, and hungry hawks flying overhead eager to snatch me from the water. Since many of my days are like that, I have come to accept that it is normal for me to be challenged by the dragons of:

- *Pressure* from having more to do than I can do in a day
- *Fatigue* when I have no time to rest and much is expected of me
- *Disappointment* when people do not meet their commitments
- *Anger* at being forced to do things that I do not want to do
- *Impatience* when things do not get done as fast as I would like
- *Defensiveness* if someone disagrees with my ideas
- *Competition* to get the best for my family and me

You may say *Me Too!* to some of these dragons, and *Not Me!* to others. You might add other of you personal dragons to the list.

At first glance, these seem like negative feelings that I should try to eliminate. An alternative is to be happy about them by accepting *what is* as normal, and understanding that my feelings are not "wrong" or "bad." They are just messages that tell me to: (1) look at change differently, (2) make new choices, or (3) ask for help. Asking for help is hard for me. But it is an effective antidote to feeling pressured, tired and disappointed. Feeling angry or impatient are clear messages that I should take a new approach because the current one is not working.

Shifts in thinking also help if I feel defensive (listen to feedback from those who care), competitive (win-win creates new possibilities), or sad for a loved one (a chance to show that I care). Everything that happens to you today is normal, including reading this book and experiencing the thoughts and feelings it causes. Enjoy them and tune into the messages that your feelings are sending to you.

Pain Is Unavoidable, Suffering Is a Choice

When the dragon of physical pain bites, our suffering (if any) will be determined by the difference between how we feel about the pain, and how we want to feel.

Sam Suffring and Paul Payne are salesmen for Happy Products. They finish work one Friday afternoon looking forward to their favorite weekend sports: fishing for Sam and golf for Paul. But life has some unplanned changes in store for them. For Sam, the change is a "honey-do" project in the backyard. Saturday morning just before leaving for his favorite fishing hole, Sam's wife asks him to lay a brick patio in the garden. He does not want to do it, and pleads to delay the project until a future weekend. But she is adamant and forces him to start the project. Sam is angry. This is not what he wanted for the weekend. The fishing trip is canceled. It is boiling hot as he starts the job. The work is miserable and he complains every step of the way. He drops a brick on the back of his hand and hears a bone snap. Sam goes to the hospital and the doctor says, *"Yep. It's broken,"* bandages the hand, and gives him two aspirin to ease the pain.

On the same Saturday morning, Paul is about to leave for the golf course when Pete, captain of the Happy Products softball team, calls and begs him to play with the team. Pete says, "Paul, if you don't play we'll forfeit the game." Paul responds, "But I'm a lousy player, and I have other plans. Please get somebody else." Finally, Paul agrees to play and reschedules his tee time. It is a boiling hot day and the score is tied. Paul is on third base with one out in the bottom of the seventh inning. Pete hits a fly ball to right field. Paul tags up at third, races down the line, and slides head first toward home plate. The catcher is waiting for the throw, and steps on Paul's hand just as it touches the plate. The umpire yells, "*Safe!*" and Happy Products wins the game. Paul is the hero, but his hand still hurts. He goes to the hospital and the doctor says, *"Yep. It's broken,"* bandages the hand, and gives him two aspirin to ease the pain.

Sam and Paul go to work Monday morning, each with a broken hand. Sam suffers as he relates the story of a miserable hot day laying bricks, and the pain of his broken hand. He tells the sad story over and over, but no one listens. Paul, on the other hand, is a hero. Sure his hand hurts, throbbing in pain at times, but people laugh and celebrate as he tells the story of how he scored the winning run for the Happy Products team. Paul's broken hand is the symbol of a hero. The pain is ignored as he proudly shows everyone his bandaged hand. Some people listen to Paul's story several times and cheer every time.

Neither man can avoid the pain of his broken hand. Sam could choose to show pictures and tell everyone about the work-of-art patio he built over the weekend. Instead, he chose to suffer in addition to the pain of a broken hand. Paul could have told everyone about the stupid catcher who stepped on his hand. Instead he chose to celebrate victory, and laugh about his broken hand. Pain is unavoidable, but the dragon of suffering is easily tamed.

Nature's Amusement Park

The struggle to achieve what we want may extract a price that is higher than the value of the prize. Changing what we want may be a whole lot easier.

Whether we embrace or ignore nature, it changes at its own pace without feeling hurt or hostile. In the backyard garden where I was struck with the inspiration to write this book, I struggled to keep the hillside immaculately groomed. The junipers were trimmed into pleasing shapes, all within proper boundaries. The climbing roses were espaliered neatly along the picket fence. The weeds were meticulously removed. And ivy was trimmed to grow exactly where it should grow. But nature did not care how I wanted the hillside to look. The ivy, junipers, roses, weeds and flowers kept growing in their own directions, and at their own speed. Each spring and summer weekend for almost twenty years, I labored to groom that hillside. I enjoyed the sunshine, but resented the hours spent on this *"have-to"* chore. There were many other things I would rather be doing.

Eventually, I decided to simplify my life by eliminating *have-to's*. The hillside was one of the first to go. I just stopped grooming it. Amazing things began to happen in just a few weeks. Purple morning glories blossomed magnificently each morning with the roses on the fence. Wild strawberries grew everywhere. Previously, I thought they were weeds. Another vine-like weed that I removed from the junipers weekly bloomed profusely with glorious white trumpet flowers.

My life is simpler now. The only change was my view of how the hillside should look. I did not change any plants, and Mother Nature certainly did not stop growing what I had previously considered to be weeds. My "weeds" are enjoyable. Several guests have complimented me on the natural beauty of the hillside garden that no longer requires intense weekly maintenance. Life is not concerned with the dragons of what we like, what we want, or how we feel. Some things we say we want may not be worth the price that we would be required to pay to get them.

It's Too Hot!

Even if things are not like we want them to be today, they are still okay because we can change the way we see them.

I joined my wife on a "fam cruise" for her new job selling group cruises. She went to Miami a few days ahead of me for training classes, and I flew there on the Saturday morning the cruise began. Waiting in the baggage area at Miami International Airport for my luggage to be unloaded from the plane, I spoke with the Hispanic cruise guide. I said: "You have a great job. It must be fun to meet people every day who are leaving on exciting cruises." She answered: "Yes, mostly. But some people always find something to complain about. They complain the plane was late, the baggage handlers are slow, it's too hot, it's too expensive, they can't understand me, or it's too crowded in Miami."

I think of her response whenever I feel like complaining. The dragon of petty complaints serves little purpose beyond spreading frustration, discontent and depression. Complaints do not make the plane arrive on time. They do not make baggage handlers unload the plane faster. They do not reduce or increase the temperature. They do not reduce the cost of a cruise. And they do not improve intercultural communications. However, the dragon of petty complaints might reduce crowds because nobody likes being around chronic complainers.

Petty complaints are purposeless judgements of good and bad based on *how the world is* versus *how we would like it to be*. They do not change anything. The complainer does not really intend to change anything. However, we cannot be optimistic about the future until we believe that everything is okay today just the way it is. Accepting the world as it is in the present moment (it cannot be any other way) brings peace and happiness. When we rise above our minor annoyances, we recognize and enjoy the wonders of the moment—in this case, a cruise to the Caribbean. Everything is okay in our lives. Or it soon will be when we focus our energy and creativity on enjoying *what is.*

Shakespeare Again

Each moment of each day will reveal wondrous new beauty and meaning if we look for them.

I am amazed by each new performance of a Shakespearean play that I have seen multiple times before. The words are exactly the same every time, but the actors' interpretations are new. Subtle shades of meaning I had not understood before emerge each time I see a play. Furthermore, thousands of people who attend the same performance take away different impressions than I do. Sometimes I am stimulated by a play, and other times I am disappointed by the same play. Is Hamlet a courageous conqueror of emotions, or a tragic coward? How can there be such a wide range of interpretations when the words and scenes are identical? Could it be the real meaning is not in the play or the actors? Maybe it lies in the nuances inside me as the actors reenact the same scenes I have watched many times before.

Everyday life is similar. Another day cleaning the house or garden. Another business meeting to improve customer service or increase sales. Another phone call from a family member. Another traffic jam on the beltway. Life in a rut, the same things over and over again, arouses the dragons of boredom and emptiness. When we dwell incessantly on infrequent vacations, major triumphs and big holidays (regardless of whether they are in the past or the future) we miss the ordinary yet incredibly special moments that are happening today.

The boredom dragon disappears, and the emptiness dragon is filled when we savor the rich nuances of difference in *"I've done this before."* New meanings, new possibilities, new lessons, and new scenery emerge when we look for them. *Wow, I've never seen that before!* The fifth time we see *Hamlet,* the scenery that surrounds the 100th traffic jam on the same highway, and the conversation during the $3{,}000^{th}$ dinner with our family are new experiences unlike anything we have ever done before. Each day offers rich possibilities if we look for the changes instead of treating today as though it were exactly the same as yesterday.

Life Is a Jelly Bean Jar

When we accept the dragons of uncertainty and complexity as normal, chaos and anxiety cease to undermine our happiness.

The simple act of choosing a jelly bean from a jar, which used to be simple, has now become complicated. Like jelly beans, life also seems to be more complex than ever. There are so many choices, and we cannot be sure what each choice will bring. Since President Reagan made them a national treasure in the 1980s, jelly beans have become popular and plentiful. As a young boy, I remember just five jelly bean flavors. I liked the cherry, lemon and orange ones, but not the lime or licorice ones. Today, there are over 100 flavors to choose from. The colors are baffling, and I get confused over which color jelly bean has the best flavor. For example, I did not like green jelly beans as a boy. But the new green jelly beans are apple flavor. When eaten with a dark red (cinnamon) jelly bean, the combination tastes like apple pie.

One new flavor I like is coconut jelly beans, which are white. Unfortunately, peppermint jelly beans, which I do not like, also look white. When I pick a white jelly bean, I never know which flavor I will get. The uncertainty is unsettling. I used to like the lemon flavor of yellow jelly beans. Now pineapple, banana and popcorn jelly beans are yellow too. Fortunately, I like all of those flavors. The color of some jelly beans is not appealing, so I tend to avoid trying them. An inner voice beckons me to try the unknown jelly beans. But I am reluctant to try new jelly beans.

It seems like I have made a big problem of simple jelly beans. How can we enjoy eating jelly beans when picking a color is such an uncertain experience? Similarly, we can never be sure what flavor (results) we will get when we pick a jelly bean from the jar of life. However, we can enjoy any flavor we get, if only because we have learned not to pick that color again. Sometimes we may find a wonderful jelly bean by accident, like the red jelly beans with green speckles (Bloody Mary flavor with Worcestershire and Tabasco). They are *good.* Maybe we should experiment with a handful of new colors?

Tiddley Winks

Let's eliminate the self-imposed constraints and excessive complexity that sabotage our happiness.

When I was a youngster, my friends and I played tiddley winks for hours. Tiddley winks is a simple game. Just flip the chip into the cup. But we made it complicated by negotiating:

- How many points does it take to win?
- Who goes first? And, if you go first, will I get my last turn?
- Do I score points for just hitting the cup?
- Can I get more points by putting a bigger chip into the cup?

These seemed like reasonable questions, but they caused many arguments and interfered with the fun of playing.

We miss important opportunities in our lives while, figuratively, playing tiddley winks with the dragons of self-imposed constraints and unrealistic expectations. For example, my wife, two daughters and I made a cross-country trip when the girls were young. We had no deadline to arrive in San Diego, but I set a goal to drive 600 miles per day to finish the trip in four days. I was upset by a truck accident that delayed us two hours and forced me to drive late into the night. I also said no to my wife's suggestion that we visit the Grand Canyon. It was out of the way and would add a fifth day to the trip. My obsession with an unimportant goal caused us to miss one of the most awesome sights in the world. We just visited the Grand Canyon for the first time last summer, thirty-four years after that auto trip.

Too often we make life more complicated than it is. The questions we asked about tiddley winks have parallels in our relationships and our jobs. Instead of enjoying each day, we are concerned that someone may get more opportunity. We may worry about reaching a goal. Or we are upset when we do not finish everything on a things-to-do list. We create artificial restrictions, set unrealistic or unnecessary goals, and fret about insignificant details. Meanwhile, wonderful people and events pass by unnoticed and unappreciated. Such self-imposed barriers are avoidable hurdles on the road to happiness and success.

Typing Class

Resistance to learning is a roaring dragon that creates conflict and limits our success.

My dad made me take typing in my senior year of high school. It was not cool in the 1960s for high school senior guys to take typing. They took auto mechanics, woodworking, or some other manly course. Throughout the summer, my father and I battled over the issue. I pleaded that I would be an outcast among my friends if I took typing. I did not need to learn typing because I planned to be an engineer, not a secretary. He was adamant. He said: "Trust me, son, years from now you'll thank me for making you take typing." That infuriated me, but I had no real choice about taking the course. The first day of school arrived, and the dreaded typing class was the first period after lunch. Lunch confirmed my worst fears. My friends talked eagerly about their new classes. I was embarrassed about mine. Laughter broke out when I said my next class was typing. I felt ashamed walking dome the Home Economics corridor. I had been in that hallway only twice in my three years at the high school.

The classroom had five rows with five huge desks in each row for typing materials and my own manual typewriter. Sure enough, I was the only male in a class of twenty-four girls. My unexpected surprise was that twelve of the girls were varsity cheerleaders. In a high school with 4,000 students, I was not in the social group with the cheerleaders. I casually knew just a few of them. However, the attention I received during lunch periods quickly changed from the "weirdo who took typing" to the "lucky one in the class with the cheerleaders."

I was unhappy when I resisted the idea of learning to type. Too often we resist changes over which we have little control. We get angry. We argue. We fight to avoid doing the things we do not like. However, *the way it is* may be even better than *the way we want it to be*. Today, as I type this manuscript on a computer almost forty years later, I appreciate my dad's genius in forcing me to learn to type. Reluctantly, I thank him. I still do not know much about auto mechanics, but I will never forget Dee Dee, Sue and Marjorie.

The Price of Rage

Uncontrolled anger cripples our chances for success. More effective responses are acceptance or trying a new approach.

Conflict sometimes causes me to leap to anger, unaware of how the anger affects those around me or the damage I do to myself and others. Like a drag racer accelerating from zero to 100 miles an hour, I can go from calm to angry in an instant. Maybe I am driving to work on the parkway when a jerk cuts me off. I get mad. I retaliate by screaming through the window of the car. I accelerate my car, and cut him off to get even. Both of our cars jump the median strip and collide head-on with traffic in the other lane. In an instant three people are dead, including me, and a fourth is crippled for life.

This obviously did not happen to me. But it did happen to four people at 6:30 one sunny spring morning on the George Washington Memorial Parkway outside Washington, D.C. Is it really important when someone cuts us off on a highway, or annoys us in another way? Is it worth our life? Is it worth destroying several families? Of course not. The sobering thought is that I drove past the spot of the accident at 6:25 that morning. If I had hit my snooze alarm just one more time, I might have been an innocent victim of someone else's road rage.

Reflecting on the tragic consequences of the anger those two drivers felt that morning, it is easy to see that many of us react in similar ways when we resist *what is*. The anger and frustrations we feel and the retaliatory actions we take against family, friends or business associates are an attempt to prove *I'm right*. The anger does not feel good. It blocks reason and does not produce what we want in our lives.

One technique that is effective in taming the dragon of rage is to hesitate for an instant whenever we feel angry and say: *"My life is over because of this incident!"* Suddenly, the person or event that is the root of the anger will seem trivial. The unfortunate incident or thoughtless action of another is easier to accept. We enjoy a sunny morning, even if someone thoughtlessly "cuts us off" on the highway of life.

Dysfunctional Pelicans

When the dragon of failure breathes its hot fire, don't let it scorch you. Instead, roast a marshmallow and savor each failure as a new beginning.

When my wife and I vacation in the Caribbean, I enjoy relaxing on the balcony of our time-share in St. Maarten watching pelicans dive for fish. They soar into the air, and fly in circles searching for fish. When they see one, they crash dive several feet deep into the water. Sometimes they catch the fish. But most dives they come up empty, and must try again. While watching them, I do not see any sense of failure in the empty-billed pelicans. They do not chastise themselves for a poor dive, or feel less of a pelican because they have no fish.

Fear of failure is strictly a human trait. We expect to succeed at everything, and are unhappy when we do not. But what if there is no such thing as failure? What if it is not reality at all, just a concept we invented to judge our results? Pelicans do not seem unhappy when they do not get a fish. We humans often feel guilt, sadness or regret when we do not achieve our goals. We complain about bad luck, blame someone or something else for our results, and become afraid to set new goals. Can you imagine pelicans excusing their fishless dives by saying the water was too cold, the fish was not fat enough, or the wind blew me off course? What if they quit diving because the chance of getting a fish was so small? Pelicans do not care about missing a fish. In pelican talk they probably just say: *I see the lesson. Next dive I'll adjust for the wind blowing me off course.*

Happiness and satisfaction lie in striving! Making the equivalent of our next dive for a fish the best it can be. Accepting the lessons that come with "no fish this time." Expecting perfection, the equivalent of a fish on every dive, measures our personal worth in terms of perfect results. No fish this time means we failed. Maybe it is just not true. Maybe we can be successful and happy even if we do not achieve all of our goals on the first try. Nothing is so bad that something good will not come from it. Look for the good in everything that you call "bad."

Life Is Like Bowling

Tomorrow's success is shaped in the crucible of today's difficulties. Today's challenges strengthen our resolve and sharpen our skills.

Each frame is a new day, each game a new year. The fall league is just a phase in our life. We get many turns at the alley, and we watch others take their turns too. Some days we get a strike. Ten big problems disappear on our first try, like pins scattered across the alley. Everyone cheers and we get a big score. More often, our first try eliminates some problems but several remain like stubborn, wobbling pins. So we try again and the problems disappear. We earn a spare, and teammates congratulate us. But some days life gives us the equivalent of a 7-10 split. There is no easy solution. We give it a good try, but the problem is still there. Like missing a 7-10 split, nobody cheers. Sympathetic friends say: "That was a tough one." But mostly they say nothing. The score is low, and we feel as though we have lost the game. We have a choice to feel bad about the score, or continue bowling. Either way, the next game begins in the first frame with a zero score.

The zest of life is the changes that test us each day. Perfect days are as rare as 300 games. And even if we bowl a 300 game, the next day still starts at zero. Similarly, happiness and success lie in solving the problems that life delivers. It is easy to get into situations that seem impossible. They happen all by themselves without our help. A 7-10 split is not a disaster, it is an opportunity. Those who watch are thrilled when we pull it off.

The trip to the bowling alley is more important than the score. Enjoying our lives is more important than our results. Some excellent bowlers allow a 7-10 split to ruin their whole night. But a problem in one day does not affect the next day unless we let the dragon of today's disappointment interfere with tomorrow's success. The joy of life is not *not getting* into trouble. The joy is *getting out* of difficult situations and, in the process, learning new skills and seeing new possibilities. Today's problems are lessons for tomorrow. Each day is exciting in its own way, even if all of our problems are not knocked over.

Afraid to Succeed

Fear of failure is a huge obstacle on the path to success. Winners are not afraid of failing, losers are.

Occasionally, I am asked why I started my own company. The real reason is I was bored working for a big company. I managed 120 people, earned a top salary, and had excellent executive perks including a company car. And I was bored. All day long I pushed paper from desk to desk, solved personnel issues, and analyzed sales and budget figures. Rarely did I have an opportunity to participate in a creative project. Preparing proposals for new clients was the most imaginative work I did. Periodically, I talked about starting a new company, but my wife did not think I was serious. Deep inside I did not believe in myself either. What if I failed?

One day I mentioned the idea to my oldest daughter while she was filling out college applications at the kitchen table on Sunday morning. I told her I was thinking about starting a new company, but was afraid I would not earn enough to pay for her college tuition. Her response was insightful: "Go for it, Dad. You've never failed at anything you've ever tried." For weeks, her words rang in my ears each time that boredom crept into my thoughts. I decided to do it, and the rest is history.

Starting a new business has been a rewarding and exciting experience. In between satisfying successes, running a company is frustrating, demanding, frightening, disappointing, discouraging and overwhelming. But never boring. I suffered through a well-paying but boring job for several years because I was afraid to fail. The fear of failure overpowered my feelings of boredom and restlessness. The fear of failure kept me from succeeding. Clearly, my choice for a long time was to be bored in a comfortable job, rather than to risk failure.

Most of us are unhappy and restless when we are bored. But too often we would rather allow the fear-of-failure dragon to lock us in the dungeon of boredom, than to risk a major change that might not work. Happiness returns when we either consciously choose to enjoy being bored, or choose the risk of a daring new adventure.

Riding Fear

The fear of failure can cause failure. Let's not let fear suck the energy and creativity we need to succeed.

My wife and I went horseback riding on a beautiful fall afternoon with two friends. They were novice riders, while my wife and I had been riding for several years. The keeper at the stable where we rented the horses, apparently thinking I was a strong rider, gave me a big stallion to ride. I was intimidated by the horse. As we rode on wooded trails through colorful autumn trees, I was afraid. The stallion must have sensed the dragon of fear inside me. Near the end of the ride, we galloped in a five-horse column with the guide leading. My stallion did not like being the last horse in the column, so he pulled out to pass the other horses. I tried to hold him back instead of allowing myself to enjoy the exhilarating ride that was about to begin. My body communicated fear to the horse, and his response was to run even faster.

I lost rhythm with the horse and knew I was about to be thrown, which was my worst fear from the start. As I bounced on the horse's back, the horrible image of a bloody accident crossed my mind. I just wanted to get off the horse without being dragged through the forest with my feet in the stirrups, or getting kicked in the head by the horse. I removed my feet from the stirrups and flew off the horse, landing in the brush on my head and shoulder. I was shocked and dazed, but not seriously injured other than scratches and bruises.

Fighting the horse while I struggled with my fear of falling contributed to my being thrown from the horse. Fear is a fascinating dragon. Thoughts of fear not only rob us of our happiness, they can directly cause the very event we fear to become reality. I spent my imagination and concentration on fear, rather than on enjoying the ride. With a stallion as my teacher, the ride was another lesson in the futility of fear.

My Image of Me

Judgements of our body are dragons that reduce our happiness. Often, the judgements have little basis in reality.

The contestants in a male beauty contest were asked to appear on stage in an outfit that was appealing and flattering. They each strutted across the stage, and flashed a card with two scores from zero to ten. The first score rated their outfit (recall they *choose* the outfit), and the second rated their physical attractiveness. The audience simultaneously rated the contestants in the same two categories. The difference between the scores holds a lesson for us.

One contestant, a handsome man in his early thirties with a dark suntan, rated himself 6.5 for looks and 10 for his flowered mid-thigh bathing suit and tie-dyed pink tee shirt. The audience rated him 9.5 for looks and only 2.0 for the flamboyant outfit. When asked about the low score he gave himself for his physical appearance, he said: "My waist is too big, and my biceps are too small." In the same contest, a six-foot-three, thin and partially bald contestant gave himself a 10 for looks. Asked how he scored himself a perfect 10 compared with men like Tom Cruise, Mel Gibson and Brad Pitt, he answered that his body rated a 10 because it worked flawlessly. The men used different standards to judge their bodies. One man's opinion was based on judgements of small deviations from a standard of perfection, while the other's opinion was a liberal evaluation of how well his body functioned.

Judgements rule our actions and influence our happiness. Too fat, too thin, too big, too small, too tall, too short, too weak, too bald, too whatever. But we do not see what is real. We see just a personal perception of reality based on the standards we use to judge ourselves. Your standards are different than mine. But either of us can change our standards at any time. We can learn to enjoy our bodies, use them vigorously, and ignore what other people may or may not think.

Your body may not be everything you might want it to be, but it is the only body you will ever have. Therefore, you may as well like the body you have been given.

Scuba or Seance

Choose your attitude independent of events around you. Stress or laughter, complaints or joy, conflict or teamwork, status quo or growth. Which you do choose?

The dragon of smashed expectations taught me a lesson one cold February when my wife and I vacationed in Key West. It was a perfect opportunity to be unhappy, if that was what I wanted to be. Everything a vacation might need to justify my being disappointed and miserable was present:

- Key West recorded cold temperatures (forty-two degrees at noon)
- My scuba diving trips and water sports were canceled
- We paid a high-season price to be there for just four days
- I hate cold weather—that is why we vacation in February!

We seriously considered returning to Washington, D.C., early because it was so cold in Key West.

After complaining about the weather vociferously and observing that our complaints did not change the temperature, we took a different tact. Accept the cold and make the best of it. We bought sweatshirts instead of tee shirts. During a tour of Earnest Hemingway's home, we spent more time inside the house than in the beautiful gardens. And we enjoyed Irish coffee instead of piña coladas at sunset on the foot of DuVal Street.

Our most courageous adventure, however, was participation in a three-hour seance in a haunted house. Those three hours produced lasting memories we never would have experienced if the weather was warm like we wanted it to be. The seance was the highlight of our vacation. We would have missed it and several other wonderful experiences if we persisted in judging the Key West weather to be bad, and complaining about it.

We judge things as "bad" when they are not like we want them to be. An alternate view for such situations is to accept *What Is* and make the best of it. *"So what, now what? How can I enjoy and learn from this situation?"* restores happiness most of the time.

Right and Wrong

Right *and* wrong *are measures of what we think should be, rather than inherent characteristics of events, circumstances or people.*

Some saw the controversial Vietnam War of the 1960s and early 1970s as "right," an opportunity for the United States to defend freedom and democracy. Others saw it as "wrong" because so many innocent people were killed, families were torn apart, and destruction was everywhere. As a naval officer I supported the Vietnam War, and was angered by my fellow Americans who threw rocks at me when I was in uniform. Several close college friends died in Vietnam defending the freedom of speech those protesters used so liberally. Was the war "right" or "wrong"? Unquestionably it was both.

Today, I might be on the other side of an issue like Vietnam. But I would not throw stones at people who held different beliefs. Instead, I would try to understand their beliefs. Today, I admire Muhammad Ali, who opposed that war publically, refused to be drafted into the Army, and forfeited the Heavyweight Championship of the World for his beliefs. I despised him at the time. Now I understand his point of view, and respect the courage it took to stand for principle, even though his principles were radically different than mine.

The right-to-life versus pro-choice clash is a similar issue. Each position is "right" or "wrong" depending on your point of view. Maybe it would be more effective to set aside judgements of right and wrong. Perhaps our time and passion would be better invested to understand the two points of view; and the intense hopes, fears and pain that each view embodies.

Too often our perceptions of *right* and *wrong* become dragons that obliterate the possibility of resolution, progress and unity. When that happens, choices are made (like rock-throwing or blowing up clinics) that may be regretted long into the future. Absolute judgements of *right* and *wrong* can be roadblocks to career success, family unity, and personal happiness. Instead, respecting the alternative views of others leads to new levels of happiness, peace and success. And those are the things most of us say we want in our lives.

Storms and Icebergs

Spend your time, creativity and energy wisely. Unlike tangible resources, they cannot be saved for another day.

The story of the *Titanic* has captivated our attention for almost a century. Imagine yourself paying thousands of dollars for a luxurious cruise on the maiden voyage of a "ship that God Himself couldn't sink." And then seeing the ship sink as you watched from a rubber raft in a cold ocean. Most of us would call that a bad day!

Like the *Titanic* crossing the ocean, we encounter icebergs, storms and waves as we take life's voyage. The next harbor is a goal we are striving to achieve. Icebergs, storms and waves are the inevitable problems that occur in our lives, obstacles that block the pathway to our goals. Who could possibly enjoy the storms of bankruptcy, divorce, disappointment or failure; or the icebergs of serious accidents, sickness and death? Yet during our eighty-year voyage through life (more or less) each of us will experience several of these events. Since we never know when one of them will occur, it may seem that we have no control over the serious challenges that abruptly appear in our lives like icebergs and storms.

When we lose sight of goals or forget to enjoy the ocean crossing one exciting wave at a time, every small change appears enormous and there seems to be no end to them. We wish for calm seas and clear sailing and it feels like the ship might sink. Then, when the really big icebergs and storms of life toss us around the ocean, we may feel like giving up. But the storms always disappear, and the icebergs always melt away. The sky always clears, and the voyage across the wide ocean of life continues one day at a time.

It is up to each of us to enjoy our life's voyage including the icebergs, storms and waves. Instead of feeling lost in the daily changes, think of unwanted change as an event that will have minor importance and short duration relative to our eighty-year voyage.

Closing Thoughts on Being Happy Today

Our life expectancy is about 27,500 days. Today is just one of those many days. Let's enjoy today's share of happiness and success whether it be large or small.

As a boy, dinner was a chore whenever we had broccoli. I hated broccoli, but was I was not allowed to leave the table until I ate it all. My mother told me that someday I would like broccoli, as she watched me struggle to swallow the last horrible mouthful. I did not see how that could be possible. Today I enjoy broccoli steamed or raw. What changed? Why did it change? When did I choose to like broccoli? Could I make other things change in the same way?

You have just read vignettes about jelly beans, broken hands, Shakespeare, pelicans, bowling, and other routine experiences. The common thought is that *happiness is a choice* independent of events, people and changes. There is no magic happy pill. You are the only one who can make you happy. Conventional thought says happiness will come if we have lots of money, own a big house, have fun, our children are successful, and other external things. Unfortunately, those thoughts produce stress (how much money is enough?), rivalries (whose house is bigger?), anger (why do they disagree with me?), disappointment (when will my child "learn" about life?), boredom (what can I do next to have fun?), and pain.

Choosing happiness produces different experiences: laughter, peace, contentment, a willingness to share, and optimism about the future. We choose happiness when we bring joy into sadness, peace into conflict, understanding into confrontation, abundance into poverty, and gratefulness into loss. Happiness is good medicine. It contributes to good health. Although the changes in our lives and the dragons they arouse are not pleasant, every one provides useful lessons.

Poignant moments occur infrequently. In this book, I share the special moments in my life with you. You have had similar moments in your life. Good or bad, we cannot make those events happen again or pretend they never happened. Happiness does not mean everything is perfect. It just means we choose to be happy with *what is.*

-----Essential Tip #2-----
LIVE IN ABUNDANCE
~ There's Plenty For Everyone

The test of our progress is not whether we add more to the abundance of those who already have much, rather that we provide abundance for those who have little.
— Franklin D. Roosevelt

Abundant Stamps

An attitude of abundance is a practical life strategy. In the long run, we get more of what we want with abundance thinking, than with scarcity thinking.

When the cost of mailing a first class letter changed to thirty-seven cents, I went to the post office to purchase one-cent stamps to augment our remaining thirty-six-cent stamps. There were over thirty people in line, most of them with the same idea. I waited over twenty minutes to buy the 40 one-cent stamps I needed. As I neared the counter, a man several people ahead of me in line bought $20 worth of the one-cent stamps. I was angry that he had bought so many, fearing there would be none left for me. Then he tore the sheets of stamps into blocks, and gave them to everyone in line, including me. The line disappeared almost instantly. His wonderful attitude of abundance saved thirty people twenty minutes each for just $20!

Abundance is a belief there is plenty in the world for everyone. With an attitude of abundance, we willingly share resources and help each other even though our goals and perspectives differ. On the other hand, an attitude of scarcity produces very different results. When things change, we hear the scarcity dragon scream: "*there won't be enough for me*" and we scramble to get ours before others get theirs. We compete fiercely rather than help each other like the generous and thoughtful man in the post office.

Abundance is not necessarily exotic vacations, large houses, fancy cars, or the other trappings of material wealth. Too often the pursuit of wealth and material goods spawns an attitude of scarcity: *I don't have enough yet* or *I'm afraid I'll lose what I have*. Just as often, wealth and an attitude of abundance complement each other: *There always will be enough, so I'll share what I have with you and others*. No matter how much or how little we may possess, an attitude of abundance always produces more happiness and success for ourselves and others than an attitude of scarcity. People remember the generous things we did not have to do for a long time.

Scarcity dragons are everywhere, even in affluent communities. They drive people to jealously protect everything they have to keep their "fair" share. The scarcity dragons would have us believe that there is not enough love, time, resources or opportunity for everyone. With that belief we are reluctant to trust anyone. Even our spouse, family, friends and employer. We fight to retain our possessions; guard our position, power and authority; and resist change. Scarcity thinking does not work because other people respond in the same way. When we compete with each other, we actually produce scarcity and reduce our collective happiness and success.

An attitude of abundance means being grateful for what we have, instead of envious of the things we want and the people who have them. An attitude of abundance tells us that we are never alone. Others are here to help. We trust each other. And, working together, like magic there is enough for everyone. In my experience, the few times my attitude of abundance has been exploited by others are inconsequential next to the help I have received, and the joy, peace and satisfaction that abundance thinking has brought into my life. This chapter shows how an attitude of abundance will create more love, more resources, more time, and more opportunity for you and everyone else. It provides precious tips to help you transform scarcity into abundance in your life. The transformation begins with an attitude of abundance, the belief that there is enough for everyone.

Narcissism

It is not true that you want the same things that I want. The possibility for abundance lies in the differences between what each of us want in our lives.

Like Narcissus, the mythical Greek who became entranced by his own reflection in a lake, fell in and drowned, we think that others want what we want and drown in fear that there will not be enough. It is a subconscious belief that everyone values what we value. It is not true, but that belief stimulates an attitude of scarcity. The wonderful reality of our world is that we each want different things, and value different things. Those differences create possibilities for abundance thinking that work for everyone's benefit.

Consider buying an apple for fifty cents. The grocer values fifty cents more than the apple, and the consumer values the apple more than fifty cents. The simplicity of the transaction is elegant. The consumer and grocer each achieve different goals. In an attitude of abundance, the grocer knows there will be more apples and the consumer knows there will be more money. Millions of people with different goals cooperate by shopping in grocery stores. Grocers cooperate with distributors, and distributors cooperate with farmers so we can enjoy an apple for fifty cents, if we wanted one. The transaction could not occur if anyone in the chain had an attitude of scarcity. If we thought there was not enough money, we may not buy an apple. If the farmer or grocer felt they could not deliver enough apples, they would not sell one for fifty cents. Thousands of people would rush to compete with each other to buy apples.

While we usually have an attitude of abundance toward apples, there often is an attitude of scarcity toward opportunities and resources. Many believe there are not enough for everyone. As the world changes, scarcity dragons push us to pursue things that are less important than the happiness, love and trust we say we want. By contrast, an attitude of abundance and cooperation produces prosperity for everyone, each of us achieving success *because* others are successful. We all will prosper beyond our biggest dream when, in an attitude of abundance, we ask each other: "How can I help you succeed?"

Awesome Results

An attitude of abundance does not mean settling for less. Rather, it means having everything we imagine as possible, plus everything we create by working together.

To me, Bill Gates, founder of Microsoft and one of the richest men alive, illustrates the awesome results that abundant thinking produces. Despite the U.S. Justice Department's ruling that "Microsoft Wields Monopoly Power," his attitude of abundance has made a huge positive impact on our world, and simultaneously produced great wealth for himself, his associates, and others. His dream since the 1960s was *a computer on every desk and in every home*. He envisioned personal computers (PCs) as the path to that dream at a time when PCs were shipped in mail-order kits for home assembly. He left Harvard (as he says: "began an extended leave of absence") to program PCs. The Microsoft Disk Operating System (MS/DOS), which has evolved into Windows, demonstrates abundance thinking and belief in a dream. IBM offered him millions for MS/DOS, but he decided a small royalty per PC would be better. Apparently, potential abundance in the future was worth more to him than the dragon of instant rewards.

In his books *Business @ the Speed of Thought* and *The Road Ahead*, Bill Gates encourages us to participate in the still expanding Information Age. He openly shares his vision for the future because he sees abundant opportunity for everyone. That concept is inspiring! The opportunities for you and I to be successful in the Information Age are limitless. If my business and similar businesses succeed, then the entire computer industry prospers. Microsoft grows when other companies prosper and the economy grows. Bill Gates shares resources under the Microsoft Partner Program in yet another demonstration of abundant thinking. My company provides solutions to clients, while Microsoft develops efficient software tools. We cannot succeed without each other. Mr. Gates' attitude of abundance stimulates me to act abundantly too. In our changing world, abundant opportunities are everywhere for all of us to share.

Passed Over

When it seems like the door of opportunity was slammed in our face, a new set of opportunities is just beginning. Look for them.

As a youngster my dream was to join the Navy and become an admiral. After nine years as a naval officer, I was "passed over" for promotion to lieutenant commander, the fourth rank from the bottom. Nine of ten officers in my category were promoted. I pored over the ten-page promotion list several times before I accepted that my name was not there. The message I heard was: *"You're in the bottom ten percent. The Navy doesn't want you."* The twin dragons of disappointment and depression devastated me. It hurt. At thirty years old, I was being told to change my career. What would I do with my life now? Obviously, becoming an admiral was out.

Even though I was promoted the next year, I was embarrassed that I had been passed over. Grieving and still angry at the Navy, I resigned as a naval officer. Stimulated by the change forced by the Navy's action, my career took an unexpected turn. In evaluating alternatives, I found that opportunity was abundant even in apparent failure. After three months of looking, I found a job that applied my education, skills and Navy experience. The starting pay was twice my salary as a naval officer. That company taught me how to manage large projects for government clients. Three years later, I became vice president of a fifteen-person computer company where I learned small business operations and software applications. Next came four years with an aerospace company where I learned marketing, sales, and financial management.

Each job provided new opportunities and taught me valuable lessons. They were the stepping stones to success. None of the success would have been possible without the opportunity of being passed over, even though being passed over did not feel like an opportunity at the time. Opportunity often arrives in a package that we do not like at first. The most important opportunities in our lives may arrive wrapped in the ugly rags of failure.

I'm Happy for You

Celebrate someone else's success, and others will celebrate yours.Help someone else succeed, and others will help you succeed.

My company lost the competition for a five-year, $15 million Navy contract. We were among the five finalists and lost. Two other losing companies protested the contract award. Both protests were rejected. I sent a congratulations card to the president of the winning company. He called and scheduled a lunch to discuss potential business opportunities. He said he had never received a congratulations card before from a company who had lost a competition. It is hard to predict where our relationship might go, but for sure it will be different than if I had been among those who protested his victory.

What does it cost to celebrate the successes and achievements of family, friends, coworkers and even competitors? Very little. And the potential rewards are enormous. Applauding their accomplishments with an attitude of abundance creates joy in their lives and in ours. It empowers us. When we hold an attitude of abundance in times of apparent loss, we feel genuine happiness for the victories of others.

Celebrating the success of family, friends and coworkers builds an environment of success, and focuses attention on things that work. When we celebrate successes every day, we build a mental inventory of things that work. When problems arise, we reach into that inventory to find proven ways to solve today's problem. Focusing on failures and weaknesses, the "half-empty glass," creates the opposite. It builds a mental inventory of things that do not work. And when a new problem comes up, we freeze in inaction because the only memories we have are the dragons of past strategies that failed. Do not try that again!

Celebrating success works especially well for parents. Celebrate the small accomplishments of your children, let inadequacies slip by unnoticed. You may find that celebrating a "B" in math actually moves the grade to an "A" next grading period. Successes are abundant every day when we look for them and celebrate them! And the celebration just may produce more success tomorrow.

What About Sports

Compete on a friendly basis for small things, and synergize on important matters. Synergy creates abundance, and competition sharpens performance.

You may ask: "Win-win is a great theory, but how can the Seattle Seahawks and Pittsburgh Steelers play win-win in the 2006 Super Bowl? Two NFL teams can't both win the Super Bowl." Pro football is exciting because the players give 100 percent on every play. The blocking is intense, pitting the offensive line's brawn head-to-head against the defensive line's agility. The knowledge that any play could make the difference between victory and defeat was win-win for millions of us who watched, no matter which team we favored. Unfortunately, the dragons of hostility and disappointment flourish when the sole standard for success is winning, rather than an exciting game well played.

The dragons of competition are tamed when we appreciate the excellence on both the winning and losing teams. Win-lose thinking sprouts in an attitude of scarcity about the opportunity of playing in the Super Bowl. Two teams achieve that feat every year, and only one will wear Super Bowl rings. It certainly is not a scarcity of resources based on the salary the players and owners earn. Did the Buffalo Bills really lose when they scored fewer points than the New York Giants, Dallas Cowboys (twice) and Washington Redskins in four consecutive Super Bowls? No team before or since has ever appeared in four consecutive Super Bowls. The Bills' frustration at losing four Super Bowls could easily be a celebration of prolonged excellence.

Few of us participate in pro-level sports competition. Yet many of us compete each day like it was a Super Bowl against our spouse, family, coworkers and employers. The blocking is often the most violent in our closest relationships, even when there is no penalty for helping the runner. Can you win if your family and friends lose? Is it possible for you to win if your employer loses? Will you win if your community loses? It would be absurd to ask: *"Who won in your marriage today, you or your spouse?"* If you both did not win today, then you both lost!

Win-Win Works

Win-Win strategies create opportunities that cannot survive in an environment of competition. Those extra opportunities produce abundance for everyone.

My company and a competitor received separate government contracts to develop solutions for a research problem. During Phase I, we both demonstrated the viability and value of our respective technical approaches, which were quite different. We offered an over-arching architecture, while our competitor designed several innovative data processing tools. We felt that we would win the Phase II contract, a contract ten times larger than Phase I, because we saw architecture as more important than tools. Our competitor, of course, felt the opposite. The Phase II contract award was delayed for months as our companies competed like two scarcity dragons to determine who would win.

Finally, we discovered the client liked both Phase I approaches and could not decide which to pick for Phase II. Win-win thinking tamed the dragon that blocked us both from reaching our goal. Viewing opportunity as abundant, we teamed with our competitor and broke the logjam by submitting a joint proposal. The new contract was awarded in two weeks. We gave or former competitor a substantial subcontract to develop the processing tools. It was win-win-win-win: the client won, we won, our competitor won, and you won as a taxpayer.

When we abandoned our *win-lose* strategy, both companies won. Following that award, a synergistic relationship grew which enabled us to pursue other opportunities that neither company could perform alone. Working together with an attitude of abundance, we added to each other in synergy rather than subtracted from each other in competition.

Synergy means 1 + 1 is more than 2. By combining your best with my best, we can produce much more than we could individually. The synergy of win-win relationships is stimulating and empowering. It is just plain fun! Win-win thinking produces such respect, teamwork and creativity, that together we see abundant opportunities that neither of us would imagine alone.

Abundant Time

Time abundance brings peace. Time scarcity produces stress.

Our culture is obsessed with time. Everyone seems to be in a hurry. In the late 1800s when someone missed the stage coach, they waited a week in a frontier town until the next one came. Today, we are frustrated when we miss a Metro train that runs every six minutes. Some people are angry if they miss an elevator. Internet shopping. Nine-minute oil changes. Instant glue-on nails. Microwaveable Minute Rice, apparently a minute is too long to wait for rice. Time scarcity is rooted firmly in our minds. Abraham Lincoln, Mother Teresa and Michelangelo got the same twenty-four hours each day that you and I get. When we live by the clock, we forget that it is always "now." Every second we spend waiting, worrying or rushing is a second gone from our lives. Are such moments enjoyable? Actually, waiting and rushing do not cause stress, attitude does.

Time abundance is especially challenging for me. I fill my life so full of activities, that I have no time for life's inevitable unplanned changes. I have a things-to-do list that schedules my day in half-hour segments. I enjoy crossing out items. I update the list every day as the last task before going home at night. The list adds structure to my day, and I rarely forget a commitment. But I have noticed that the list stresses me. It stimulates my time-scarcity dragon. I have damaged relationships by prematurely ending a meeting saying: "I'm out of time, it is time for the next item on my list." My weekends also are time-cluttered. I have a prioritized list of golf, haircuts, household chores, and writing this book. Such lists are a time-scarcity dragon that inhibits enjoyment of the moment. Peace enters my life when I use the lists as a guide for what might be done. Anything not finished is left for another day, or I scratch it from the list and forget about it altogether.

Do you have time to savor vignettes about living in abundance? If you do, great! Read on. If not, examine your time priorities. Do you run them, or are they running you? If you *choose* something that is a higher priority, put this book away. It will be here next week, or next year when you can *choose* to invest your time to read it.

Are You My Friend?

An attitude of scarcity causes us to mistrust people who act or believe differently than we do. Maybe we should trust them more because they have so much to teach us.

How would you feel if you arrived home tonight and found an alien from another galaxy in your house? Would you be afraid it might hurt you and your family, or steal your possessions? Such thinking is based in part on an attitude of scarcity. Alternatively, would you trust the alien? Would you be eager to meet creatures from different worlds who might teach us a new way of living? That response stems from an attitude of abundance. Too often, we treat people who look differently, speak differently, or hold different beliefs as if they were aliens. Your spouse, children, friends or coworkers may look like aliens at times.

We each must answer the fundamental question: *Is the world a friendly place*? Those who say *YES* will deal with "different" people in one way, while those who answer *NO* will deal with them another way. In an attitude of abundance, the initial response to "different" people and ideas could be trust instead of fear. We could believe our family members are friendly, strangers are friendly, the government is friendly, and the aliens we meet will be friendly too. We could assume that aliens will treat us kindly. Such an attitude of abundance may appear naive since it leaves us open to pain and loss. But my experience with an attitude of abundance has not been pain and loss.

People often surprise me with their unique ideas and generous heart. When it appears that someone has tried to harm me or exploit my generosity, it usually is because they were thoughtless. Worried about scarcity, they focused on getting something for themselves and, in the process, inflicted pain on others. In the few times that someone intentionally violates my trust to achieve their goal, I do not feel like I have lost. I am happy he or she has achieved their goal and sad for the world because, if we had both won, the world's score would be twice as high. Our global score is running very low these days. Maybe we should focus abundance thinking on the aliens we live with and work with every day.

The Goose That Lays Golden Eggs

An attitude of abundance is patient. It knows that seedlings we plant today will grow into our future abundance.

The scarcity dragon caused the poor man in Aesop's fable to kill the goose that laid golden eggs. He killed the goose to get all of the eggs today, thereby leaving himself poor for the rest of his life. No more golden eggs. Each of us simultaneously is the goose who lays golden eggs, and the man or woman who decides how to treat the goose. Each of us has the ability to produce the golden eggs that will fulfill our dreams, and deep down we know that teamwork produces golden eggs by the dozens. Unfortunately, an attitude of scarcity sometimes causes us to choose short-term gratification over future happiness and success. The dragon of impatience shouts in our head: *"I want it all. And I want it now.*" We are reluctance to be content with what we have today, while we invest in tomorrow's golden eggs.

When our daughters first went to school, my wife decided she would go to college. She enrolled as a special student in the College of Charleston because she lacked the credentials for regular admission. She did homework with the girls every night. I supported her by doing extra housework, and by helping with science and math. Four years later, we attended her graduation ceremony in the Cistern. Dressed in the traditional white gown, she carried a red rose and won awards for excellence in English literature.

The investment of four years' work by the entire family has paid huge dividends. My wife and I have found that when we nurture our relationship, golden eggs (health, relaxing vacations, gratifying home improvements, and entertaining adult toys) flow naturally. However, when we drift away from each other and feel isolated, neglected or used, the golden eggs stop coming. Thoughtfulness, understanding, sharing and acceptance rejuvenate our relationship. Such attitudes of abundance restore the love, the patience, and the passion that are so vital for a thriving relationship. When we take care of our relationship goose, the golden eggs follow in abundance.

Little Leagers

Don't let the fear of losing arouse the scarcity dragon. In competitive situations, appreciate performance excellence in ourselves and in others.

The newspaper reported that a father was sentenced to forty-five days in jail for threatening to kill a Little League manager who took his son out of the game after two innings. He was quoted as saying: "How dare you make my son into a two-inning player." As a young boy, I played Little League baseball every spring for several years. Each game day was an intense adventure. Butterflies fluttered in my stomach hours before the game started. I looked forward with great anticipation to the thrill of the game. But the dragon of fear attended the games too. What if I struck out? What if I made an error in a crucial play of the game? Both of which I did frequently.

During the games, some parents yelled at the umpires and criticized players who made errors. The final score seemed more important than learning the game. Being especially susceptible to criticism, I acquired an out-of-balance focus on results from those games. Winning was all important. The goal was to beat the other team, rather than enjoy the game. Other parents applauded good plays, laughed at errors, and savored the spirit of the game. They cheered when a young batter stepped up to the plate and hit a bloop single, when a pitcher struck out the side with a blazing forty-mile-per-hour fastball, or when an outfielder closed his eyes and still caught the ball. Good plays were celebrated no matter which side made them. Their attitude of abundance was focused on enjoying the game, learning how to play, and helping the boys grow. Those parents knew there would be abundant future opportunities to play the game seriously if baseball was to become a career.

What are we teaching our children by our reactions to games: fear and disappointment because the objective is to win, or happiness and joy in celebrating outstanding performances and good tries?

The Famous Deposit #11

An attitude of abundance values differences between ourselves and those we love the most.

My wife and I are different. Those differences are simultaneously the source of our abundant relationship, and stimulation for our scarcity dragons. In almost forty years of marriage, I have had multiple lessons in appreciating our differences. Maybe the most challenging lesson was balancing the checkbook for my wife's fashion clothing business. One month, deposit #11 showed up as we processed the accounting records. The deposit was $223, but no sales receipt was attached. Where did the money come from? When asked about deposit #11, my wife reluctantly acknowledged that she made it up. She had created the deposit solely to reconcile her checkbook with the bank statement. My first reaction was anger. How could she do that? We cannot run a business that way! The episode triggered my fear of failing and being broke (scarcity view of opportunities and resources).

Fortunately, after a few minutes, I realized that deposit #11 really reflected one of my wife's greatest strengths: an unwillingness to be bound by conventional practices. That strength has produced many wonderful moments in our relationship. I also realized that she had invented the deposit because she was afraid of my adverse reaction to an unbalanced checkbook. That was the aspect of the situation for which I was responsible. As soon as I willingly accepted an out-of-balance checkbook, she became willing to ask for help and stop creating deposits from nothing. Our bank probably would not be so understanding if we overdrew the account. But that would be just a small pothole in life's highway.

Appreciating differences is vital in abundant relationships. The willingness to see value in other points of view, to accept that each of us sees the world uniquely, is the basis for synergy. My wife and I often laugh about "deposit #11." It reminds us that, by combining our strengths, we have produced abundant results that far exceed what either of us could have accomplished alone. Who knows how big deposit #12 will be?

Taxes and Tithes

An attitude of scarcity produces scarcity. When everyone is taking, there is no one left to give.

Most of us have an attitude of scarcity toward taxes. We feel that we work hard to earn what we get, and we should be able to keep more of it. In my case, the President and the Governor of Maryland take (I do not willingly give) more than fifty percent of my income for federal and state income taxes, Medicare, FICA, property tax and sales tax. The scarcity dragon causes me to resent surrendering such a large part of my income to support welfare, special-interest and other programs that I do benefit from or even not agree.

On the other hand, I do not tithe either. Tithing is giving ten percent of our earnings to benefit others as an expression of gratitude for our well-being and success. The giving could be in services, goods or cash to a church or charity. It also may be helping a needy family, or being a big brother. I give money, goods and time to United Way and several other of my favorite charities, but the sum is less than ten percent of my earnings.

Is it possible that our taxes are higher than they should be because we do not tithe? Are taxes high because of our attitude of scarcity? It seems that many of us would rather "let the government take care of them," then to directly support those in need. Statistics show that the number of registered churches, synagogues, mosques and other tax-exempt houses of worship in the United States is about half the number of families enrolled in federal welfare and social aid programs. If each congregation (that means you and me) would help just two families currently on the welfare roles, we might eliminate welfare programs completely and reduce income taxes substantially. The point is, instead of giving ten percent tithe and offering our time and resources in an attitude of abundance, we pay absurdly high taxes with an attitude of scarcity. Fifty percent in taxes is five times what the Bible suggests that we give in tithe.

The Pizza Dragon

If we erased the belief that there is not enough, many of the compulsive habits in our lives would disappear.

Pizza symbolizes my continuing struggle with the dragon of scarcity. I will eat pizza pie with any toppings, from green peppers and pineapple, to double cheese and anchovies, to the works. At times, I have been compulsive about pizza. It began when I was eight years old and my bedtime was 9 p.m. Occasionally, my older bothers and sisters, mother and father would have pizza delivered to the house at 10 p.m. to eat while they watched television, a new technology in the early 1950s. When I had breakfast in the kitchen the next morning, I would see the empty pizza boxes near the garbage can. I felt left out. I was angry that I did not get my share. No one thought of me. Those mornings were the birth of my scarcity attitude toward pizza.

My compulsion may seem amusing, but I have to admit it is not possible for me to eat just one piece. One Saturday night, my family took me to an Italian restaurant for dinner. I ordered a large pizza and devoured the entire pie by myself, all eight pieces. I was sick for hours and could not unbuckle my belt. As a teenager, four friends and I saved money for a pizza binge. In competition to see who could eat the most, we gorged ourselves on pizza until we just could not stuff down another bite. In two hours, the five of us consumed eight pizzas. Since I ate more pizza than my four friends, I did not have to pay a share of the bill (a large pizza was $1.25 then). Even today when we serve pizza at an employee meeting, I eat four or five pieces when most people have two or three.

I am abundant in most areas, but I have an attitude of scarcity about pizza. I have to get mine before others get theirs. That attitude does not work well in my life, since pizza contributes to my widening waist line. And I feel guilty about eating it, even though I know there is plenty of pizza in the world. Just knowing that pizza is a trigger for my scarcity thoughts has helped me tame the pizza dragon. Is there a similar dragon in your life that stimulates an attitude of scarcity?

Fishing Limits

An attitude of abundance will drive us to want more so we can share it with others. On the other hand, it might be the scarcity dragon pushing us incessantly to get more.

A friend invited me go fishing for striped bass in his boat on the Chesapeake Bay. He explained that the limit was six fish per person, and each fish had to be more than twenty inches long. We had a great day on the water, and the bass were plentiful. The twenty-inch "keeper" criteria was not a problem. We threw back any fish that was even close to twenty inches, being careful not to damage their mouths as we removed the hook. After several enjoyable hours, we reached our limit of twelve fish. He caught more than I did, but that was expected since I am an inexperienced fisherman.

We moved to another area of the bay, and trolled for bluefish, which had no catch limits. Near the end of the afternoon, my friend had a violent strike on his line. He carefully brought the fish from the bottom to the boat. Keenly aware that I did not want to be the cause of losing this trophy fish, I was careful in bringing the fish aboard with the gaff net. It was a forty-one-inch striped bass, our thirteenth of the day. After the fish was stored in the ice chest with the other twelve, my friend seemed to be uncomfortable. He wanted to keep the fish, but knew it was over the limit. I was troubled about keeping the thirteenth fish, but I saw how proud he was of the trophy bass. He kept the fish, and nothing more has ever been said about the incident.

That trophy bass reminds me of the dragons of desire and excess that push me to get more for myself. The "more" dragon is insatiable. It never has enough. It always want more and bigger. Simultaneously, that wonderful day on the bay is a reminder to be grateful in an attitude of abundance for what I have achieved, the people who help me, and the people I am able to help. I must remind myself frequently to be clear that the reason to expand my success is to help others. There is no limit on success when our motivation is to assist others. My goal is to be successful by helping others become successful.

Giving Just a Little

Amazing results are achieved in our communities and our world when we each give a little bit in an attitude of abundance.

An employee in my company was diagnosed with lymphoma, a cancer that had spread throughout his body. In his mid-forties, he was married with two sons. Massive chemotherapy was his main treatment program. Early in the treatments, he came to work in the morning and got his treatment in the afternoon. He was tired the next day, but was committed to delivering a good day's work. As the treatments became more intense and his strength wore down, he took off the day after each treatment. Finally, the treatments became too much. No longer able to work, he submitted a claim for long-term disability insurance. Our insurance carrier rejected the claim as a prior existing condition. The insurance company from his previous employer disallowed the claim as a new condition.

His coworkers, learning of the situation, decided to contribute an hour each month from their annual leave to cover his absences. They enrolled others, including me, to contribute. Soon the contributions equaled his monthly pay. During the entire disability period, he and his family received a full paycheck twice every month because of our employees' attitude of abundance. Unfortunately, he survived for only six months. Many employees attended the funeral to honor their coworker, and support his widow in her time of sadness. The funeral service was touching. The widow and children were surrounded by loving family and friends.

The coworkers felt good about their giving. They were reassured knowing, that if they got sick, they too would be supported. The small contribution each individual made, one hour of leave per month, was minor. The importance of the combined contributions to the family was priceless. Opportunities for us to make similar contributions are plentiful in our families and our communities. The dragon of scarcity deceives us into believing that small contributions make no difference. The reality is, when we all make a small contribution in an attitude of abundance, the combined results literally change the world.

Closing Thoughts on Living in Abundance

To attract abundance, be abundant. An attitude of abundance will draw people to you who are abundant and together you will share abundance.

The table below identifies results that an attitude of abundance and an attitude of scarcity toward love, time, resources and opportunity create inside ourselves, our families, our careers, and our world. If we say we want the things in the abundance column, why do we give in so easily to the scarcity dragon? In our rapidly changing world, proof is everywhere to justify an attitude of scarcity or an attitude of abundance. TV shows, newspapers and movies tell sad stories of crime, conflict and deceit that seem to prove that love, opportunity, resources and time are scarce. However, the same sources report teamwork, sharing and human triumphs that confirm the power of abundant thinking.

		An Attitude of Abundance Creates	An Attitude of Scarcity Creates
Love	In Ourselves	Gratitude & Celebration	Apathy & Loneliness
	In Our Families	Compassion & Respect	Separation & Anger
	In Our Careers	Cooperation & Teamwork	Conflict & Envy
	In Our World	Harmony & Empathy	Bigotry & Hatred
Time	In Ourselves	Patience & Calmness	Pressure & Stress
	In Our Families	Kindness & Understanding	Broken Commitments
	In Our Careers	Agreement & Consensus	Stress & Frustration
	In Our World	Acceptance & Appreciation	Prejudice & Ignorance
Resources	In Ourselves	Generosity & Sharing	Isolation & Greed
	In Our Families	Plenty & Giving	Hoarding & Anxiety
	In Our Careers	Risk-taking & Affluence	Cut-throat Competition
	In Our World	Peace & Resourcefulness	Crime & War
Opportunity	In Ourselves	Confidence & Imagination	Fear of Failure
	In Our Families	Synergy & Trust	Jealousy & Selfishness
	In Our Careers	Teamwork & Creativity	Rivalries & Bankruptcy
	In Our World	Global Prosperity	Haves & Have Nots

An attitude of abundance creates everything we say we want, while an attitude of scarcity produces what we say we do not want.

Which do you believe? Which do you want? An attitude of abundance nurtures creativity, enhances success, and provides peace in our lives:

• ***Abundance of Love.*** Knowing there is enough love for everyone helps us accept others with understanding and empathy. Those who are close to us feel our acceptance and, in return, accept us as we are. An attitude of love abundance actually creates love and acceptance in our lives.

• ***Abundance of Time.*** Believing that we have time to complete all of the important things produces calmness and serenity. People sense the calm, and tasks are completed efficiently and correctly the first time. An attitude of time abundance actually creates more time in our lives.

• ***Abundance of Resources.*** Even if we find happiness in satisfying our greed, lust or hunger, the happiness lasts a fleeting moment before we need more. When people resist our efforts to get more, conflicts arise. On the other hand, helping others leaves us satisfied and encourages people to share their resources with us. An attitude of resource abundance actually brings abundant resources into our lives.

• ***Abundance of Opportunity.*** When our goal is to grab power or possessions, we feel inferior around people with bigger opportunities, higher positions or more power; and superior around people who have less. Opportunity depends on who we are with. An attitude of abundance enables us to live with consistent values from day to day. An attitude of abundant opportunity actually creates new opportunities in our lives.

An attitude of abundance not only affects today, it determines the happiness and success we will experience tomorrow. It might seem that with an attitude of abundance, we would not save for a rainy day. Actually, the opposite is more likely. Today's abundance carries into tomorrow. Surrendering to the dragon of scarcity today will cause scarcity tomorrow because we become afraid to take the risks necessary to produce future abundance. *Living in Abundance* is the foundation of our future happiness because, with that attitude today, we willingly and courageously stretch for tomorrow's happiness.

-----Essential Tip #3-----
Stretch to Tomorrow
~ Reaching Beyond Our Grasp

I always undertake that which I cannot do, in order that I may learn how to do it.
— Pablo Picasso

Struggling Butterflies

No matter where we are in any job,relationship or hobby, reaching the next level requires us to risk change.

Since my wife raises Painted Lady butterflies, our gardens have an array of host and nectar plants. Butterflies flutter from flower to flower on the nectar plants, and lay eggs on the host plants. Looking carefully, we find tiny larvae crawling on the host plants. My wife cuts branches from the host plants, and puts them in a see-through box. We watch the larvae break out of their cocoons and become young butterflies. One batch of larvae was unusual. Most broke free easily from their cocoons. But one larvae struggled. For hours it made no progress. In sympathy, we helped it break free from the cocoon with a toothpick. It appeared to be healthy, but the next morning it was dead. We later learned that butterflies break from the cocoon by stretching their wings to become strong enough to fly. Some need to struggle more than others. Like butterflies, we grow through our struggles too.

As the world around us and the people in it change, the dragons of doubt coax us to stay in our comfort zone. They convince us to avoid change by exaggerating the risks. But there is little lasting happiness and no real success in the comfort zone. Success and happiness lie in stretching today for what we want tomorrow. Not entirely for a better tomorrow, but because stretching produces joy and self-esteem today. We each have an image of how we are. Mostly we are content with what we have, but want more. For some, happiness may be wealth or power, for others travel or excitement, for still others health or peace.

One effective way to create the future is to listen to the feelings we have today. Feel the security or fear, joy or frustration, satisfaction or restlessness. Those feelings tell us *where we are* versus *where we want to be.* They tell us *what to change* and *how urgently it must be changed.* Feelings carry us through a five-step growth cycle:

• ***Step #1 - Contentment.*** “Things are great! Don’t change a thing. I want more of this.” Feeling this way, we take no new actions and what we have today is approximately what we will have tomorrow.

• ***Step #2 - This Isn't Enough.*** "This is disappointing (or frustrating, or boring). I don't know how to change, but I know I don't like what I have." Feeling this way, we may change, but we are not quite ready yet.

• ***Step #3 - Fear of Change.*** "Things must change! But what will work? One possibility is too hard, another takes too long, and a third costs too much. What if change doesn't work?" Frozen in doubt, steps #2 and #3 are repeated until our willingness to risk exceeds our fear of change.

• ***Step #4 - Willing to Risk.*** "Okay, I'll give it a try. I've got to take a risk even if I don't know which choice is best. I'll stretch past the doubts and fears." With this attitude, the changes we consider are stimulating and exciting, but rarely are the ideas risky at the life-threatening level.

• ***Step #5 - Growth.*** We try something new and our first result is: "That didn't work. Things are better, but not what I want. I'll get help, and try again." The second try improves things. We see possibilities we did not see before. We feel the growth. The third try is better still. It is working! We keep working, and finally get it right.

• ***Step #1 - At the Next Level.*** Then we say: "Things are great! Don't change a thing. I want more of this." Feeling this way, we will take no new actions and the new something we have today is about what we will have tomorrow. We are back at step #1, and the stretch cycle begins again.

Usually, multiple stretch cycles are happening in our careers and family lives concurrently. Moving to the next level is not having no doubts or fears. Rather it is using doubts and fears to our benefit. Acknowledge them, embrace them, even enjoy them. Doubts and fears are signs that we are stretching to a new level. Is it time for us to risk reading these vignettes about stretching. It is a small risk. Or is it? The following vignettes explore the five steps in the stretch cycle.

Farewell to Security

Stretching may seem like a dragon, but stretching has given us the only real happiness and growth we have ever known.

To get to where you are today, you have stretched through many changes. I have too. At three years old, I abandoned the comfort of my biological mother to leap into the loneliness of an orphanage, and the uncertainty of adoption into a new family. I did not choose that stretch, but the experience gave me a deep determination to take care of myself. At six, I left home to risk a strange new place called school with boys and girls I did not know. I learned reading and writing, and how to make friends. At fourteen, I ventured from familiar friends in middle school to the intimidating atmosphere of a multi-racial 4,000-student high school with seniors who drove cars. The result was meeting my wife, more learning, and preparing for big risks.

At eighteen, my father told me to stop dating the girl who would later become my wife or leave the house. I moved out to demonstrate my independence. Ready or not, I have been responsible for myself ever since then. At nineteen, I left my hometown to go away to college and live in a fraternity house where no one told me what to do. I made mistakes, and I experienced tremendous individual growth. At twenty-one, I gave away the freedom and independence of being single to get married and become the father of two beautiful daughters. I stretched to find the joy of sharing life's dreams and challenges with another person, and began learning lessons of unconditional love.

At twenty-four, three years after my college contemporaries had graduated, I left the comfortable academic surroundings of graduate school to become a naval officer and go to sea on ships. I gained practical engineering skills, leadership abilities, and valuable professional contacts. At thirty-two, I resigned as a naval officer, leaving the security of wearing a uniform every day to face the uncertainty and results-or-else pressure of the business world. My reward was in-depth management experience, a wide network of business contacts, and financial growth. At forty, I abandoned the financial stability of working for a large, stable company to ride the thrilling roller-coaster of self-employment. Two years later I accepted responsibility for the job security and benefits of employees. I gained the opportunity to make a difference in the world and build financial assets. At fifty-nine, I am relinquishing my knowledge of computers and business to write stories about happiness and success. Beyond the pleasure of clarifying my beliefs, I am not sure what the result will be. Time will tell.

The most significant advances you and I have ever experienced in our lives have followed exciting stretches. Some we chose, and others were forced upon us. In fact, given a choice, in several cases I would have chosen almost any path besides the stretches that I was forced by others to take.

Without a doubt, however, stretching through each new change took me to a new level, a more stimulating and satisfying level of living than I knew before I stretched. Several stretches still lie ahead for me. I can feel the dragons of doubt and fear raise their menacing heads as I think about my new stretches. Two of biggest stretches are retirement and leaving the safety of living to brave the ominous and mystical uncertainty of death.

Every minute of our lives is a choice between stretching for a new level of satisfaction, or accepting safety in the comfort zone of what we already know and already have. The choice that takes us to new levels of freedom, security and happiness (if that is what we want) is a stretch that leaves safety and security far behind. One of the most meaningful freedoms we can give ourselves is the freedom to fail.

Screaming Apathy

The same job, same hometown, same hobbies can be too comfortable for too long. Avoid the sad lament: "Someday I will..." by stretching today!

A song by Alabama tells a story of an old man in a rocking chair who says: "Someday I'm goin' to climb dat der mountain!" To me it is a sad song about a man who wanted to risk something new, but resisted stretching to do it. Unless he left the chair and stretched with every ounce of strength and courage to climb "dat der mountain," he may die wishing and wanting. Could he reach the top of the mountain? Maybe, maybe not. But reaching the top is less important than the climb.

The comfort dragon tells us what we have today is good enough. We should be happy with it, and not try for more. The dragon tells us to stay where it is safe, and do exactly what is expected. But doing the expected all the time is dull. What would life be like if we did what everyone wanted us to do for our entire lives? Go to school, graduate and get a job because that is what our parents expect. Get married, have children, and be a good partner because that is what our spouse expects. Teach the kids skills and manners, help them in school, and be a safety net because that is what they expect. Be dedicated and efficient in our jobs, contribute to our communities and favorite charities, vote in elections, be loving grandparents, and eventually retire and die because that is what society expects.

After doing everything that everyone expected every day, I would die of *screaming apathy!* Why? Because I never really lived. I never really chose my life. I never stretched for something that was uniquely me. I never reached the top because I was never willing to walk near the edge where I might fall off. I would never taste sweet success because I would never have risked bitter, crushing failure.

By stretching for a dream, by going all out when people say we are crazy, by persisting when everything and everyone tells us to quit, we escape *screaming apathy.* We tame the comfort dragon when we stretch to reach what seems beyond our grasp, what lies outside our comfort zone.

Winning the Lottery

It would be wonderful if wishing made things happen. Unfortunately, wishing is not enough, stretching is required to achieve the goals we set.

The wishing dragon makes the lottery look like the answer to all of our problems. You may want to win the lottery, but you cannot win unless you buy a ticket. Many people do not buy lottery tickets because of the outrageous odds, which are *135 million* to one in the Virginia "Big Game" where I occasionally buy tickets. I certainly do not suggest that you rush to buy hundreds of lottery tickets. Rather, consider that when we wish for things in a fairytale way (like winning a big lottery), they cannot come true. We must stretch to buy a winning ticket. Consider the following lotteries which most of us say we want to win:

• ***Rewarding Careers Lottery.*** We want careers that yield high pay and self-fulfillment. Tickets in the Rewarding Careers Lottery are new skills, education, and being team players. The odds are 20-to-1 against earning over $100,000/year (about five percent of the population earn over $100,000 per year according to the IRS). Even so, buying tickets in the Rewarding Careers Lottery has more favorable odds than any state lottery.

• ***Healthy Body Lottery.*** We want healthy bodies and a long, vigorous life. Tickets in the Healthy Body Lottery are healthy eating, exercise, adequate sleep, and avoiding tobacco and drugs. Odds in this lottery are 2-to-1 if a healthy body is measured by living past age seventy-eight, the average life span for American men (eighty-one for women). The odds are 4-to-1 (my guess) if a healthy body is being vibrant and energetic into our seventies and eighties. Clearly, odds in the Healthy Body Lottery also are much better than any state lottery.

• ***Happy Marriage Lottery.*** Those of us who are married will say that we want a happy marriage. Happy Marriage Lottery tickets (from a male view) are flowers, compassion, listening and thoughtfulness (partial list) toward our spouse. The odds in this lottery are about 6-to-1. Over half of all marriages end in divorce, and many of the remaining marriages are unhappy. I guessed at the numbers. But certainly the odds in the Happy Marriage Lottery improve when we buy tickets regularly.

• ***Loving Family Lottery.*** We want loving families. Loving Family Lottery tickets are acceptance, giving, understanding, and reaching to help (partial list) family members. The odds are higher than the Happy Marriages Lottery (say 10-to-1) since some marriages may not produce a loving family, and very few broken marriages can produce a loving family. Still, the odds in the Loving Family Lottery are more favorable than any weekly Lotto.

Our everyday thoughts and actions buy tickets in the lotteries of life. Are we buying "caring tickets" in the Happy Marriage Lottery, or "sexual affair tickets" in the divorce lottery? Are we buying "exercise tickets" in the Healthy Body Lottery, or "high-fat donut tickets" in the heart attacks lottery?

Buying tickets in the important lotteries of life is a stretch. It is hard to do these things, and the rewards are not immediate. But the stretches eventually produce awesome prizes. We can have almost anything we wish for, but fulfilling the wish requires stretching. Not by wishing the goals were simpler, but by stretching to reach them. Not by wishing for no changes in our lives, but by developing the skill to deal with continuous change. Not by associating exclusively with "good time" friends, but by sharing encouragement and support with friends who have high expectations and a commitment to career and family goals that is consistent with our goals.

If we are not buying tickets in the most important lotteries of our lives, then why are we surprised when we do not win the grand prizes?

Life Is a Candy Counter

So many possibilities, so many choices. But each choice requires that we stretch to grasp the new "candy bar."

Each afternoon, a small boy went to the candy store, gave the owner a quarter, and asked for the same candy bar he bought yesterday. When he grew tall enough to see over the counter, he was shocked by the variety of candy bars he could have selected. Our lives are like the boy at the candy counter. Eating the same candy bar is comfortable, but it may produce boredom, monotony and depression in our lives.

Life has so much variety, so many choices. It is unfortunate to miss any of the adventures because the dragons of comfort and fear stop us from tasting new experiences. How much do we miss by saying *NO* to things we have never done because we have never done them, we do not know how, or we are afraid to try? If not today, when will we stretch to make new choices? Maybe the real questions should be: *Which new candy bar will I choose today? And which one tomorrow*?

As you consider selections on the candy counter of life, imagine how each choice will taste. Your mouth may water if you like the imagined flavor. But you will never know until you taste it. So pay the money and take the candy bar. Take the chance. Occasionally, the nuts and caramel will be exactly what you want, and sometimes you will not like the flavor. In any case, you will no longer be guessing about the flavor of the candy bar. You know how it tastes.

I had a "candy counter" experience with wine. For years, I drank inexpensive wine, and made a random choice when the waiter brought the wine list in a restaurant. Red wines with meat and white wines with poultry and fish was all I knew. Even that was wrong. Then my wife and I took a wine-tasting course. Now I know what I like and do not like, and why. Having clear criteria for picking a wine has extended the fun of dining out. To create joyous tomorrows, stretch to try something new today, even if the something new may not taste good the first time.

My First Dives

Fear and fumbling accompany any new adventure. Expect them. Laugh about them. As we practice, fear and fumbling disappear.

I recently enjoyed my 200th scuba dive on a Caribbean vacation. Despite four-foot seas, my entry into the water and return to the boat were smooth, and I relaxed while exploring coral reefs and the wreck of a freighter. My first dives were quite different. Classroom lectures and an eighteen-foot-deep pool did not prepare me for diving in a quarry on a cold December morning. Nervously, I was putting on equipment for my first dive when the instructor told me that my air regulator was backwards. Embarrassed, I removed and reversed the regulator. I never made that mistake again. Shivering in the twenty-five-degree temperature even in a wetsuit, I waited on the dock for my turn to enter the water. When it came, I waddled to the edge in my fins, slipped on the ice, and fell helplessly into the water. As I began to perform the qualification exercises with the instructor, I was scared and breathed rapidly. Thirty minutes later, not finished with the exercises, I ran out of air and aborted the dive.

My second dive was a little better. Careful to avoid the ice, I jumped in the water with perfect form. But my tank was not fastened properly, and it came off. But I did not run out of air that dive. The next day on my third dive, I was about to enter the water when my dive buddy noticed that I had forgotten my weight belt. Most divers take a career to make the mistakes I made in my first three dives.

My diving experiences are typical of anything new. The first dive I was afraid, the second apprehensive, and the third just uncomfortable. The dragons of fear and embarrassment were with me on each dive, but I tamed my response to them. You may have had similar experiences. Remember learning to drive? Excitement helped you through the fear and embarrassment. The emotions you feel today when you drive are very different. Some people never overcome those fears and never learn to drive. The unique emotional dragons you have conquered (or not) during new experiences is what makes you *you*. The stretches you make (or do not make) today determine who you will be tomorrow.

No Quick Fixes

Even sudden good fortune is not enough to permanently change our lives. Only stretching will lift us to lasting joy and success.

The lottery in my home state recently passed its twentieth anniversary. Since the multimillion-dollar grand prize is paid incrementally over twenty years, the first winners have received all the money they will ever get from winning the lottery. Winners from the first year were interviewed and asked how, after twenty years, winning the lottery affected their lives. About half said, on balance, winning the lottery had been a negative event in their lives. Several were bankrupt. Most winners reported uncomfortable notoriety, frequent solicitations, and constant pressure to buy goods and services after their "good fortune" was announced. One man said winning the lottery was the worst thing that ever happened to him. It was a fire-breathing dragon that scorched his entire life. After twenty years of annual lottery payments, he was divorced and penniless. His professional contacts and skills had atrophied because he thought he would never have to work again. People expected him to give them jobs, not the other way around.

There are no shortcuts to the things we really want, no quick fixes for the fundamental challenges in our lives. Personal growth, physical fitness, loving families, and economic stability do not come easily. They are built through thoughtful and consistent stretching. Consider my study habits in college as an example. Sports, bridge and horse races were more fun than studying. So I compensated for lack of study during the semester with all-night study binges before finals. Usually I did well. But today I remember little from those courses. All-nighters worked if success was good grades, but quick-fix studying was useless if learning was the standard for success. Similarly, financial gains obtained with little effort generally provide only brief satisfaction. It seems that earning money is as rewarding as having money. Earning the money produces self-esteem. Stretching is its own sweet reward. When we successfully grab the golden ring that we stretched waaaaaay out to reach, the ring and the pleasurable memory of stretching are satisfying for a long, long time.

The Balance Beam

Great success requires us to conquer fear over and over again, learning from each try.

The women gymnasts in last summer's Olympics were inspiring, especially their performances on the balance beam. They twisted, jumped and somersaulted with abandon, seemingly with no fear of being hurt. Those young women had practiced gymnastics most of their lives. Every one of them had fallen off the beam many times. The commentators told how one gymnast injured her back in a fall, and another hit her head on the beam. They recovered physically and mentally to compete in the Olympics, and perform like nothing had ever happened. Some gymnasts won gold, silver or bronze medals. Most finished with no medal, and a few fell off the beam at the Olympics too. But they all survived. The dismounts were especially exciting because so many of them lost points by missing the landing after a double flip with a full twist. From my comfortable seat on the couch, I wondered why they did not do just a single flip, or eliminate the twist to guarantee a perfect landing every time.

Life is like the balance beam and we are Olympic gymnasts. The margin between mediocrity and success is stretching to tame the fear of failure. Success does not know how many times we have failed, or how afraid we may be about failing again. Success insists that we give 100 percent every time we are on the beam. Yes, success hangs on every step and we could fall at any time. But even if we did, we still would feel the excitement and joy of full-out competition.

Whenever we risk change in our lives, we move away from the center of the beam and feel out of balance. Is it bad to be out of balance? No, but it is uncomfortable. We naturally are afraid of being out of balance and want to get back to our comfort zone. Would we risk the equivalent of a double flip with a twist in our careers or our family life? Maybe we should. Maybe that is what will be required to win the gold medal for personal happiness and career success. Living close to the center of life's balance beam without stretching for out-of-balance experiences limits the medals we will win.

What a Fluke

There are no coincidences, good luck, or bad luck. Rather we stretch (or not) and put ourselves in situations where the results we want are possible (or not).

On my fifteenth birthday, my dad and I went fishing in our eighteen-foot runabout near Jones Beach Inlet on Long Island. My birthday is in late June so it was a warm, sunny afternoon. I wore a bathing suit and took my shirt off to get a suntan. My feet dangled in the water over the side of the boat as I fished and enjoyed the day. On the other hand, my dad fished intensely. He lifted his pole every few seconds to see if a fish was nibbling. Suddenly, my tackle appeared to catch on the bottom, and I almost lost the fishing pole overboard. When the pole began moving back and forth, it was clear however that I had caught a big fish. My dad, worried that I would lose the fish by bringing it up too quickly, yelled: "Don't horse it! Don't horse it! You've got a big one!" But there was no danger of losing this fish. My calm fishing style had allowed the fish to swallow the bait "hook, line and sinker." The fish was hooked in its belly, not its mouth. It was a fifteen-pound, six-ounce fluke, the second largest caught that year in the local fishing contest. The fluke was too large for the gaffing net, so we lifted it into the boat with the oars. Then we put the oars, gas can and tackle box on the fish to hold it on the bottom of the boat.

Why was it me who caught the fish? How could I land it despite being an inexperienced fisherman who essentially was asleep? My dad said it was just plain luck. I would like to believe it was how I fished. While I stretched to enjoy the sunshine, the fish struck the line. I did not move the pole every few seconds, but left the bait for the big fish to swallow. I chose to be there that day fishing in that manner, and my choices produced a big fluke. Sometimes high-probability events happen, and other times low-probability events happen. But everything that happens, happens because we consciously or unconsciously put ourselves in position to achieve our goals, or to miss them.

The Dragons That Hold Us Back

Tame the dragons of self-doubt and you will achieve high levels of career success and personal happiness.

Imagine what these six beliefs might produce in a person's life:

- Belief #1: I don't have enough contacts to start a business.
- Belief #2: I can't speak in public, nobody will listen to me.
- Belief #3: Marriages can't last forever because people change.
- Belief #4: Success isn't easy. W must work hard to reach goals.
- Belief #5: If it's worth doing at all, it's worth doing perfectly.
- Belief #6: I can't change the mistrust and poverty in the world.

These beliefs were dragons that stood between me and the changes that I needed to make to achieve my biggest goals. At one time or another, I believed each one of them. I still believe some today. I thought *that's the way I am* or *that's how the world is* until an unusual event changed my belief.

Belief #1 stopped me from starting my own business for a long time, until the bureaucracy of a big company became boring. That boredom, coupled with another belief—*It's better to try and fail, than not to try at all*—propelled me past my fear. Scratch #1 from the list. Belief #2 caused me to avoid public speaking whenever possible. Until one day, forced to speak in public on many occasions, I began to enjoy the exhilaration watching large groups listen to me. Scratch #2. Belief #3 was a barrier to enjoying a close partnership with my wife. I clung to my marriage because I was afraid to be alone. I was afraid that our relationship could not last because we are so different. Until, separated for a year, I realized that differences were the strength of our marriage. The very traits that annoyed me about my wife were the same things that I loved. Scratch #3. I am still trying to eliminate the other beliefs.

It is likely that you have a similar list of self-limiting beliefs. What are they? Write them down. Such beliefs, when written on paper, lose their mysterious hold. It is incredibly powerful to acknowledge self-limiting life views and begin to eliminate them from our thoughts, relationships and actions. All it takes is a stretch to tame the dragon of limiting beliefs.

Jump Right In

When the dragon of fear roars, ask yourself if it is real or is it imagined. Imagined fear is like being afraid of the bogeyman. Stretch right through him.

As a young boy, I was afraid that a bogeyman (I never heard anything about bogeywoman) would jump from the dark and grab me, even though I had never seen a bogeyman. Since then, I have learned the best response to a bogeyman fear is to ignore it, jump right in, and enjoy the excitement. When I was eight, my family moved to a waterfront home on Long Island. My dad and oldest brother had boats moored at the dock. But I was forbidden to go on my dock or the neighbors' docks since I could not swim. I was embarrassed because my friends played on their docks. They knew how to swim. Some took boats out to go fishing by themselves. Under severe peer pressure, I sometimes ignored the rules and got into trouble when I was caught on my friends' docks.

At nine, I learned to swim without a lesson. One summer day, I was cleaning our boats with my dad when he picked me up by the seat of my pants and threw me into the water, clothes and sneakers included. I have been able to swim ever since. My mom was furious at him for the risk he had taken. But what was the real risk? In the short term, there was a one-in-a-million chance (a bogeyman fear) that I might drown while my dad and brother watched from just ten feet away. In the long term, the risk was much higher that I would fall into the water when no one was around. Not knowing how to swim, I might easily have drowned. That was a real risk. Drowning seemed to be one of my adopted mom's greatest fears. However, it seems to me she mistook a bogeyman fear for real danger when my dad threw me into the water.

As an adult, I am no longer afraid of the bogeyman. However, I find that many of my fears are not based on facts and reality. They are the adult equivalent of being afraid of the bogeyman. If a bogeyman fear is holding you back, jump right in and swim with him.

Zest of the Moment

Joy and happiness lie just on the other side of your fears. Stretch through the fears to bring them into your life.

After three rounds of a member-guest golf tournament, my partner and I were tied for first. The first playoff hole was a 510-yard par five. All four of us were on the green in three strokes. I was fifteen feet from the pin, and the only one who got a handicap stroke on the hole. Our first opponent sank his putt for a birdie. So I was putting to win the tournament. Two hundred people around the green watched as I studied the putt. I was shaking, afraid to miss. What if I missed the putt so badly that I could not make the next putt to tie? Evan as my dragons tried to frighten me, my mind shifted to: *This is a super experience. Make it or miss, a fabulous moment.* The zest of the moment was exhilarating as I putted and watched the ball drop in the hole. Thirty years later, I treasure the zest of that moment more than the victory.

Tee shirts that say *NO FEAR* are misleading. Fear is unavoidable. How we handle the dragon of fear determines how much of life's joys we will experience. Is it possible for fear to be enjoyable? Could it be an asset? Like other emotions, fear is a subconscious message meant to help us. It warns us of physical danger or emotional pain. Fear causes us to stop and think about our actions because the outcome is unclear. Excitement is essentially the same physiological message. We look forward to an experience even though we are unsure of its outcome. Tame the dragon of fear by transforming it into excitement.

Examine each fear. Is it real or a bogeyman (imagined) fear? My fear of putting was clearly a bogeyman fear. There were no lasting adverse consequences of a missed putt. The joy of making a clutch putt far exceeded the disappointment of missing it. However, driving on a highway while a car passes going ninety-five weaving in and out of traffic is a real fear. Imminent danger is present, and defensive action is required for survival. To tame the dragon of fear, embrace your fears. Tune into the intense fears that bubble up whenever you face change. Are they are real or bogeyman fears? If they are bogeyman fears, change them into excitement and stretch to enjoy the zest of the moment.

Taking a Risk

Success begins with small stretches consistently and carefully practiced. Little stretches before big ones.

My efforts to learn country-western dancing have pleased my wife, and dancing together is fun. However, I am afraid that I will embarrass myself because I do not know the steps, and I have a poor sense of rhythm. When I probe this dragon, I find it is clearly another bogeyman fear. Dancing mistakes do not produce real physical or emotional danger. So I gallantly transform the fear into excitement, stretch onto the floor, and do the best Two-Step, Waltz, Watermelon Slide or Mambo Shuffle that I can. Turning fear into excitement does not magically produce the coordination or rhythm I need to dance, but a huge breakthrough has occurred:

#1 - I have acknowledged I do not know and am willing to learn
#2 - I have chosen to risk something I have never done before
#3 - I have taken action to learn things I do not know, and
#4 - As I persevere through mistakes, eventually I will *KNOW*.

My Two-Step sometimes has three counts, and I only know a few spins and turns. Sometimes I move left when everyone else moves right in the Mambo Shuffle. But I will not quit. My wife and I go to a group lesson once a week, and open dancing on Saturday night. I am getting better. Even I can see the progress. The dancing blunders I make today are at a more advanced level than the blunders I made six short months ago. I even lead assertively (sometimes), and build new sequences from the Two-Step moves that I learned individually.

Each day of the twenty-first century will challenge us to learn something new. Learning is an incremental process that takes longer than we expect. Each new "knowing" is just the point-of-departure for the next learning adventure. The key to moving to the next level of family, professional and spiritual success is the four steps above: acknowledge that you do not know, embrace the fear and risk a new start, take the actions ro learn, and work through the inevitable difficulties that a first attempt at anything new always produces.

Nothing Is Important

Nothing *is a powerful action in many circumstances.*
The patience to do nothing *is a big stretch for many of us.*

Whatever the problem, *nothing* might be the answer. The answer may not be to do *something*. Many of us seek security in prestigious positions and material possessions, when *nothing* might provide the security we want. *Nothing* separates the earth from the sun. It protects us from being fried by the sun's million-degree temperatures. *Nothing* is why horror movies are so very popular. They are *something* exciting while we watch, and *nothing* when they are finished. Sometimes, the ultimate stretch may be to accept *nothing* as a solution. A dream is *nothing* in the current reality. But having a dream and stretching to reach it may be more rewarding than achieving the dream. A lottery ticket is usually *nothing.* When we purchase the lottery ticket, we are not buying a multimillion-dollar prize. Rather we are purchasing a daydream about what might be if the ticket was a winner.

Nothing is why I wrote this book after thinking about it for over a year. As I write this vignette, I do not know if this book will ever be published. And if it is published, would anyone buy it? Many people tell me: *"You can't write a best-seller!"* The dragon of skepticism has a picnic in my thoughts: (1) telling me that writing this book is wasting time, (2) tantalizing me with other things I might do with the hours, and (3) reciting hundreds of reasons why the book will never sell. Maybe the dragon is right. Odds favor its prediction, since about one in a hundred new authors get published. But other voices say: *Go for it!* Publishing this book is a dream even if it turns out to be *nothing*. Even if the book is never published (*nothing*), I had the awesome experience of writing it, of thinking these thoughts. Yielding to the *It won't work* message of the skepticism dragon would be depressing. Even when such doubts are accurate, they produce depression and despair. Those doubts destroy our happiness in the moment, and jeopardize the possibility of future success. *Nothing* is important! Even if our biggest dream does not come true, pursuing it brings joy into our lives.

Manure Piles

Some day you may be lucky enough to have your worst fears come true. It probably will not be as disastrous as you feared. Laugh at the experience.

Anytime we stretch to try something new, we risk landing in life's manure piles. As a teenager, I attended a boarding school in upstate New York, and worked on a dairy farm to help pay the tuition. I had never seen a cow up close until my first day on the farm. Grumbling after a 4 a.m. wake-up call, I went to the barn for the morning milking. First, we herded the cows from the fields into the barn. A fascinating experience, since cows are a blend of stubborn and docile. When the cows were in the stalls ready to be milked, as the newest member of the crew my job was to clean the gutters. There was a special shovel for the job, twelve inches wide with two-inch sides. It fit perfectly into the gutter under the rear ends of the cows. I shoveled manure and urine into a wheelbarrow, wheeled the sloppy mixture to the manure spreader by the barn door, and dumped the mess in the spreader. The ramp to the manure spreader was a ten-foot-long two-inch by twelve-inch wooden plank.

The fear dragon was with me that morning. These were new surroundings for me. I wanted to impress the old hands on the crew, and I was afraid of looking stupid. The third time up the ramp, the wheelbarrow slipped off the ramp, manure spilled on the ground, and I fell into it head first. The milking crew laughed for twenty minutes, confirming my worst fear. My clothes were ruined. Even after two showers, the stench was still on my body. Despite that horrible experience, I enjoyed working on the dairy farm. Nothing is sweeter than the rich flavor of warm milk fresh from a cow.

In the forty years since it happened, I have laughed many times about falling in that manure pile. The incident did not affect my choice not to be a dairy farmer. Most dairy farmers at one time or another have had similar experiences. There is a high probability that we will fall into the proverbial manure pile when we stretch to try anything new. The manure pile does not hurt, and falling can produce some of life's most precious moments and valuable lessons.

11 Hours to 22 Minutes

Fighting the resistance dragon is a frustrating battle. Embrace him instead, and you will enjoy the major challenges in your life!

One summer I spent four weeks at a camp. The group had ten troops with twelve boys in a troop. Each day, each troop was assigned a chore like cleaning the latrines, policing the grounds, washing dishes or building a campfire. Washing dishes was the most onerous chore, more disliked than cleaning latrines. The resistance dragon struck our troop the first time we were assigned the chore. The inspector rejected tray after tray of dishes. We washed some of them four times. After three painful hours, we finally finished the breakfast dishes about 11 a.m.

Our troop ate lunch grumbling about the morning and dreading the afternoon. We washed the lunch dishes with even less passion and took about three and a half hours. The dinner dishes took another three and a half hours. We missed the campfire and went to sleep whining about a horrible day: eleven hours spent washing dishes. Our performance was notorious. No other troop had taken as long as we had.

The next morning at breakfast our troop leader suggested that we volunteer to wash dishes again. He agreed the chore had been painful, and said we could do better. We did not believe him. After considerable persuasion, we agreed to the stretch and were assigned the dishwashing chore. Everyone in the camp giggled. When breakfast was over, the troop leader organized us into teams and planned tasks for each team. With better teamwork and a positive attitude, we finished in an hour. Next day we were recognized as the honor troop, and were exempt from chores. Each time we were assigned the dishwashing chore, we became more efficient. By the end of three weeks we had moved from notorious to legendary: we washed the dishes in twenty-two minutes. After lunch one day, the other troops lined the walls of the mess hall to watch us. We were spectacular as a team, having transformed the pain of resistance into the joy of accomplishment. It started with just a small stretch to do a chore we hated. By taming the dragon of resistance, teamwork and practice produced fun and success.

His Sweat, My Chills

Great performances in theater, sports and business are 100% stretch with no energy expended on thoughts of yesterday's performances no matter how good or bad they were.

My wife and I waited fourteen months for Saturday night front-row seats to see *Phantom of the Opera* on Broadway in New York City. When the night of the performance arrived, we took our front-row seats looking up at the theater stage. Our anticipation and excitement were so thick you could cut them with a knife. In the scene where Christine strips the Phantom's mask, Sarah Brightman and Michael Crawford stood just fifteen feet from our seats. Sweat ran down Mr. Crawford's face, chills when up my spine. Even though they had performed that scene thousands of times before, their dedication and passion shined through. It appeared as if they stretched to give 100 percent in every performance, no matter how big or small the crowd.

When asked how life is going, too often we respond "I'm hangin' in there." The response is a bit sad because the zest of life is more than just "hangin' in there." The zest is going 100 percent, and letting "it all hang out!" Taming the dragons of hesitation, doubt, second guesses, and any remembrances of past failures and past successes.

Does intellect set us free from the dragons, or is it emotion? Maybe both. Too much of either can be a barrier to going 100 percent. Unbridled passion is exciting, but emotions may obscure the goal. Seeing the goal clearly and knowing how to achieve it produces confidence. On the other hand, excessive analysis of alternatives paralyzes us, and inhibits the actions required to reach the next level. The conflict is like a high-performance car racing with the brakes on. The brakes are smoking. The gas mileage is terrible. And the results are poor. Whatever we choose to do, joy and success lie in stretching without fear or reservation. Going 100 percent enables us to enjoy life's exciting roller coaster ride every minute of every day. It enables the legendary performances each of us is capable of producing.

Just 108 Feet

If you listen to them, critics will become dragons that stop you from stretching to reach highest levels of happiness and success.

Orville and Wilbur Wright's first flight in the fall of 1903. For more than a decade, they had worked in a Dayton, Ohio, bicycle shop to design a heavier-than-air flying machine. Each fall they traveled by train and boat to Kitty Hawk, North Carolina, to test the latest flying machine in the sand dunes. Their first *successful* flight lasted a minute and was just 108 feet long, less than the wingspan of a Boeing 747. Naysayers said things like:

> *"Who cares about contraptions that fly 108 feet and crash."*
> *"That toy won't amount to much even when it works."*
> *"Don't they know that we can never fly like the birds."*

Today, 100 years later, those "toys" fly around the world at the speed of sound, and carry passengers and cargo to places the naysayers never heard about. Alexander Graham Bell with the telephone and Thomas Edison with the light bulb probably heard similar criticisms. They could not have imagined the cellular phone networks and high-intensity lights that we have today any more than Orville and Wilbur could have imaged today's jet planes.

When people say that today's new technologies have this or that limitation, I think of Orville, Wilbur, Alex and Tom. The Internet is similar. In the early days, naysayers said it was a novelty for e-mail and advertising. They claimed it would never be much because of lack of bandwidth and security for important functions. But it is more fun to focus on the possibilities of what might be tomorrow rather than the limitations of today. The Internet may be the communications medium that enables peoples of the world, with varied culture and education, to exchange beliefs and knowledge in a way that lifts our world to a level of trust and cooperation that has never been achieved before. Look for ways to make it happen. In this abundant world, there are limitless opportunities if we stretch to find them, even though our early attempts may be limited and disappointing.

Closing Thoughts on Stretching For Tomorrow

To achieve all that is possible in your life, ask a question to which the answer probably will be NO, try something that may not work, and try again when it fails.

Last Saturday my twelve-year-old grandson skied on snow for the very first time at the beautiful Wintergreen Resort in Virginia. I took the first-time skiers' lesson with him since it had been nearly five years since the last time I had skied. At first he had difficulty latching his skis, but I was able to help him through that problem. He fell four times during the lesson and, like most new skiers, struggled to get up. He was frustrated by how hard it was to stand up after falling. When the lesson was over, we skied Potato Patch, the easiest of the green slopes at the resort. He fell nine times on the first run. We took nearly an hour to complete a 2,000-foot run that had a 200-foot drop. But he was open to more stretching.

After dinner, I watched his five-year-old brother while he insisted on one more ski run with his mom (my daughter). They returned to the lodge about 9:30 p.m. After several tries, he finally negotiated Potato Patch without falling, and moved on to the more difficult green slopes. After a few tries, he also skied those slopes without falling. He ended the night with several runs on blue slopes. My daughter told me that falling on blue-slope moguls had ended his eight-hour skiing marathon. Wow, I am impressed with my grandson's tenacity. He moved through several levels of frustration and skiing ability in a single day, and really wants to return to the slopes as soon as he can.

We cannot become what we want to be by staying like we are. Stretching is growing. As infants, we learned to walk by struggling to stand up. We held on to the furniture, wobbled a few steps, and fell down. Since at that age we did not know the dragons of frustration like my grandson, we got up and tried again. Eventually, we wobbled but did not fall. Then we did not even wobble. Soon we were running.

Learning is an essential step in growth. We obtain lasting happiness and satisfaction by stretching to achieve a goal. Boredom, frustration and an unwillingness to stretch, make instant gratification seem attractive. It is easier to stuff the *I don't like this* feeling with work, food, alcohol, drugs, gambling, sex and other obsessions than to acknowledge that something must change. But the price of overindulging in pleasing but destructive habits is high.

No matter how good, bad or boring today may be, there is little chance that tomorrow will be the same. Is it worth stretching today for something that may not happen tomorrow? Is tomorrow's possibility an adequate reward for enduring a stretch? For example, when I consider the minuscule possibility of this book being successful, I think about quitting. But to conclude that I am wasting my time would be placing a higher value on the result (publishing a book) than the effort itself (writing a book). Maybe the stretch itself is the reward.

I offer you this challenge: *stretch each day to do something that scares you and may shock others*. Whistle as you walk through your house. Shake hands with and smile at a stranger. Compliment people who sweep the floors at your work place.

Helen Keller said: "Life is a daring adventure or nothing at all." Her optimism and courage in face of her disabilities is an extraordinary example of our human ability to transcend limitations. Her courage stands as convincing testimony that each of us can achieve our goals by stretching to reach them. Small stretches to learn, and big stretches to achieve our biggest goals. The green slopes, then the blue. Eventually, like my grandson, we will be able to jump the moguls of life.

Part II

Our Relationships
Why Do It Alone?

We are separate beings, yet we play together
in the Universe like instruments in a symphony.

Outrunning the Bear

Since success and happiness depend on the quality of our relationships, it is worthwhile to invest in improving them.

Two campers woke up when a grizzly bear wandered into their campsite. One camper quickly put on his sneakers. The other said: "You can't outrun a bear." The first camper answered: "I don't have to outrun the bear. I just need to run faster than you." Too many of today's relationships seem like an effort to outrun our relationship partners, leaving us alone to wrestle with the changes that we all face. Why do we struggle alone when it would be so much easier to achieve success by working together, even when we are escaping the grizzly dragons of change?

In my relationships, my dragons interact with the dragons of my relationship partners. Similarly, your dragons interact with your partners' dragons. The interactions may be cooperative or competitive, helpful or hurtful, pleasant or confrontational, loving or intimidating. Some dragons that we think we see in others actually are reflections of our own dragons in our partners' lifestyles.

Everyone has a wide variety of relationships. We all have relationships with ourselves and our parents, and current and former friends. Almost all of us have relationships with siblings, a spouse, child(ren), relatives, co-workers and merchants. Some of us have relationships with multiple spouses (past, present and future), teammates and competitors in sports and business, and therapists.

We have relationships with people who are alive and dead, people who are close and far away. The relationships may be intimate, casual or ignored. But relationships are inescapable. Since relationships are so important to our happiness and we have so many of them, there is a huge return on any investment we make to improve them.

We can improve our relationships *no matter what* other people do by changing the only thing that we absolutely control: *ourselves*. For example, even though my biological and adopted mothers and fathers are dead, I will have a relationship with them in my memory as long as I live. The good news is that I can change that relationship at any time just by changing the way I remember them. I can remember the kind, loving things they did to nurture me, or I can remember the times when I felt mistreated. Similarly, we can cease trying to change our spouses, children, friends and others with whom we have a relationship. Instead, we could choose to be a fabulous marriage partner, a loving daughter or son, a caring parent, a loyal friend, and a helpful business associate. Hopefully, our spouses, parents, siblings, children, co-workers and friends will see our proactive example, and respond with similar behaviors. Whether they do or not, the surest way to improve our personal and professional relationships is to improve the contributions we make to those relationships.

Your most significant contribution to your relationships is not what you say and do. Rather it is who you are and the values you demonstrate in the relationship. If you conveniently change your values in an effort to be liked or to manipulate others, inevitably they will see through the thin veneer to your inner character. On the other hand, when the things you do and say are based on consistent values, they are likely to appreciate the benefit of having a relationship with you even if they do not share your values. They will recognize that you stand for something special; and when they want that something, they know they can find it in a relationship with you.

The following vignettes show how you can improve relationships by taming: (1) the independence dragon, a dragon who tempts you to go it alone; and (2) the manipulation dragon, a dragon who leads you to think that you can achieve your goals by changing others. These two dragons will breathe destructive fire on your closest and most precious relationships if you let them. The good news is that the dragons of independence and manipulation are easily tamed—if you really want to tame them.

College Reunions

Partners in effective relationships achieve mutual success by willingly giving help and gratefully accepting help.

Recently, I had lunch with a fraternity brother whom I have not seen in thirty-five years. Jokingly, I said I had not stayed in touch because I did not have his e-mail address. During lunch he told me about brothers he had seen at reunions. I was invited to those reunions, but never went. The *too much to do* dragon kept me from continuing my relationships with them. As we talked I realized I had ignored a valuable resource by thinking I could be successful on my own. He is a broker who helps companies prepare for changes in ownership…ownership of my company will change before I retire. He spoke of a brother in Georgia who developed data mining tools, and wanted to market them to the government…my government clients need data mining tools. Another brother is a government executive in Washington…I work hard to get audiences with such officials.

Why do we think *independence* is best, even when we see that the most effective relationships in a changing world are interdependent? They involve both giving and receiving. Interdependence produces the trust and harmony which are so vital in relationships. The alternatives, independence and dependence, are much less effective. Independence produces competition and conflict, while dependence spawns low self-esteem and frustration. Today's emphasis on independence seems to be a reactionary attempt to reject dependent relationships. We are angry when a relationship partner tries to dominate us. We resist when they manipulate us, and we become resentful when they tell us what to do.

Independent people may give to others, but they are reluctant to accept help. Dependent relationships also are sub-optimal since one partner surrenders his or her individuality by continuously receiving, but not giving help. A dependent partner craves help and becomes angry if it is not provided. In interdependent relationships, giving and receiving are valued equally. Although values and goals may differ, the partners in an interdependent relationship each know what to expect from the other as they travel their intertwined pathways of life.

Who's Leading?

More than ever before, the success of today's relationships depends on both partners sharing the leadership role.

As poorly as I dance, I like to lead. It generally works okay as long as my wife is willing to follow my lead. Being the better dancer, she sometimes asks if she can lead to show me a new dance step or combination. That works well too, as long as I know in advance and accept that she will lead us across the floor. What does not work is a weak lead on my part, or my wife taking the lead without prior agreement.

Similar to intricate dance routines, rampant change injects more pressure and complexity into today's family relationships than ever before. Decades ago marriages were based on breadwinner-homemaker relationships (leader-leader) where the husband was expected to earn the income, and the wife was expected to care for the children and the home. Divorces were rare. The world is not that simple anymore. The roles of breadwinner and homemaker no longer are gender specific. Furthermore, one breadwinner is often not enough. Two incomes may be required to make financial ends meet in the household. It follows that each spouse also must be a homemaker to ensure the relationship succeeds and endures.

To further complicate family relationships, many of today's homes are built with the pieces from previously broken relationships: former wives and husbands, stepchildren, weekend visits by children from previous marriages, and alimony and child support payments. It is not a surprise to anyone that these rebuilt relationships are more stressful. Such awkward relationships, combined with demanding traditional family roles, are uncomfortable for both partners. The dragons of over-work and haunting memories of failed relationships are common. The success of today's complex relationships, especially intimate ones, depends on both partners understanding and accepting multiple roles and responsibilities. The most effective relationships are those in which both partners are leaders in caring and giving.

First Prize Is Nothin'

Our relationship partners deserve our appreciation and support even if they don't do what we want them to do.

For several years, my job as a naval officer was directing nuclear submarine refueling overhauls. The planning was detailed, the training and dedication of the workers was extraordinary, quality controls were meticulous, and everyone did their best. Safety was paramount in everyone's mind. However, a common waterfront witticism was: *First prize is nothin'—second prize is worse.* Superior performance nearing perfection was expected from everyone, every time. Rarely did anyone get recognition or rewards for high performance, but everyone noticed if something was less than perfect. An elaborate investigation (referred to as a "Critique") was conducted when anything went wrong. The last question in the critique was: "What will you do to ensure that this never happens again?" That is always a difficult question when personnel error is the root cause. Sometimes it is impossible to answer.

For the most part, relationships are not as explosive as a nuclear reactor. Yet many of us treat them that way. When our relationship partners do everything that is expected, little is said. No compliments, no thank you's, no appreciation. But when they fail to meet our expectations, they receive an instant critique, blunt disapproval or a cold shoulder. The criticism dragon takes control of our hearts and our tongues. We expect that criticism will change others, stop them from repeating the behavior that triggered our disfavor. But it rarely does anything more than damage the relationship. Light praise and heavy criticism do not build trust and respect.

Our relationship partners need to hear our appreciation, even if their response to change is not exactly what we would like. In such situations, help and compassion are more effective than criticism. In effective relationships, first prize, second prize, and all the other prizes, are understanding and acceptance. Therefore, influence your relationship partners by expecting them to do their best. And, no matter what the results, trust that they did the very best they could under the circumstances. Don't you always do the best you can do?

A 50-50 Deal?

Unconditional giving works much better than score-keeping in our most important relationships.

For a year of our 35-plus-year marriage, my wife and I separated. She lived in downtown Washington and I lived in our house in the suburbs. I wanted to live together while we reconciled our differences. But my wife insisted that she was not ready to work on the marriage because she needed to work on herself. At first I was upset she was not working on our relationship, but I reluctantly accepted her wishes. We dated frequently during the separation. I consistently expressed my intent to be together. I could have abandoned her. After all, I felt she had abandoned me and our relationship. Actually, the separation gave me time to appreciate my wife and work on my issues. My firmness kept us focused on staying together, while her firmness helped us face the issues that caused us to separate in the first place. Both were essential in preserving our marriage.

Too often we treat intimate relationships as if they were business transactions. We find ourselves saying: "This isn't fair. It's time for you to do your part. I gave in last time." But what if a relationship is not an equal partnership; *not* a fifty-fifty deal? The unfortunate problem with the fairness dragon is that it leads to score-keeping. One partner may think (s)he gave in three times while the other partner conceded once. But the partners often are using different scoring systems. Like one football team counting a touchdown as ten points for our team and five points for the other team, we value concessions we make for more relationship points than the concessions our partner makes, and vice versa.

Another pitfall in viewing relationships as a fifty-fifty deal is that sometimes a partner just does not have fifty percent to give. Overwhelming changes like health issues or job worries might be draining our partner. If I cooked dinner two nights in a row and my wife is exhausted from a hard day, she does not want to hear that it is her turn to cook. In such cases, compassion works better than score-keeping. A quiet dinner at a restaurant would be much appreciated. Effective relationships are a 100-100 deal. Each partner gives 100 percent of what they can every time!

Why Won't You Change?

Change is a door that can only be opened from the inside. No matter how hard we knock, our partner may, or may not, choose to open the door.

When I walk down a dark city street at night, I worry about an unpleasant relationship with an assailant. I imagine him jumping out from an alley, putting a gun to my head, and saying: "Your wallet or your life." With no one around, I would have to take his threat as serious. But I would try to change him. I would have two goals: keep my wallet and make him go away without hurting me. His goal is to get my wallet, and probably thinks I have no choice. Actually, I have at least three choices: (1) give him the wallet and hope he goes away; (2) refuse to give him the wallet and hope he goes away; and (3) attack him to scare him away. I do not know which choice I would make. In the terror of the moment, how could anyone know what would work? Even if I gave him my wallet, it would not be because he forced me to. It would be because I felt it was the best way to achieve my goals in the transaction. After I make my choice, the assailant will do whatever he chooses. He might kill me no matter which choice I make.

In this fictitious relationship, the assailant and I both defend our "doors-to-change" vigorously. He cannot open mine and I cannot open his. Invoking the dragons of coercion, manipulation or guilt will not force someone to change if they do not want to change. We might be so persuasive, so threatening, or so strong that others choose to do what we want. But it is always their choice.

Since we cannot force a relationship partner to change, the only dependable way to improve our relationships is to change ourselves. It is hard to change ourselves, however, because changing requires us to accept at least partial responsibility for making the relationship the way it is today. But the part we are responsible for is precisely the part that we can change! When we open our "door-to-change" by changing ourselves, our relationships grow without limit. It starts with you and me. Each of us can open our door to change and keep it open, no matter what others do.

Master Puppeteers

Quit trying to change others. Tame the dragon of manipulation by accepting others just as they are.

As I held my new grandson in my arms, it occurred to me that we learn as babies to manipulate relationships. My grandson cried when his diaper was wet, or when he was hungry. Not knowing the cause of his discomfort, I tried various things until his crying stopped. You and I learned the same way when we were young. Before our first birthday, we had discovered that crying got a response (or not). When we were hurt, we found that we received compassion and sympathy (or not). As we grew older we experimented with other behaviors like seriousness, smiling, laughing, sadness, cooperation, aggression, asking questions and expressing feelings. We made judgements that some behaviors brought acceptance in relationships, and other behaviors caused us to be rejected. Some behaviors gave us what we wanted, and others did not. We judged behaviors as good or bad, and adopted the "good" ones as habits in our relationship patterns.

As adults, we still may be using those behaviors like puppeteers to manipulate relationships. We are adept at pulling strings to make our spouse, children, family, friends and coworkers do what we want them to do. Since they resist, we must be either very subtle or very strong as we pull the strings. Sometimes the more intimate a relationship, the more frequently we pull the strings. Most string-pulling is gentle, but it may be as frightening as an assailant holding a gun to someone's head. Do you remember any of the following puppeteering techniques being used on you? Maybe you have used some of them yourself:

• ***Helpers*** use support to manipulate relationships. They control others by compulsively doing nice things. Helpers think they will get their way if people like them and everyone is happy.

• ***Browbeaters*** intimidate to manipulate relationships. They display a temper, get angry, or issue blunt commands to get their way. Most people are afraid of browbeaters.

• ***Inquirers*** use information to manipulate relationships. They ask questions until everyone knows the facts, especially facts that support the conclusions they want. Usually, inquirers think they know the answers before they ask the questions.

• ***Party People*** create excitement to manipulate relationships. Always having fun and suggesting new activities, party people control others by drawing them into the excitement. Party people are frustrated when others do not want to "have fun."

• ***Sad Sacks*** solicit pity to manipulate relationships. Sad sacks believe that people only offer help and compassion if they feel sympathy. Sad sacks tell heartbreaking stories about amazing bad luck, and they often suffer from debilitating sicknesses.

• ***Wallflowers*** withdraw or remain aloof to manipulate relationships. They control people by ignoring them. They think that if we see someone alone in a corner, we will be drawn to them. Wallflowers frequently find themselves alone.

These and other puppeteer techniques can become dragons in our relationships, especially when we are unaware that we are using them. Looking at my past, I see the conflict, resistance and pain I have caused by trying to manipulate others as an inquirer or browbeater. And I am surprised how often people resist what I think are good ideas. Puppeteer habits originate from a lack of trust, a belief that we must manipulate others because we cannot get what we want through open and honest approaches. Discarding these concealed techniques for changing others will bring the acceptance, love and synergy that we want into our relationships.

Manipulation creates resistance in others. Resistance cannot exist without at least a small perception of being manipulated.

Hot Tub Relationships

Partners in effective relationships value differences. Differences are treated as strengths and they are used to erase weaknesses.

For my fiftieth birthday, our family spent a week together on the Outer Banks of North Carolina in an awesome beach house with a hot tub. The gift I requested from my wife and two daughters was written views of *What Is Possible for the Stieglitz Family*. We read and talked about one of the views each evening as we lounged in the hot tub. The four of us are very different individuals, each with different and unique strengths. After listening to the four views, I realized that we had spent too much of our most precious and passionate energy trying to change each other, rather than understanding and benefitting from our core differences. That is changing. We now see and appreciate differences as the strength of our family. They are the source of the synergy that enables us to contribute more as the Stieglitz family than the sum of our achievements as individuals.

Too often differences are treated like dragons in a relationship, when they should be a source of strength. We expect relationships to provide more than we would have alone. The *more* lies in our differences. When relationships seem like less (less fun, less stimulating, less satisfying), it may be because uniqueness has been compromised for the sake of the relationship. Or because differences between the partners are not being recognized and appreciated.

Effective relationships, on the other hand, are synergistic. They multiply the joy and happiness of the partners by joining differences in an expansive manner. In that way the relationship produces more joy, more happiness, and more success than the partners would experience individually. Contrary to the rules of math, a synergistic relationship is like 1 + 1 = 3, or 11, or 57. Differences are the fuel that propels relationships toward mutual success and personal happiness for the partners.

Make a List, Check It Twice

To improve the most important relationship in your life, work on the only thing over which you have total control: yourself.

Let me recommend a foolproof technique to improve the most important relationship in your life. You choose the relationship: your spouse, son, daughter, parents, friend or business associate. Make a written list of the things you want most from him or her. The list can contain as many items as you like. Just be sure each item is specific enough for him or her to understand clearly. Put this book aside while you make the list and continue reading when you finish.

Review the list carefully. Is it complete and specific? Check it at least twice. Put a star next to the three items that, in your opinion, are most vital for improving the relationship. Memorize those three items, and throw the list in the garbage. Do not show it to the person that you selected as the most important relationship in your life. The three items you starred are the three things you most need to give to that person. That is how you must be in the relationship. If you want support, be supportive. If you want excitement, be exciting. If you want tenderness, be tender. Love is giving what we want most to receive.

Attempting to change your partner creates a dragon because your partner probably will try to change you too. When I performed this exercise for myself, I chose the relationship with my wife as the most important in my life. The three items I starred were:

(1) I want her to listen and understand what I really say,

(2) I want her to share my favorite activities with me, and

(3) I want her to accept me as I am since I do the best that I can.

I was amazed when I reversed these three items and realized how infrequently I listen to my wife, how few of her favorite activities I share, and how seldom I give her compassion and acceptance. My willingness to give these things to her has improved our relationship immensely. On both sides! It demonstrates again that *change is a door that can only be opened from the inside.* I can only change me, and only you can change you.

Three Essential Tips On *Relationships*

Relationships flourish when we focus on improving ourselves, rather than compulsively trying to change others.

A friend of mine over the last thirty years has been through four divorces and married five times. The stories she tells at cocktail parties about her ex-husbands are compelling. The first was...; the second did...; the third always...; and the fourth would not...! After hearing her passionate and humorous recitations, most listeners agree that any reasonable woman would have divorced such men. While her stories are convincing, but they are irrelevant in her fifth marriage. The relevant factors are the contributions she may have made (however small) to the failure of the previous marriages, the ways that she may (or may not) have changed in the past thirty years, and possibly her criteria for picking husbands. Those factors persist in her fifth marriage. Fortunately, those are precisely the things that she can change, even though she cannot change her ex-husbands or her new husband.

The rapid pace of change we are experiencing in the twenty-first century offers many exciting new opportunities to form and nurture lasting relationships that will unlock the door to successful careers and joyous families. In times of change, our relationships are more likely to be rewarding when the things we say and do are based on consistent values. You know what I stand for, and I know what you stand for. We easily recognize the worth of our relationship, even though our values and beliefs may differ. When we treasure such differences, neither of us feels compelled to change the other. In this vein, the three essential tips for building and maintaining more effective relationships in the twenty-first century are:

• ***Give Love Freely:*** Love is giving the things we want most for ourselves. "Freely" means unconditionally. Expecting nothing in return. With no judgement of those to whom we give love. The vignettes in this chapter describe the power of love to build lasting, fulfilling relationships, even with those who may have hurt us in the past.

• ***Be Open & Honest:*** Successful relationships require more than honesty. They require openness to tell all the truth, all the time. Telling just part of the truth damages relationships in the long term because the message we send is that our partner is too weak to deal with the whole truth. The vignettes in this section provide tips on increasing the level of honesty, openness and trust in our most important relationships.

• ***Say* YES!** *YES* says beautiful things! Everything we are today, and everything our relationships are today, are the sum of the *YES*es we have said. We are not, and our relationships are not, all of the *NO*s that we have said. The vignettes in this section provide tips about saying *YES* to the people we love, even when it sounds like a *NO* because of a more important *YES* in the relationship.

These three tips on building relationships will provide perspectives and strategies for your relationships that you might not have considered before. Ponder them carefully because they may help you produce trusting, effective and lasting relationships with the people you most want in your life.

-------Tip #4-------

Give Love Freely

~ Love Spoils If We Hoard It

What the world needs now is love, sweet love. It's the only thing that there's just too little of.
— Burt Bacherach

The Greatest Gift

Our most vital needs are satisfied when we give love freely. Even if those we love do not love us back.

A good friend visited our home and brought a gift: a train set with polished wooden tracks and cars. Taken back by the unusual nature of the gift, I hesitantly said: "Thank you." With obvious joy in his eyes, he said: "The best gifts are ones I like to receive myself." We played with the train set on the floor as we reminisced about childhood memories. He gave a great gift that night. More than a train set, it was love. A present is just an object. But in these hectic times, expressions of love, given freely, are special gifts. Thoughtful acts of kindness, investing time to help a colleague, or bending to accommodate a friend's needs, are offerings from the heart more precious than any tangible present.

Fire-breathing dragons are instantly tamed by love. Giving love without expecting something in return was a huge change for me. For most of my life, love was reserved for God, and family and friends who pleased me. I am awestruck as I begin to see how much more there is to love. The paradox of love is *the more we give away, the more we have.* Giving love freely transforms our hearts and minds, the way we live, and the world around us.

Love is the things we do, the laughter and tears we share, and the dreams we pursue. The kind of love we give determines how we treat each other and our world. Unconditional love values the intrinsic worth of *people,* while conditional love values the *things* they do or have. We do not exist apart from each other. The vignettes in this section describe love in terms of acceptance, forgiveness and support. They illustrate that giving love freely produces the happiness, peace and success we want by taming the dragons of judgment, anger and competition.

What Is Love, Anyway?

Love is a feeling inside, rather than a trait or characteristic of the thing or person being loved.

Unfortunately, I cannot give you a precise definition for love. How could I when love is so many things that no single human could possibly know them all? The love we each know is merely the tip of a limitless iceberg. The English language uses a single word to describe *love*. Other languages have different words to convey different types of love. For example, I understand that Greek has four words for love: *agape* is a free, unconditional love; *storge* is a nurturing, mentoring love; *phileo* is a friendship or partnership love; and *eros* is a physical, sexual love.

The English word *love* is widely misunderstood because it is used in many contexts to define diverse relationships with people and things. For example, saying we love…

- *God* which implies worship and reverence
- *Ourself* which implies confidence and self-esteem
- *Our mother and father* which implies honor and gratitude
- *Our spouse* which implies intimacy and devotion
- *Our children* which implies generosity and hope for the future
- *Our family and friends* which implies comradery and synergy
- *Customers and coworkers* implies cooperation and teamwork
- *Our job* which implies dedication and satisfaction
- *Our possessions* which implies pride and ownership
- *A pretty day* which implies peace and beauty
- *The World Series* which implies excitement and enthusiasm
- *A delicious meal* which implies satisfaction and enjoyment.

The emotions surrounding love span a broad range of feelings and attitudes. But are they different? Notice that in each case, the "love feelings" originate inside our heart and mind. They are not traits or characteristics of the person or object being loved.

Extend that observation to the concept of unconditional love. If I love my wife more than I love a beggar on the street, it is only because she satisfies my conditions for love while the beggar does not. That is "conditional" love. Unfortunately, the conditions can become dragons in our relationships because they compel us to withhold our love not only from beggars, but also from those we claim to love the most. Unconditional love for a beggar would not manifest itself in the same form as unconditional love for my wife, but love can be given freely and unconditionally in both cases.

As a Christian, I believe Jesus Christ loves me no matter what I do, even if I am a beggar on the street. I cannot begin to comprehend His limitless love for me until I experience unconditional love for others. You may hold different religious beliefs, but the highest ideals of your religion undoubtably embody an analogous concept of love for all mankind. When we near the end of our journey on earth and reflect on life's most exquisite moments, physical possessions and temporal achievements will be remembered very much less than tender moments of unconditional love with those whom we really care about. It is the unconditional love we gave and received that will be remembered with sweetness, warmth and gratitude as long as we live.

Lunch with Mom

Unconditional love is courageous. It conquers every challenge and every fear, and expects nothing in return.

When I was three, my biological mother died of leukemia. She was diagnosed with the disease soon after I was born. What a change it must have been for her to shift from the joy of my birth to the reality of death. My most vivid memory of her was a day we spent at home. She was in bed and unable to get up. My dad was at work and my brother was in school. With a big smile I remember to this day, she asked me to make lunch. I felt loved and trusted as I went to the kitchen. Of course, I made the only lunch a three-year-old knows how to make: peanut butter and jelly sandwiches, and milk. I carried the lunch up the stairs to the bedroom on a tray, being careful not to spill the milk.

My mom and I talked as we ate lunch on the edge of her bed. I do not recall what she said to me or what I said to her, but I do remember that she spoke softly and lovingly, smiled as she listened to me, and looked beautiful. She wanted nothing from me. Instead she gave me the awesome gift of unconditional love despite her exhaustion. She died soon after that day, and that lunch is my last remembrance of her. It is a picture I treasure as the most vibrant and perfect love I have ever experienced. Her life may have ended, but her love is alive today.

Love is motherly trait. Unconditional love is, however, a choice. Facing the dragon of death, my mother chose to give love freely. There were other choices. She could have told me how sad she was for dying so young, her remorse for mistakes she may have made, her need for compassion, or grief for the events in my life that she would miss. Maybe she felt all of those feelings while we were eating lunch. Such feelings would have been normal. But if she felt those feelings, she did not communicate them to me.

Unconditional love is brave. It has knows no boundaries and no fear, even the fear of death itself. Unconditional love does not possess others, nor will it be possessed. Unconditional love is its own reward, sufficient unto itself. I am sure my mother's last minutes on earth were filled with great joy because she invested them in unconditional love.

I Love Champagne

Love is a joy to be near. It brightens our days, reduces our stress, and supports our dreams.

No, not the bubbly cocktail. I mean Champagne, our green and yellow parakeet. He has been with us for nineteen years now, an incredibly long life for a parakeet. Three months ago he was very sick, lying on the bottom of his cage twitching. My wife took him to the veterinarian, who said that he had suffered the parakeet equivalent of a stroke. The veterinarian suggested that we put him to sleep and end his pain. But Champagne had always been so feisty in fighting back from life-threatening injuries and sicknesses. I was not willing to be the one to snuff out his last breath. He never quit, and he did not quit this time either. We fed him sugar water three times a day with an eyedropper, and he pulled off yet another miraculous recovery.

Champagne has been a joy in our house for almost two decades. He has tamed his dragons (if he ever had any) and helped me tame mine. He brightens everyone's days. He says "I love Champagne" in a cheerful, squeaky voice that instantly makes people fall in love with him. He says "Merry Christmas" every day of the year, even the Fourth of July. I think the only phrase he really understands is "Let me out," which he says standing at the door to his cage. Occasionally we let him out. He enjoys flying, even though he is nearly blind and sometimes crashes into a wall. The best he can do today is crash land on top of his cage. He shakes it off and infectiously says: "I'm so cute. I'm so cute." If reincarnation exists and Champagne comes back as a man or woman, I look forward to being close to that spirit in human form. We have all met people who are like Champagne, although they are rare. No matter what happens, they are a joy to be with.

Footnote: Subsequent to this vignette being written, Champagne died about two months past his twenty-first birthday. But not before being recognized officially by the Guinness World Records® as the "Longest Lived Budgerigar (Parakeet) in Captivity in the USA."

He Ain't Heavy, He's My Brother

Sometimes love means just being there to give support, resisting the urge to jump in and fix a friend's problems.

By *just being there* at a crucial time, my brother helped me tame the dragons of loneliness and fear. When our mother died, our father left us in an orphanage. My brother, eight years old at the time, went to the adolescent section, while at three I was put in the nursery section. The orphanage was the loneliest time of my life. My darkest days. I slept in a long, narrow, austere room with twenty small beds on each side. The nuns were very strict, and I was constantly reprimanded. One year at the orphanage seemed like eternity to me. But Friday afternoons were like Christmas because my brother visited me. Every week he would bring an Oh Henry candy bar, and we would play and talk together for an hour or so as we ate the candy bar. Fridays were the only bright spot in my otherwise dark memories of the orphanage.

No matter how thoughtless or rude my brother may have been in the years that followed, no matter what happened or did not happen in our relationship, I never forgot those Oh Henry candy bars. For my brother's fiftieth birthday, my gift to him was a box of Oh Henry candy bars to repay a forty-two-year-old debt. He was obese and died prematurely at age fifty-eight. Several people who attended his funeral gave me an Oh Henry candy bar because they knew that was my best memory of him. I am forever grateful to my brother for *being there* when I really needed a friend. It was an unmistakable expression of unconditional love.

Often a friend or family member, someone we love, just needs us to be there. *Just being there* is hard, because our natural inclination is to help. We think we have a solution for the problem, and offer help even when it is not requested. We volunteer answers, even though no questions were asked. Such help does not build lasting, trusting relationships. The message we send when we offer help without being asked is: "You are incapable of solving your own problems." No one likes to hear that. *Just being there* means listening with compassion, performing acts of kindness, and giving help only when asked.

I'd Give My Life for You

If we let them, the dragons of everyday routine will tear us away from the most important relationships in our lives.

Like most fathers, my relationship with my daughters is precious. They are my priority. I support them in achieving their goals, and claim that I would sacrifice everything for them. *I would give my life for you* is how I feel about my daughters. Like a movie hero I imagine myself fearlessly rescuing them from a fierce dragon. A romantic notion. And true too. Fortunately, it is unlikely that any of us will have a chance to demonstrate our love so dramatically.

However, in reality, we lay down our lives for our children one minute at a time each day. Sharing time is giving our lives to the people we love. When we get sucked into the changes that surround us and are too busy to be with our children, we surrender to the dragons of the less important. What choice did I make when my pretty five- and six-year-old little girls asked to play with Daddy? "Maybe later, I have to work now" was often my response. That response was stealing me from them because something else was more important. Work will wait while we share a sunset or a rainbow with our children. But, the sunset and rainbow will not wait while we work. I tried to justify work as a necessity to provide a comfortable home for my family. As I look back and see how often I chose work, I realize the real reason for my choices was the positive strokes my ego received from work. Those strokes were stronger than the strokes I gave myself for being a loving father.

I would make different choices if I could relive those years. Like you, I have heard that lament many times from many people. I heard it back then too, but my choices did not change. Finally, the lesson is clear. Today, my priority is to support my wife, daughters, and other family members. My daughters are grown now, and they have chosen to live far away from my home. I accept their choices unconditionally and will support them whenever, however, and wherever they want me to. What do you choose as the top priority in your life? To what or whom do you give your life?

Loving a BMW

Insomuch as you have done these things unto the least of My brethren, you have done them unto Me.
Matthew 25

A BMW was side-swiped. The driver got out screaming about the damage to his "beemer." When the policeman observed that the man's arm had been severed in the crash, he gasped: "Oh no! Where's my Rolex?" Rolex watches and BMWs are often cited in jokes about materialism. But caring about a BMW, a Rolex or other possessions is not intrinsically bad, and sacrificing prized assets is not a prerequisite for effective relationships. However, the high importance we attach to possessions can awaken the WIIFM (*What's In It For Me*) dragon and become an obstacle to forming new relationships and building old ones.

Which, if any, of your possessions would you be reluctant to share with a friend who needed it? Would you loan your car to a stranger if he or she had an emergency? Answering the question for myself, the WIIFM dragon would cause me to wonder if I would get the car back undamaged. By taming the WIIFM dragon, I find sympathy for his or her plight and find ways to help.

Consider a more difficult challenge: Would you invite a homeless stranger to spend the night in your home if it was freezing outside? I would sooner lend him my car than let him sleep in my home. Again, the WIIFM dragon would ignite my fear of losing my house, or my life. Our tendency is to ignore strangers rather than to help them without expecting something in return.

What might happen if we conquered our dragons and helped the "strangers" in our families, in our neighborhoods and at our work sites? First, a stranger might become a friend. Second, we might learn from them. And third, we might feel good about by the giving experience. Forming new relationships is surprisingly easy when we open ourselves to being friendly. All it takes is an open-hearted smile, a small gesture of understanding, and a genuine commitment to being friendly.

Too Busy to Help

Happiness comes more easily from giving time to your most important relationships, than from doing things.

My brother called me at work one winter afternoon about 5 p.m. He asked me to pick him up at his apartment about ten miles from my office, and drive him to a hospital about two miles from his apartment. He had been struggling for a week with a respiratory infection, and the doctor recommended that he go to the hospital for testing. My first thoughts were: *"I'm too busy to leave now." "It will take thirty minutes to get there in rush hour." "I'd rather not drive in the snow,"* and *"Why doesn't he call a taxi?"* After taming those dragons, I agreed to take him to the hospital. I called my wife to say that I would be home late for dinner, and I left several important tasks unfinished on my desk at the office.

My brother was waiting anxiously in the lobby when I got to his apartment, and we arrived at the hospital about forty minutes after his phone call. As we sat impatiently in the crowded waiting room, we talked about everything from our childhood memories to the Yankees' spring training. Several times I pressured the receptionist and triage nurse in futile attempts to accelerate his examination and check-in process. The busyness dragon was feeding me thoughts like: *"I have so much to do." "This is a waste of time,"* and *"How much longer will this take?"* Finally, after a three-hour wait, the doctor took my brother into the examination room, and I left to drive home.

Minutes after I arrived home angry about what felt was a wasted night, the phone rang and the doctor told me that my brother had died from a massive stroke. Today, I do not remember any of the things that seemed so important to me earlier that night. I remember vividly the three hours talking with my brother, the last hours of his life. I almost was too busy to spend those hours with him. How often do we think we are too busy to support friends and family members? How many of us do not understand and appreciate our parents as they grow old? Fortunately, they usually do not die before the next chance we have to visit them or to help them. But one day they might.

The Power of Giving

Why do we wait for a crisis to tap into the innate power of giving inside us? Instead, we could treat each other like that every day.

On September 11, 2001, after terrorists destroyed the World Trade Center buildings in New York, a business colleague immediately left our Washington office to find his sister who worked in the buildings. Born in Kansas City, he had never traveled to the Big Apple. After several days, unfortunately without finding his sister, he returned to Washington. His most vivid memory of the trip was of how thoughtful, caring and giving everyone at "Ground Zero" had been.

When the crisis came, policemen and firemen became heroes, and food and water to sustain them was abundant. Thousands of volunteers appeared from nowhere and became a powerful, effective force when each of them gave just a little. Red Cross and Salvation Army warehouses overflowed with donations. People stood in line to give blood. The United Way's "September 11th Fund" reached its goal in just a few weeks. We cried for families that we did not even know. It was anything but normal.

The fireman, policemen, volunteers and donations were in or near New York City on September 10th too, but we all felt like we had more important things to do. Upon returning my colleague said: "I always heard that New Yorkers were rude, insensitive and pushy. They were nothing like that." Being from New York myself, I knew there was some truth in his former image of New Yorkers. Which are the real New Yorkers: the caring, giving people who were incredible in crisis, or the people with a worldwide reputation for being rude and pushy?

Buried inside each of us is the desire to help others. It flows freely in times of crisis. But somehow, in the fog of our daily routines, we set aside caring to satisfy individual needs. Often we neglect family members and close friends. A few weeks after the disaster, there was a push to get back to normal. But the old normal is gone forever. Many of us have tamed the dragons of independence and aloofness that were so ferocious on September 10th. The new normal has more of the caring and giving that helped New York through that horrible crisis.

An Esteem Bath

Unconditional love is born in our relationship with self. Our most damaging critic often is the dragons in our own head.

My adopted parents' love seemed conditional to me. When I was eleven, I was hit in the face by a baseball bat and had eight stitches. After he came home from work, my Dad asked if I was okay. When I said yes, he slapped me and said that I was foolish to be catching without a mask. My parents said I was a "good boy" or a "bad boy" depending on my grades and how well I obeyed them. But I was never good enough. They always told me how I could be better. My pain was intense since, even when I was away from my parents, the "I'm not good enough" dragon in my head mercilessly told me that I should be doing better, that I should be doing more. The "self" was missing from my esteem. It was driven by others.

When I became an adult, I needed an "esteem bath" because my image of myself was measured by results and what people thought of me. Fortunately, my biological mother and grandmother had taught me unconditional love when I was small. I was able to reconnect with that love, acknowledge my strengths and weaknesses, look into the mirror, and love the man who stood before me. It was a gigantic relief.

Our willingness to accept others is the outward manifestation of the unconditional love we feel for ourselves. We cannot love others unconditionally when we place conditions on loving ourselves. We cannot accept others when our mental dragons constantly push us to give more, do more, and be more. We tame those dragons by accepting ourselves when things are not perfect. The voices in our heads become friends who comfort and love us unconditionally. They build our self-esteem by providing a compassionate assessment of our results.

The relationship we have with ourselves is the foundation of all relationships since we cannot love others more than we love ourselves. Each of us is our own best friend. Quiet moments alone are special times to connect with our unique qualities. To enjoy being yourself with no conditions is an *esteem bath* every bit as soothing as any sauna or hot tub.

Conclusion Jumping

Don't let a small misunderstanding damage a great relationship. Nothing requires you to participate in every argument to which you are invited.

At three years of age, my oldest daughter left the lights on in her bedroom. I switched them off and asked her to please turn them off in the future. Next day the lights were on again. With rising frustration, I sternly repeated my request that she turn the lights off. The third day, the same thing. Concluding she was ignoring my requests, I yelled at her and insisted that she do what I asked. She began to cry and blurted out: "But Daddy, I can't reach the light switch. Mommy turns them on for me." I had misunderstood her discomfort with my first and second requests, and failed to notice that the light switch was too high for her to reach. I was embarrassed to discover that she was too short to reach the switch. The event of the lights being on had not changed, but the emotions I attached to the event changed radically with that new information. It was instantly okay that the lights were left on.

The "jump-to-conclusions" dragon breathes scorchingly hot fire on our closest relationships. Things are not always as they seem. The misunderstandings produced when we jump to conclusions damage great relationships. Our relationship partners often become defensive in response to our conclusions, and pointless arguments follow. The events in our lives are completely separate from the emotions we attach to them. For example, an event you find incredibly humorous might be depressing to me.

We cannot change events that happen in our relationships and our lives. But we have complete control to change how we feel about those events, and how we treat our relationship partners. The events can never change, but the emotions we attach to them can change. Give your relationship partners the benefit of every doubt. *Every* doubt. Accept what they do no matter what it seems like. You might find that your relationship partners cannot reach the proverbial light switch.

Just Listen

Empathetic listening is caring enough to allow our partners unravel their own concerns and satisfy their own needs.

One day my wife called me at my office obviously upset about something. I answered the phone just as a meeting was starting and listened as she explained her problem. I acknowledged her with "oh no" and "that's too bad." With business associates in the room, I could not offer solutions for the problem, nor did she ask for any. When she finished, she said: "Thank you for listening. You were a big help" and hung up. I was shocked. I had not said a thing. I just listened, but she was grateful for my help. That day I learned that listening is helping.

Listening is one of the most loving gifts we can give, whereas the "I know the answer" dragon pushes people away. When we listen empathetically, we hear the small differences between our experiences and those of our relationship partners. Such insights are a solid basis on which to build trusting relationships. By listening, we send the message that: *I respect your ability to solve your problems.* Empathetic listening gives our relationship partner time to explain their concern fully *to himself or herself.*

Empathetic listening means using our eyes to see body language, as well as our ears to hear words. By seeing what others are feeling in addition to listening to what they are saying, we gain a more complete appreciation of their hopes and dreams, fears and concerns.

Empathetic listening does not mean agreement, it means trying to understand. It means we are not: (1) evaluating what is said in terms of our own experiences, (2) judging what is said against what should be, or (3) probing to determine how we can fix the problem. In the short term, empathetic listening may take more time. But in the long run, empathetic listening is easier, and it takes far less time than correcting misunderstandings and repairing damaged relationships. It would be fabulous if everyone could see the world through our eyes and be in touch with our feelings. Since they cannot (and neither can we), our loving gift to our most important relationship partners is to just listen by taming the "I know the answer" dragon.

The High Price of Conditional Love

The human need for approval drives people to fear judgements. Our judgements become barriers to the healthy relationships we want in our lives.

In 1995, the Chief of Naval Operations, the highest ranking officer in the U.S. Navy, committed suicide reportedly because he was accused of wearing campaign ribbons that he *might* not have earned. He was justifiably proud of the respect and admiration he had earned as the "sailor's admiral." On that day, however, his need for acceptance by others (conditional love) and his fear of rejection by those he cared so much about apparently were stronger than the love of life itself. It seems unlikely that he would have taken his own life if he had believed that the sailors would have accepted him unconditionally even if he did not deserve the ribbons.

The judgements we make of others are conditions on our love. When there are such conditions (i.e. conditional love), a natural human response for our relationship partners is to hide today's shortfalls and conceal past events that might be embarrassing. Forced to live in such an atmosphere, the need for acceptance and support drives people to be defensive and afraid. In extreme cases, the fear of our judgements can drive them to end our relationship.

Conditional love pushes people away. If an important someone in your life seems distant, it may be because the love you are giving has too many conditions and demands. The fear-of-criticism dragon spends enormous energy erecting defensive walls. How different would we be if we could be ourselves without fear of rejection and judgment? What if we knew we could try anything without being judged a failure if it did not work? It is probable that a world full of unconditional love would be a world without fear. And the energy and lives we waste today on that fear could be directed toward new achievements.

How long into the twenty-first century will we wait to put unconditional love, acceptance and trust into our relationships, including international relationships? It starts by *YOU* and *ME* giving unconditional love to the most important people in our lives.

You Did Great!

Consistently positive feedback builds confidence and fosters a healthy willingness to take risks.

I was always proud of my youngest daughter's athletic accomplishments. She earned varsity letters in three high school sports, was all-county in two of them, and received an athletic scholarship to a prestigious college. One high school softball game stands out in my memory. She was the shortstop. With bases loaded and one out, the batter hit a ground ball to the second baseman who flipped the ball to my daughter at second. She touched second to get the force out, and relayed the ball to first for a double play to end the inning. Everyone cheered as the team ran off the field.

On the sidelines, I took my daughter aside and explained how, by dragging her foot across second base differently, she could cut a half second off the pivot which might be crucial for a future double play. A week later, in the same situation, the second baseman tossed the ball to my daughter who dropped it for an error. When she came off the field, I asked what had happened. She answered that she was thinking about the new footwork I had suggested, and took her eye off the throw. My intent was loving, but the dragon imbedded in my suggestion was: *You aren't good enough the way you are*. Of course that was not how I felt. Nor was it the message I wanted to send. *You did great!* was my intended message.

Positive feedback is a powerful tool for building relationships, much more effective than negative feedback disguised as help. Positive feedback celebrates each little victory, while negative feedback often transforms small shortcomings into huge dragons. When faced with new challenges, people who have received consistently positive feedback reach into their memory to create a solution rooted in past successes. Conversely, negative feedback instills vivid memories of past mistakes and failures. The dragon of things that did not work freezes people in inaction: *Don't try that again, it didn't work well the last time*. Make positive feedback the loving rule in your relationships with yourself and your family, friends and colleagues at work.

Just One Kiss

It is comforting to know we can be ourselves within our family, confident that we are loved unconditionally.

Since the very first day I met my wife, I have been attracted to her gusto, her auburn hair, and her pretty face. We met when I was a senior and she was a sophomore in high school. The first time I saw her, she walked up to me in the park where I was playing stickball, sat on my lap, and kissed me. She said it was because she was "dogging" for a sorority, but I knew it was an excuse to meet me. As I got to know her better, I fought the dragons of conditional love as we explored common interests, family histories and differences. I wondered if she would be enough? Could I find someone better? That was over forty years ago.

In choosing a life partner, love begins as conditional. But it must become unconditional for the relationship to last forever. The love is at first conditional because the partner must have a pleasing appearance, compatible personality, and interesting experiences and activities to share. Romance blossoms when partners accept each other and thirst for moments together. Romantic partners are attracted by what they see in each other today. But what happens when they change? When they age and beauty, hair, health, figure or physical strength are gone?

My wife and I have been together most of our lives. I have changed many times, in many ways, over the last four decades. Some changes were for the better, and others were not. My wife has changed too, although in different ways and at different times. When did my love for her become unconditional? When did I begin to love her instead of her gusto and beauty (both of which she still has)? I cannot identify the instant in time. But I know if our love was still conditional, I suspect we would be divorced today. I will love my wife no matter what she does, no matter what happens. I will not try to change her.

When romance grows into marriage, the partners do not surrender their uniqueness. Instead they combine their love and talents to face life's challenges and enjoy life's small adventures. Together they find the courage to venture into a future that offers no guarantees, with the confidence that it will be a festival of joy. From just one kiss.

Here Come Da Judge

If a friend's actions seem self-centered or illogical, instead of judging ask about the changes and pressures they are facing.

A usually productive and reliable employee was working on a high-priority software project. We were in a crucial phase and had discussed what needed to be done. He acknowledged his assignments. Several hours later, I returned to check progress. Little had been done. I was upset and explained in sharp, direct words that he needed to finish his part of the project quickly. Again he seemed to understand his role and its urgency. Two hours later, I returned to find that he still had completed almost nothing. Furious at what I judged to be indifference and incompetence, I was about to explode when he began to cry. He blurted out that he had discovered that morning that his mother had cancer and was expected to live only a short time. Immediately, my anger and frustration evaporated. My focus shifted from judging his performance to forgiveness and empathy. The project did not seem so important anymore.

Too often the judgement dragon deludes us into thinking we know all the facts, which we never do. We wear the wisdom and robes of a Supreme Court justice as we issue final judgements: good or bad, right or wrong, worthwhile or worthless. We act as if we hold a book of laws and rules that defines the truth in all matters. When we judge others, our judgements get in the way of acceptance and we cannot love them unconditionally.

Judging the choices of others does not work in either business or personal relationships. If the choices of our relationship partners do not appear "right," it is because we do not fully understand their goals and constraints, and the changes they face. The closer people are to the core of our lives (like children, spouse or parents), the more likely we are to judge them and think we know what they should be doing. Judgements damage relationships because they reduce the value of our relationship partners. Unconditional love is a suspension of judgment. It means to forgive, to accept *what is*, and to understand our relationship partners as they face a changing world in their own way.

The Unforgivable

Forgiveness is a precious gift we give to ourselves. Hate is like swallowing a poison pill and expecting someone else to die.

The news reported that, over two years after the crime, a man was convicted of a brutal rape-murder of a twelve-year-old girl. As the judge sentenced the criminal to die, the girl's father yelled at the murderer: "I want to be there when the juice runs through your body. I want my eyes to be the last eyes you see. Just like your eyes were the last eyes my little girl saw."

As a father, I feel his pain and empathize with his overwhelming grief. He probably went to the prison to watch the man be executed. But was that revenge "sweet"? Did the father feel better after the murderer was put to death? Maybe, maybe not. But seeing the man executed did not return his daughter to life. And it is unlikely that the revenge he wanted and the hatred he felt reduced his loneliness.

Hatred and anger toward another person or an unwanted change are fierce dragons. Their grip on our hearts allows the other person or the unwanted change to continue to hurt us. Forgiveness is a gift we give to ourselves, not something we withhold from the person who did or said something that hurt us. The dictionary defines *forgiveness* as: *To cease to feel resentful or anger toward someone.*

Forgiveness does not pardon or condone an unpardonable act. Rather, it is letting go of resentment and hatred to move on with life.

When our energy and creativity are spent in resentment and hatred, little is left to create happiness for ourselves and those around us. Feelings of anger and revenge reduce our ability to make rational choices, and jeopardize the peace and joy in our lives. The point is not to eliminate capital punishment or to pardon people who commit brutal crimes. The point is to forgive with love. Mahatma Gandhi told us The weak don't forgive. Forgiveness is a quality of the strong.

Forgiveness is an essential ingredient in healthy relationships. It also may be the most refreshing form of revenge.

You're Okay

Acceptance is easy when people are like we want them to be. The challenge is to give love freely when they aren't.

My grandmother came to visit our family for the Christmas holidays when we lived in Boston. Three recently returned Vietnam veterans lived upstairs in the apartment building. They enjoyed hearty parties and invited us to attend a gala Christmas celebration. I went early and stayed late, while my grandmother and wife stayed just a short time. I had several drinks and it was the only time in my life I have smoked marijuana. After staying at the party from two in the afternoon until eight at night, I staggered back to our apartment. My family was finishing dinner after waiting hours for me to return home. Bumping into walls, I found my way to the kitchen, reeled to the kitchen sink, and threw up. My wife was shocked and angry. My grandmother helped me into the bedroom, where I fumbled to take my clothes off and went to bed.

Even in my drunken state, I knew that my grandmother was not pleased with me. She may have been concerned that I was developing a drug and alcohol problem. But she never mentioned the incident. Not that night, not the next day, not ever. I knew she did not condone my behavior, however she accepted me with love and trusted me. I learned two lessons from that embarrassing incident. The next morning, my aching head and upset stomach were refresher training in avoiding indulgence. But the biggest lesson was about unconditional love.

It took me years to appreciate the power of what my grandmother did that night. I was not as accepting or loving in similar situations as a dad. I could not resist the dragon of fear for my children. That dragon threatened horrible things. So I delivered judgmental lectures instead of trusting my daughters' ability to learn from their results just as my grandmother had trusted me. Unconditional love is accepting and forgiving. We each learn from our results, or we repeat them. Either way, no one has anything to prove or to change. You are okay just as you are. Even if you throw up in the kitchen sink.

Closing Thoughts on Giving Love Freely

Love, forgiveness and acceptance tame the dragons of frustration and fear that appear in our lives whenever we face change.

The navigation system in my car was built to give unconditional love. I tell the system where I want to go, and it tells me how to get there. Sometimes I do not follow the directions that it gives me. I take my own route and ignore the system's instruction to: "Turn right at the next intersection." Without judgment, the soft voice in the navigation system calmly tells me to: "Make a U-turn when permitted." Even after I disregard that suggestion and several others, the system simply adjusts and continues to provide the best directions based on where I originally said I wanted to go. If someone blatantly ignored multiple suggestions that I offered, I would be angry. But the navigation system is confident in its directions and does not know anger. Without judging or rejecting me, it unconditionally continues to help me.

When we accept ourselves with unconditional love, we gain the power to accept others and the power to give love freely. We naturally treat others with respect and dignity, and expect to be treated the same. We do not abuse others psychologically or physically, or allow others to abuse us. Conversely, when we cannot accept others, it may be because we reject the part of ourselves that we see in our relationship partner. Love is the core of our being and acceptance is our natural tendency. But it is not easy to love and accept others when the dragons of change cause us to be afraid of being rejected, afraid of being hurt, or afraid of not having enough.

Acceptance and love are especially challenging when they seem to tell us to watch a child, relative, friend or coworker struggle with life's changes. Unconditional love and acceptance may mean allowing them to make what we call mistakes. Too often, we jump in and solve their problems, even though we would resent such help if it we forced on us. Unconditional love enables us to allow struggling relationship partners to discover their own path through difficult changes using the abundant resources that lie inside each of us. *What the world needs now is love, sweet love. It is the only thing that we have too little of.*

----Essential Tip #5----
Be Open & Honest
~Throw Away the Secrets

Upon the friendly fields of strife are sown the seeds that on other days, on other fields, will bear the fruits of victory.
— General Douglas MacArthur

Thanks for Asking

Openness and honesty areclear signs of strength, courage and self-esteem.

Each fall I participate in the "Longest Day of Golf" to benefit the National Multiple Sclerosis Society. The objective is to obtain pledges from family, friends and business associates, and play as many holes as possible from sunrise to sunset. The typical pledge is a few dollars per hole. This year our foursome set a goal of raising $25,000 for MS, which meant I had to ask more people for pledges. I find it difficult to "ask for the money." But I solicited a business associate whom I was reluctant to approach in previous years. I told him we generally play about seventy holes. He pledged ten dollars per hole. When I thanked him profusely for his very generous pledge, he said: "No. Let me thank you. My sister suffers from MS, and anyone who helps MS is helping my family." A new relationship grew from that moment of openness and honesty we shared. We understand each other better.

Openness and honesty are vital in healthy relationships, especially when the world around us changes so frequently. Honesty means that everything we say is the truth. Nothing is manipulated, conveniently forgotten or hidden in a feeble ttempt to mislead. Openness means we express exactly how we feel about transactions and the relationship. Everything, all the time, without any fear of rejection or retribution. Openness and honesty push the nagging dragons of doubt, confusion and misunderstanding out of relationships.

We build trust when we say sincerely: *I'm afraid of... I'm not sure if... I was wrong when... I need... I'm sorry I...* Such vulnerable words leave us open to a variety of responses from our relationship partners. But openness and honesty are certainly not weak. Rather, they are unmistakable signs of courage, strength, high self-esteem, and clear personal values. Openness and honesty demonstrate unconditional love, and build a solid foundation for lasting relationships.

Most us want relationships that are cheerful, rewarding and fulfilling. We are stimulated by passionate discussions of ideas, hopes and dreams. We are inspired by honest discussions of feelings, choices, goals and plans. On the other hand, we get bored when work, weather, sports and other people are the only subjects that are discussed. Those are interesting topics, but a relationship feels empty and shallow when we are reluctant to share with our partner what we really want, what really excites us, what we really feel, or what we really are afraid of.

Lack of openness and honesty puts a relationship in a small box. A box that has too little inside and too much outside. *Don't tell my spouse... Be sure my boss doesn't find out... We can't tell them that...* Small relationships live in fear of judgement and fear of the future. Those fears limit the peace and joy we experience in our families and careers. Often we feel we are helping others when we avoid talking about subjects that might make them feel uncomfortable. But to equate comfort with caring shrinks the relationship. Instead caring may mean challenging our relationship partners about their negative behaviors and attitudes, and appreciating and thanking them when they challenge us in a similar way.

When we are afraid of judgement and embarrassment, we reduce the value and the intimacy of our relationships.

We create a true safe space in our relationships by encouraging our relationship partners to be open and honest, to really know us, and to allow us to know them. It is amazing how often, when we open up and tell a friend about a problem, the problem gets smaller and a viable solution appears just because we have talked about the problem openly and honestly. The vignettes in this section are about being open and honest about our past, about discussing our needs openly and honestly, and about building effective relationships through openness and honesty.

Precious Secrets, Precious Pain

Secrets stop us from enjoying our closest relationships. Being open and honest sets us free.

The year I spent in an orphanage was my biggest secret. For decades I was ashamed that my biological father "threw me away." I felt he did not want me because I was worthless. Being adopted by my grandfather was another secret. I felt secure, but not wanted or loved, in my adopted family. For decades, I changed the subject when people spoke of their childhoods. That my wife was pregnant when we were married was a another big secret. For years I spent enormous time and energy hiding these secrets. But running from my secret dragons left me feeling tired and angry. I was afraid of being scorched if one of my big secrets got out. Keeping my precious secrets became survival itself.

I was painfully wrong for a long, long time. In reality, my secrets kept me from having close relationships and experiencing the joy of intimacy. You have read my most precious secrets in this book. Nothing has been held back. There are no more secret dragons in my closet. I feel lighter. My secrets may seem benign to you. Most people feel that their secrets are darker and more serious than anyone else's secrets. You may feel that it was easier for me to share my secrets than it would be for you to reveal yours. Maybe you should reconsider. The price of a lifetime of joy and peace is a brief struggle with secrets.

Like me, you may have kept secrets all your life because you did not want people to know your past. You may have lived in fear that somebody might find out and reject you. You may have held painful secrets close to your heart as if they were precious gold. But with each lie to protect a secret, we blow off self-esteem. Soon we have done so many cover-ups that no self-esteem is left.

Actually, if your experience is like mine, you will laugh at your old secrets. I joke that I do not have a family tree, I have a family vine. My grandfather is my father. I am my uncle's brother, and my cousins are my nieces and nephews. Writing about my secrets in this book has been painless. In fact, *thank you* for letting me release the last remnants of the precious pain I have carried inside for over fifty years.

Fishing with Dad

Openness and honesty are not about *the relationship, they* ARE *the relationship.*

Fishing with my adopted dad, who actually was my maternal grandfather, was a source of many intimate moments. When he retired, I was a teenager. Fishing was his favorite hobby, and he took me along several times a year to fish for fluke and flounder. We would leave our home in Freeport, New York, in the morning in an eighteen-foot boat with a thirty-five-horsepower outboard motor. The trip to Jones Inlet near the Atlantic Ocean or one of his private fishing holes generally took about an hour. We would fish quietly into the early afternoon before heading home. We talked as we fished. I learned many significant and lasting lessons from him during the fishing trips when he openly and honestly shared his life stories and his favorite maxims:

• ***A man wrapped up in himself makes a small package.*** My dad knew the joy of giving to others versus the cost of being a one-man show. Based on what he thought were unsuccessful family relationships, he told me how easy it was to get caught in the ego-gratifying excitement of business while important life events pass by. He encouraged me not to exaggerate my self-importance, but to remember that happiness and joy come from relationships with others. Especially family.

• ***Do what others are unwilling to do, the things you like least, and you will succeed beyond your wildest dream.*** In college, my dad catered campus parties because no one was willing to serve food. While everyone else partied, he built a food service business that paid his college expenses. He said that, if I had a list of things to do, do first the thing that I liked the least. He explained that doing first what I liked best would create a feeling of dread toward the remaining tasks. On the other hand, the exhilarating feeling of completing the most unpleasant task first would be a stimulus to finish everything else. People sometimes wonder how I get so much done. It is because of the advice my dad gave me while we were fishing.

• ***Don't get your meat and bread at the same store.*** There were tears of regret and sadness in my dad's eyes as he confessed his affair with a young secretary, an unwanted pregnancy, a divorce from my maternal grandmother, and being disowned by his father (my great-grandfather). That secretary became his second wife and my adopted mom. I had heard parts of the same story from other family members, except that they told it with bitterness. My dad was genuinely sorry for the mistake he had made twenty years before I was born. He survived that mistake, made the best of the situation, and endured the pain. Sharing that pain gave me a lesson that endures today, and is serving me well as my business grows.

• ***Average people learn from their mistakes. Brilliant people learn from the mistakes of others. And stupid people make the same mistake over and over again.*** We often talked about "doing the right thing" and how to recognize "the right thing." He suggested that I look at what worked for others and emulate it in my life. He told me it was much easier to learn by watching other people make mistakes, than it was to suffer through the mistakes myself. But sometimes, he said, it is inevitable that we make a mistake and "learn the hard way." He admonished me to learn the lesson *the first time*, because it is stupid to make the same mistakes over and over. He shared with me what he judged to be mistakes in his life in the hope I would be in the brilliant category and not repeat them in mine.

Those fishing trips were intimate moments I have never forgotten. My dad shared himself openly, honestly and completely, including the most painful experiences in his life. He allowed himself to be vulnerable. But in those moments of vulnerability, I saw and felt the depth of his strength and wisdom. Hiding embarrassing moments and pain would not have been as effective in building my admiration as his openness and honesty were.

The dragon of shame would have us believe that keeping mistakes a secret will increase the respect we receive from others. The reverse is actually more likely. Respect grows for relationship partners who openly and honestly share the lessons they learned from past mistakes. Respect atrophies when we hear about the mistakes from someone else.

Ancient History

Sharing our stories openly and honestly is stimulating when the stories become the reasons for our dreams.

As a boy, I attended a church service where the minister held up a crispy new $20 bill and asked: "Who would like this?" Everyone in the congregation raised their hand to say "yes." He then crumpled up the money, threw it on the floor, pointed to the bill, and challenged us by asking: "Now who wants it?" Every hand still went up. Next he stomped on the money with his shoe, ground it into the floor, picked it up, and showed it to us. The once clean $20 bill was now wrinkled, dirty, and torn in one corner when he asked for a third time with an incredulous tone in his voice: "Would anyone want it now?" Again everyone raised their hand. He gave the money to a handicapped woman who was in a wheelchair near the front row.

He continued the sermon by saying: "No matter what I did with the money, you still wanted it because its intrinsic value was the same." He said that each of us was like that $20 bill. Sometimes in our lives, we may feel crumpled, thrown on the floor, dirty, and stomped on by a mistake we made or an unfortunate event that occurred. But no matter what has happened in the past, or whatever might happen tomorrow, our value is undiminished. We are priceless to those who love us. Our value is not in what we do, or what we have accomplished. Rather, our intrinsic value lies in *who we are* and *what we stand for*.

I am fascinated to hear how people have transformed horrible adversity into happy, rewarding lives. Their stories help me deal with the relatively minor dragons of change that creep into my life. On the other hand, it is depressing to listen to those who continuously retell stories of circumstances or past events that are still barriers to their happiness today. Victims of ancient history. Some full-grown adults tell dragon-like stories about awful childhoods that limit their success and joy today. Fifty years ago their father abandoned them. Forty years ago their mother was an alcoholic. Thirty years ago they were sexually, emotionally or physically abused. Twenty years ago they lived in poverty, and could not afford an education. Ten years ago they were unfairly fired from a job. And yesterday they stubbed their toe. They speak as though no one could possibly succeed after such adversity. Unfortunately, they probably will repeat the same stories for their entire lives. But I do not want to hear them.

On the other hand, the late Christopher Reeves was inspiring when, after an accident that left him paralyzed, he invited the world to enjoy living each day. It is stimulating to see abundant joy under such circumstances. Superman-turned-quadriplegic seemed to see more beauty in life as a cripple than he did as a successful movie star.

Being open and honest about our values and our dreams for the future is among the most exciting gifts we give each other. I am eager to hear what you stand for, the goals you strive for each day, and the new possibilities you see for improvements in our world. They interest me even though I may have different values and goals, and I may see our world in an entirely different way. The beauty is sharing our stories with each other in openness and honesty to honor our roots, accept the events that have shaped our lives, and then moving on to our goals for the future. My father put me in an orphanage when I was three. For decades that was *my story*, my reason for not trusting anyone. Now, it has shaped my vision for the future. It is why building effective family relationships is a top priority for me. How has your story helped shape your vision for the future?

The Voices in My Head

Change is born and bred in the honesty and clarity of the conversations we have with ourselves.

I feel unsettled and anxious when I am not open and honest about my needs with the voices in my head. I am in touch with four distinct voices, each with a unique personality and different perspectives:

- "Dr. Stieglitz," the analytic strategic planning executive
- "Richard," the loving husband, father and friend
- "Little Richie," my inner child, and
- "Frankendick" (short for Frankenstein), the dragon of my past failures.

You probably have about the same number of voices in your head too, although their personalities and perspectives are likely to be different.

My four voices hold town meetings to discuss today's big issues. Usually they compromise, but sometimes they fundamentally disagree about what I should do. Sometimes in risky high-pressure situations, they scream at and argue with each other. "Dr. Stieglitz" is clear about his goals and strategies, and feels compelled to make a difference in the world. "Richard" cares deeply about others, especially family. "Little Richie" always wants to have fun. He has never grown up, nor does he want to grow up. He sees life as too short to do anything that is not fun. Then there is "Frank," who is deathly afraid of failure. It seems like he has an electronically cross-indexed encyclopedia of everything that has ever failed in my life. He updates the encyclopedia every day with new stories about anything that did not produce perfect results.

A conversation among my four voices might go something like this in discussing a potential weekend task:

• Dr. Stieglitz suggests: *We must complete this extra task to be successful. I know it will take more time over the weekend, but it's very important to our goals and reputation.*

• Richard observes: *Our wife won't like it. She wants to go out for a picnic and country-western dancing Saturday night and we promised that we'd go with her.*

• Little Richie pipes in: *I don't wanna do it! Doesn't sound like fun to me, and it won't make much difference anyway.*

• Frankendick, always the voice of doom, predicts: *It will probably fail, but we've got to do it. If we don't, the client will cancel the contract and we'll lose the revenue.*

Those are the soldiers who fight on the mental battleground where I make important decisions every day.

Even though your warriors are different, you have a similar battlefield in your head. Something inside of us (call it "The ***I***") helps our voices come to terms with each other. The ***I*** is our values and purpose. When the ***I*** is clear, decisions are much easier. However, when our values or purpose are fuzzy, the ***I*** gets confused and decision-making is excruciatingly difficult. Since our voices want different things, the ***I*** cannot decide until all of them are heard.

In my case, "Frank" is dealt with quickly. Most of the time, the other voices easily discredit his exaggerated negative concerns. When he expresses a valid fear, the other three voices quickly agree, the ***I*** makes a decision, and everyone is happy. Sometimes, the vote is three to one and the ***I*** must determine why the fourth voice dissents. Maybe "Little Richie" does not see fun in the proposed decision. So the ***I*** will look for ways to make it into a game. Two against two is a tough vote. "Dr. Stieglitz" and "Frank" often align against "Richard" and "Little Richie." The question might be a chore that takes me away from the family. The ***I*** asks: *Will this chore achieve our purpose and does it support our values?*

Since the ***I*** has become clear about values and purpose, and used them in the decision process, the answer sometimes is: *No, it doesn't!* So the voices look for alternatives and the ***I*** is satisfied. Occasionally, all four voices have different opinions. Actually, that divergence is fun. "Little Richie" really enjoys it. The voices have learned that arguing is useless, so the four voices and the ***I*** unify the possibilities into the final choice. The results are fascinating. Openness and honesty about what is important resolves conflicts that otherwise might tear me apart. Firm values and clear purpose produce internal peace. They tame the voices in my head which otherwise might become dragons.

You Just Don't Understand

Effective communications depend more on how well we are understood, than on how eloquently we express ourselves.

Last night I asked my wife if she was hungry. She said "No." I was upset because I wanted to go out to a restaurant. I asked the wrong question! I should have said: "I'm hungry. Would you like to go to our favorite restaurant?" The dragon of feeling misunderstood often strikes when we do not clearly communicate our desires. We expect others to understand even when what we say is not what we mean. Remember that experts say over fifty percent of what we say is either not heard at all, or is misunderstood by the person we are talking to.

Several lines in *Gone with the Wind* have produced speculation about how the star-crossed lovers, Rhett Butler and Scarlett O'Hara, might treat each other in a Margaret Mitchell sequel. Scarlett and Rhett did not communicate openly or honestly. For example, when Rhett said: "Frankly, my dear, I don't give a damn!" he really did care about Scarlett. Or did he? And Scarlett seemed worried about the future when she said: "Oh fiddley-dee, I'll worry about it tomorrow." Or was she? It is easy to be misunderstood when we talk in riddles. Instead, Rhett might have said: "Scarlett, I'm angry. I care about you but I'm frustrated we aren't happy. What stops us from having the love that we want?" And Scarlett might have said: "I'm so worried about the future I can't concentrate. I need Rhett." These open and honest lines would have made a boring novel, but they may have produced an effective relationship.

Talking in riddles complicates relationships. The "eraser" words *however* and *but* obscure the real meaning of our communications. The statement "I love you, but your anger scares me" really means "I can't really love you because I'm afraid of your anger." Similarly, "I want to be home with you, however I have to work" really means "I won't be home because work is more important." Listen for *but* and *however* in your conversations. When you hear yourself use either of those works, mentally ask yourself if you really mean that the first part of your sentence was false.

Hold Those Tears

Sharing our feelings and needs openly and honestly strengthens relationships and builds our self-esteem.

To earn tuition in graduate school, I taught freshman Physics Lab. A girl in my lab class was not in the right college, and was not destined to be an engineer. She failed every lab report, and scored less than thirty percent on the mid-term. When I returned the exam, she sobbed uncontrollably and burst into tears. I did not know what to do to console her so I said: "Pull yourself together!" and ignored her for the rest of the class. I had no idea how to comfort someone who was feeling intense pain. Guess what happened as my daughters were growing up and became frustrated by the changes of adolescence? You guessed it. I had no idea how to deal with their tears and pain either. I was powerless to help.

Like many young boys, I was taught to hide my tears and never admit that I hurt inside. *Real men don't cry* was accepted truth among my friends and the grown men that I admired. Emotions were dragons that should be hidden. Learning the lesson well, I stuffed my real needs or ignored them altogether. Anything but cry or show emotion. But that made me like an eight-cylinder engine running on just four cylinders. I responded only to intellectual stimuli. With the emotional cylinders out of order, my engine did not run smoothly. I was uncomfortable dealing with people who felt joy so intense or pain so acute that they cried. In short, I was unable to empathize with others. When I finally got in touch with my inner pain after almost fifty years, I cried deeply. But, in acknowledging my pain, I learned to understand others in their times of need. Paradoxically, feeling my pain freed me to experience and savor the joys of life.

Why are so many of us afraid to express our needs or embarrassed to reveal our most intense emotions? Why do we feel it is weak to be open and honest about feelings? Quite the opposite is true. When we share our sharpest pains and most exhilarating joys openly, we enhance the quality of our lives and strengthen our most important relationships in our lives.

Swallowing Ball Bearings

When we stuff feelings, we are doing a massive con job on ourselves about what is really important in our lives.

Stuffing a feeling is like swallowing a ball bearing. Every time we stuff a feeling instead of sharing it openly and honestly, we swallow another ball bearing. Soon the ball bearings become a lumpy dragon of hostility and anger in our stomachs. A dragon that survives long after the causal event is forgotten. When my wife and I argue, I may bring up an event that occurred five years ago, an old ball bearing I carry in my gut. I have a high ball-bearing job with frustrations and changes every day. I may tell my wife that my day was routine, but the ball bearings I swallowed all day show in my attitude toward her.

Traumatic childhood experiences are often a source of swallowed ball bearings. For some, the ball-bearing level gets so high that they cry for no obvious reason. Tears are liquid ball bearings overflowing from our eyes. Openness and honesty eliminate ball bearings. Forgiveness and acceptance help too. When we are disappointed in something or angry at someone, the feelings can be expressed and released in a constructive way. When we are frustrated or discouraged, it is vital that we express those feelings openly and honestly.

When feelings like disappointment, anger or frustration are swallowed in one part of our life (like work), they emerge in painful and damaging ways in another part (like family). We overreact to minor provocations at home, when the real reason is repressed anger from work. The eventual price of stuffed feelings is poor health and deteriorating relationships.

Medical research also has shown that cumulative stuffed feelings contribute to psychosomatic illnesses (e.g., some forms of arthritis). To release feelings, we might say "I feel angry because..." rather than "You made me angry by...." "You made me angry" sounds like an accusation and usually elicits defensiveness responses. Whereas, "I feel angry because..." leads to open and honest discussions that resolve the issue or misunderstanding. No matter what the other person does in response to openness and honesty, we do not swallow the ball bearings.

The Masks We Wear

Intimate relationship flourishes between authentic partners, partners who have thrown away their masks.

Recently, I made a business trip to California. On the five-hour, nonstop flight from Washington to San Francisco, I sat next to a man about my age who was dressed in a suit and tie like I was. I initiated a conversation. I briefly described the business purpose of my trip to California and asked about his business. He responded: "I'm in sales" without saying what he sold or whom he worked for. I volunteered that I was looking forward to visiting my daughter, son-in-law, and baby grandson while I was in San Francisco. He said: "That's nice" without offering any information about his family.

After reading the sports section in the *Washington Post*, I was upset and sad in describing how I felt about the Redskins losing a close game the day before. He said he did not follow football. Golf was his favorite sport, and he told me that he had shot his best round ever (even par) just two weeks earlier. Being a golfer myself (but never close to par), I was excited for his success and asked how it felt to shoot even par. He spent the next thirty minutes telling me about his drives, shots from sand traps, and putts without ever being in touch with how it felt to shoot even par. I was willing to get to know him, but his mask was difficult to penetrate. If all he was willing to talk about was his golf shots, I would rather continue reading the newspaper.

Masks are coverups that extinguish meaningful relationships. Intimate relationships flourish when we remove our masks and reveal our authentic self. Here are a few masks I sometimes wear in spite of my best effort to be authentic in all of my relationships:

• ***The Mask of Satisfaction*** with what I have achieved since, if you knew my dreams, you may think I was really a failure.

• ***The Mask of Confidence*** because if you knew all the doubts I have inside, you would understand how scared and unsure I really am about the future.

• ***The Mask of Authority*** to conceal that, in many cases, I do not really have a clue what to do next. I just guess. But I do it with authority and decisiveness.

• ***The Mask of Contentment*** with what I have, which hides my doubts about the changes that lie ahead for me and my family as I enter retirement.

In reading this book, you probably have seen these more clearly than I do. You may see other masks of which I am not consciously aware. What masks do you acknowledge that you occasionally wear?

We wear masks to increase our social and professional acceptability, to create a public image. They become relationship dragons when we cling to them, and are afraid to be seen for *who we are* even in intimate relationships. As if *who we are* was something bad.

Masks that hide real and imagined fears and weaknesses come in many different forms. Some masks are physical, like makeup to cover blemishes and brighten cheeks. Wearing no makeup might be a mask of plainness to avoid being noticed. Attitudes of timidness, helpfulness or gaiety can be masks. A chip-on-the-shoulder mask might be used to conceal feelings of weakness or insecurity. Positions of authority can be masks too.

When our masks are removed, we all share the same hopes, needs and fears. That is where great relationships begin. The more open and honest we are in dropping our masks, the more likely it is that our relationship partners will drop their masks too. When I dropped my masks, I found that I liked the person behind the masks better than the masks in many ways. You probably will like the person behind your masks too.

To Crocus, or Not to Crocus

When we find ourselves disagreeing with a relationship partner, the first step to resolution is to listen carefully to his/her needs.

My wife and I landscaped our front and back yards a few years ago. I planned to plant 800 crocuses, tulips, daffodils and irises in the gardens. She did not like the idea. We discussed it a few time casually during the summer. In July, when I selected bulbs from a catalog to place the order for fall planting, she repeated her objections. We joked that our big decision was "to crocus or not to crocus." I thought I had placated her by ordering only white and purple flowers, her favorite colors. However, the discussion, now raised to the level of conflict, continued until the bulbs arrived. She refused to help me plant them, so I did it myself over two weekends. In the entire three-month drama, I never understood why she objected to planting the bulbs. The truth is I did not try to understand, because I was so intent on telling her why I wanted the flowers. Fortunately, a mutually pleasing result appeared in the spring when the purple and white flowers brightened our spirits.

Being open and honest is bi-directional. It also means hearing what others say. Until we understand each other's goals, it is difficult to find a change that will please both of us. I am surprised at how often I do not hear what others are saying. Or I ignore the clear message they are sending with their body language. *Seeking first to understand* is a challenging paradigm shift for me, a substantial change my pattern of relationships.

Insisting that others understand our point of view is a relationship dragon. Especially when, concurrently, we do not hear the feelings and needs that family, friends and coworkers express. Too often the sole objective of our listening is to gather data to build a rebuttal. By paying attention to what others say, we begin to appreciate their needs and can express our needs in context with mutual needs. When we truly listen and understand other points of view, new solutions emerge that we did not see before. There is no need to defend our position, because we are listening and thinking in a whole new way.

I Blew It!

A mistake not acknowledged is a second mistake.
Admitting mistakes is the first step toward fixing them.

My controlling nature as a father inhibited my daughters from maturing as quickly as they may have if I had given them acceptance and unconditional love. At times I was a tyrant. It took many years for me to say: "I blew it! I'm sorry. " But saying those words began the process of rebuilding our relationships. "I blew it" was not a confession intended to elicit forgiveness or sympathy. Rather, it was an open and honest expression of regret, and a commitment to be different in the future. My daughters tell me that they know I did the best I could, and I appreciate their generosity and compassion.

"I'm sorry, I was wrong" are among the most endearing words in the English language, second only to *I love you.* Saying "I was wrong" diffuses anger, ends arguments, and restores relationships. The clear message in those words is that the relationship is more important than being right. It is one thing to make a mistake that affects others, and quite another to acknowledge it. Defensively justifying ineffective actions, covering mistakes, or blaming them on factors beyond our control breathes fire on the future of a relationship. No amount of explanation can erase the effects of our actions, and explanations often dilute the trust and confidence that our relationship partners have in us.

Acknowledging that we could have done better in the past and committing to do better in the future opens the door to cooperation and understanding. Mistakes are more easily corrected today and avoided in the future when we openly and honestly take responsibility for our results.

Everyone knows that mistakes are human, a normal result of not anticipating changes or inaccurately interpreting the available data. What people find difficult to forgive is our reluctance to recognize that we made a mistake. "I'm sorry" accompanied by making new choices are very effective first steps in rebuilding the trust which is so vital in successful family and professional relationships.

Do You Trust Me?

If you are trusting, someone may take advantage of you. Be trusting anyway.

I was one of fifty-four strangers who took part in a group exercise about trust. We faced one another, looked each other in the eye, and said: *I trust you*, *I don't trust you*, or *I'm not sure if I trust you*. About fifty percent of the strangers said they were not sure if they trusted me. Twenty-five percent said they trusted me, and twenty-five percent said they did not trust me. My responses to them were about the same. The conclusion is that seventy-five percent of people who have never met me before either do not trust me, or are not sure if they trust me. And I feel the same about them. No wonder new relationships are so hard to build!

Mistrust is a menacing dragon in relationships. One effective way to create trust in a relationship is to be trusting. Trust creates trust. Studies show that when one person trusts another, the second person is more likely to be trustworthy. Similarly, if the first person does not trust the second, the second person is more likely to be untrustworthy. It seems we trust those who trust us, and vise versa.

Effective relationships are based more on trust than technique. Verbal and non-verbal communications in trusting relationships are spontaneous. Trusting partners understand each other intuitively and accept change easily. On the other hand, communications in relationships that lack trust can be strained and tenuous. Even a simple "Hello" can trigger the dragons of doubt and fear: "What does he/she mean by that?" Being in such relationships is like walking on eggshells. Each word is chosen carefully to avoid breaking the shell.

As children we were taught not to trust strangers. It seemed like good advice at the time. But too often the dragon of mistrust persists in adult relationships such as jobs, marriages, families and communities. The belief that "I don't know you, therefore I shouldn't trust you" is all too common. Unfortunately, when I mistrust you, you immediately mistrust me. Mistrust does not work in any relationship, old or new. Therefore, let us start every relationship by trusting each other even if there is little evidence to support that trust.

Troubles

How we treat people when they make a mistake largely determines how we will be treated when we make a mistake.

A manager in my company had an affair with a subordinate. Both were married. When the affair became public knowledge as affairs always do, the gossip dragons were everywhere. Morale plummeted and allegations of favoritism were rampant among the staff. Several people expected me to fire them both. Such abrupt and judgmental action seemed inappropriate at a time when they already were suffering pain, shame and ridicule. They needed a friend, not an executioner. In an open and honest "carefrontation," they were that told such behavior was unacceptable. They could continue at the company provided the affair ended immediately. They were encouraged to be open and honest with their spouses, and seek professional help to repair their marriages. After a few weeks, the gossip dissipated and relationships returned to normal. Today, both employees have left the company and nobody remembers the incident. It was a joy to see one of the couples happy together recently at a social gathering.

No one enjoys being the subject of gossip. Therefore, when we gossip about others, it says less about them than it says about our character and our need to criticize others. Compassion, openness and honesty tame the gossip dragons. Effective relationships are built by valuing people and treating them with openness and honesty, rather than reactive judgements of their actions. Others may not share our values, and frequently they feel uncomfortable with the confrontation that openness and honesty sometimes produces.

Too often problems persist when we choose the path of least resistance by gossiping about others, or rejecting them. Understanding and patience toward a troubled family member, a friend in crisis, or an unscrupulous coworker demonstrates that we are trustworthy and compassionate. People will trust us when we are open and honest, and care enough to confront them rather than gossip about them to others. *To be trusted*, it is said, is greater than *to be loved*. In fact, it appears t me that to trust freely ***is*** to love freely.

Drive-By Shootings

Relationships take time and patience. Time to explain ourselves clearly, and the patience to wait for the right moment to discuss sensitive subjects.

I had just finished reviewing the financial reports for last month when I realized I was late for a meeting. There were a few items on the reports that required discussion and changes. Just then the phone rang. It was the vice-president of a subcontractor who said that a payment was late. I agreed to look into it. Pushed by the time dragon, I burst into the controller's office, hurriedly asked why the payment was late, and added that we would discuss the other discrepancies in the monthly reports later. In a rush to get to the meeting, my tone was abrupt and harsh. It was a *drive-by shooting* as surely as if I shot at the controller with a gun from a moving car. A few hours later after returning to the office, I met with him to explain what I meant and outline the needed actions. He had spent the entire morning upset about my outburst, and wondered what the problems really were. Recovering from my rash outburst required considerable time. I was open and honest, but in a manner that damaged our relationship.

Being open and honest does not mean dumping my frustrations and problems on others. The attitude we exhibit while being open and honest counts for more than what we actually say or do. When caring and sincerity show through, our relationships are strengthened by being open and honest even if we may not choose the most tactful words. The difference between openness-and-honesty and dumping is the recipient's willingness and readiness to hear what we want to say.

Deep feelings must be discussed directly with the person at whom the feelings are directed. However, the discussion needs to occur when they are ready. If they are busy, unaware or just do not care, openness and honesty come across like an accusation or criticism. Fortunately, there are several ways that we can release our feelings without dumping them on others. They can be released effectively in silent meditation, in letters that are never mailed, or in shouts in an empty room. It is essential that our feelings be released constructively.

ASS-U-ME

Openness and honesty not only avoid misunderstandings, they lift relationships to heights that cannot be achieved any other way.

An intern gave medicine to a patient that interacted with other medications, requiring emergency action to save the patient's life. The doctor said he did not want to interrupt other doctors to ask about side effects because his performance rating might be lowered. A newspaper story told of a novice pilot in a light plane who did not ask directions because other pilots would think he was lost. The plane ran out of gas, crashed and killed two people. A friend admitted she was embarrassed to ask how to change a toilet paper roll until she was thirty years old. It started when she was eight and was too bashful to ask her mother. It continued when she was fifteen and was embarrassed to ask friends. It grew into a dragon when she was twenty-five and was afraid to ask her husband. Finally at thirty, she saw her daughter change a toilet paper roll and learned how it was done. The point is that we can look foolish for an instant when we openly and honestly ask a seemingly trivial question, or suffer consequences of the dragons of ignorance.

Open and honest questions are vital in healthy relationships. An old adage tells us that to *ASS-U-ME* may make an *ass* of *you* and *me*. We are often off-base when we assume that we know what others are thinking, how they are feeling, or what they want. Instead, we might ask openly and honestly:

- *What I heard you say is... How do you feel about .....?*
- *What do you expect from me? I see your pain. Tell me about it.*
- *You look upset. What is it? You look tense. What's wrong?*

It is uncomfortable to ask this type of question because we seem to be intruding into another's private space. What if we should already know the answer to the question? Or we are the problem? When we ask such questions, others initially might see us as pushy or insensitive. But not asking the questions risks serious damage to our relationships. When we openly, honestly and sincerely ask others about their feelings and needs, we learn more about them and our relationship flourishes.

What to Wear on a Nude Cruise

We sacrifice freedom and risk missing life's pleasures when we hide ourselves. On the other hand, openness and honesty bring joy, laughter and intimacy into our relationships.

The nude cruise that leaves from Orient Beach on the catamaran *Tiko Tiko* is a highlight for my wife and I when we visit French St. Martin in the Caribbean. The cruise is a one-day trip to a deserted island with drinks and a delicious gourmet lunch. The passengers usually are eight married couples, most returning year after year for the cruise like we do. The night before our very first nude cruise, my wife could not sleep worrying what to wear. The options she considered were surprisingly diverse: (1) wear a cover-up without a bathing suit, (2) remove our clothes on the boat, (3) remove our clothes on the beach, or (4) go "full monte" when we left the car. Our dragon, of course, was the fear of being judged and subsequently teased by the other passengers.

Few areas generate as much anxiety as concerns over how people will judge our bodies. Will they think we are too fat, too thin, too big, too small, too short, too tall, or too weak? Many of us use clothes as a mask to shield us from judgements and criticism. Our bodies remain hidden behind clothes like precious secrets. On a nude cruise there is no place to hide those secrets. Having conquered that fear, we faced a new dilemma: would our fellow passengers think we were wearing the wrong clothes for a nude cruise?

We have laughed many times about our fears since the first nude cruise. We share the story with our companions each time we return for another nude cruise. That is the exhilaration of a nude cruise: complete freedom without inhibition or worry. Just glorious sunshine, laughter and fun. I do not recommend that everyone run around naked. Rather, my point is that we may be sacrificing our freedom and missing some of life's pleasures by hiding our secrets, when openness and honesty would produce huge quantities of joy and laughter. The nude cruise has produced such joy for us, even if we still wonder what to wear.

Closing Thoughts on Being Open & Honest

When we stuff openness and honesty to avoid upsetting a friend, we limit that relationship to topics of small consequence.

In explaining the concept of being open and honest to others, I say that people who care about me tell me when I have bad breath. People who do not care, tell someone else, or they cringe at my breath and say nothing. I do not enjoy being told I have bad breath. But there is no way for me to find out except being told by a person who cares. And it probably is uncomfortable for them to tell me I have bad breath too.

Instead of openness, some relationships are like the Simon and Garfunkel song "Sounds of Silence": the partners talk without speaking and hear without listening. They talk without saying what is really in their heart. They hear family, friends and coworkers through the filter of their own experience, without listening empathetically to their partner's needs and feelings.

Instead of honesty, some relationships deal in secrets. Secrets are not bad, they just have a high relationship cost. When a relationship has too many secrets, there is nothing significant to share. Secrets suck joy from our relationships. The voice in our head screams: "Don't tell him/her that!" Therefore, when someone asks you to keep a secret, weigh carefully the cost of that secret relative to your other relationships. If the secret is about a third person, you may want to say: "Don't tell me. I don't want a secret to hide from my friend." The hidden feelings that we call secrets do not fade or disappear. They erupt later in ways that potentially damage relationships.

In these rapidly changing times, pity the person whose relationships are a mix of unloving critics and uncritical supporters. Who will tell us the truth? Our most helpful relationships are friends who openly and honestly help us tame the dragons of resentment, low self-esteem, vanity, stubbornness, etcetera. Being open and honest is risky in a relationship because there is a wall of past secrets to overcome. Once we get over that wall, however, openness and honesty come naturally; and with them come joy, passion and freedom. Openness and honesty are essential ingredients in relationships.

---Essential Tip #6---
Just Say Yes
~ It's More Fun For Everyone!

A positive attitude does much more than turn on the lights in our relationships. It magically connects us to serendipitous opportunities that were somehow absent before we said YES.
— Earl Nightingale

YES or NO

YES *powers relationships to grow beyond individual contributions. I say* YES *to you, you build on my YES, I add to your* YES, *and so on.*

During the celebration of his fiftieth wedding anniversary, I asked my Great-Uncle Bill: "How did you stay happily married to Aunt Mae for fifty years? People call her a battle axe." At eleven years old, aunt Mae intimidated me. She was six feet tall, and dominated relationships with both her stature and her forceful personality. Uncle Bill's answer was simple: "No matter what Mae asks, I answer *Yes, dear*." Uncle Bill, a strong-willed gentleman in his own right, went on to explain that he said *YES* to his relationship with Aunt Mae, not necessarily the things she asked. He said that her specific requests were details to be ironed out sometime in the future.

YES and *NO* produce different relationships. *YES* strengthens bonds and builds synergy. *NO*, on the other hand, can be a dragon that breathes fire and scorches our relationships. *NO* forces our partners to search for new ideas, new goals, new interests or new activities that allow the relationship to continue. The importance of a relationship determines how many *NO*s will be accepted before our partner abandons us to look for a more rewarding and satisfying relationship. Based on the number of broken marriages, and strained professional and family relationships that exist today in our lives, there are too many *NO*s and not enough *YES*es. That can change in the twenty-first century if we just say *YES* to each other. If we just say *YES* to relationships, and just say *YES* to change and growth.

YES and *NO* are inseparable. They always occur together. When we go to bed, we say *YES* to sleep and *NO* to activities we might do if we stayed awake. When we say *YES* to working overtime at work, we simultaneously say *NO* to the activities we might do with family and friends. *YES* is not always positive, and *NO* is not necessarily negative. Rather our *YES*es and *NO*s reveal our priorities, the things we consider to be most important in that instant of time. Is the *NO* because we are choosing a bigger *YES*, or is it a *NO* without a viable alternative (a negative choice)? For example, saying *NO* to getting out of bed in the morning is a positive choice when the objective is to give our bodies needed rest, but a negative choice when the *NO* is because we are bored or afraid to start the day.

*YES*es and *NO*s that are based on positive choices build effective relationships; while *YES*es and *NO*s based on fear, apathy or mistrust damage relationships. As you read these vignettes, consider *YES* and *NO* to be concurrent events. If you are eager to read vignettes about *Saying YES*, what motivates the *YES*. If you are inclined not to read them, what motivates the *NO*? The vignettes demonstrate that saying *YES* is vital in healthy relationships. They show how *YES* is often the start of an exciting learning experience or significant change; and they provide techniques for sorting out the bigger *YESes*. Let us say *YES* to continuing our relationship. I will continue writing, if you continue reading these vignettes.

Wind Beneath My Wings

YES *is vital in a happy marriage.* YES *to dreams and activities.* YES *to sharing the emotional and physical challenges that we encounter every day.*

About a year before our thirtieth anniversary, my wife asked that we invite our family and friends on a cruise to renew our wedding vows. The idea sounded outrageous. Who would come? How much would it cost? Who would make the arrangements? I said *YES* because she was so passionate about the celebration. Twnety people joined us on the four-day cruise. They all enjoyed the touching renewal ceremony and champagne celebration that followed. My sister-in-law's gift was a movie that chronicled the key events in our thirty-five-year relationship: meeting in high school, college graduations, several new homes, our daughters growing up, the birth of our first grandson, and holiday celebrations. Those joyous memories were created by a *YES*.

Similarly, my wife's *YES*es have been the "Wind Beneath My Wings" that lifts me to new heights. When I asked her for our first date, she said *YES*. After we dated for three years, I asked her to marry me and she said *YES*. During the wedding we each said "I do," two more *YES*es. Where would our relationship be today if she had said *NO* to any of those requests?

Longtime marriage partners often wonder where the romance and fun went. Maybe it got lost in too many *NO*s. Thirty-five years ago if my wife asked me to go shopping, I would say *YES* just to be with her. Today, my first thought is *NO* if she asks me to go shopping. I find shopping and shopping malls to be boring. But my *YES* or *NO* has little to do with shopping malls. It is about being together. *YES* says "I want to be with you," while *NO* says "something else is more important than you." After too many something elses, she may conclude that I do not really like being with her. Too many *NO*s can become a dragon that weakens the marriage and forces our partner to look to other relationships for *YES*es. Fortunately, *YES* in relationships easily becomes a habit that builds happiness and success for the partnership. Try a few more *YES*es today in your most important relationship.

YES *Produces Results*

YES *is a key that opens a treasure chest of successes.*
The positive results of saying YES *may shock you.*

I have learned that when I do not know what to say, *YES* is the best answer. In 1993, a junior employee asked if he could install a web site for my company. I did not understand what a web site was then. At the time they seemed like expensive novelties. He estimated the cost of the server, firewall, software and installation at $100,000, plus $4,000 per month in recurring telephone and software license costs. Neither he nor anyone else in the company had ever installed a firewall. I cringed at the large investment and recurring monthly expense, but hesitantly said *YES* to the project. He struggled for three months to make the web site work, and several other employees jumped in to help. The benefits to the company of my reluctant *YES* were enormous in terms of hands-on training and the start of a whole new line of business services for the company.

Recognizing the unrealized potential in others creates wonderful possibilities. Saying *YES* to a new idea builds ownership in the person who suggests it. When we say *YES,* we validate their ability, build their confidence, and strengthen the relationship. Hearing *YES* can change a person's life dramatically. You will be surprised by the results of saying *YES* to people who are committed to an idea. Those *YES*es expand our success by tapping into the unlimited potential of others.

On the other hand, the dragon of negative judgements about someone's abilities ("NO, *he can't do that*") or the merits of his/her new idea ("NO, *that won't work*") smothers success. Everyone benefits from investing *YES*es in people. The adage *He didn't know it couldn't be done, so he just did it* applies. Enormous energy is unleashed when we genuinely believe that someone will succeed, even if we do not know how. It is vital for us to say *YES* with our words, our actions, and our body language. When we acknowledge each person as a *Master of the Universe*, we can expect them to achieve their highest purpose. And they usually do. Each person and each situation has potential treasures. Saying *YES* is the key which opens that treasure chest.

I'm Not Sure

Indecision strains relationships more than NO
because it feels like NO *with added doubts.*

A friend handed me his resume and asked if there was an opening in my company for his qualifications. I responded that I was not sure, and said I would distribute the resume among several project managers to see they had an open position. Ten days later, when I responded that his credentials were impressive but no suitable opening was available, he confided that my *NO* answer actually was a relief. In the ten days, he had worried that he was underqualified, that I did not like him, and that his salary request was too high. The ten-day period of indecision obviously had been a strain on our relationship.

Indecision is a struggle between our natural desire to say *YES,* and our doubts and fears relative to possible consequences of saying *YES*. Since prolonged indecision without explanation feels like *NO* to our relationship partners, it can be a more ferocious dragon than *NO* and more dangerous than a hesitant *YES*. The intent in delaying decisions is to gather more information or avoid the confrontation of an immediate *NO*. However, the message a relationship partner is likely to receive from our indecision is: (1) we do not like their request, (2) we prefer another alternative, or (3) we doubt their ability. Our partners expect us to answer *YES* or *NO* promptly, and they deserve a prompt response too. The confrontation over indecision can become especially intense if the request is urgent, a deadline is near, or the indecision period drags on and on. A delay implies that we do not recognize or acknowledge the urgency of their need.

When you face indecision in others on urgent matters, determine the factors that support *YES* in their minds, and amplify them. If the request is not urgent, giving people time to consider all alternatives is more likely to lead to a *YES* than added pressure. Increased pressure usually pushes people to the *NO* response. Whether it is *YES*es we are giving or *YES*es we hope to receive, a quick firm response, even if it is *NO*, is most effective in sustaining the relationship.

Parties or Mountains?

We say YES *to relationships that meet our needs, even though we may not clearly know what those needs are.*

My daughter has friends with widely varied interests. One likes to party late into the night. Another spends quiet nights at home with a special-needs child. A third enjoys being in nature. When my daughter wants to "party hearty," the first friend is the person to call. To share quality time with her son, she calls the second friend. The third friend is most likely receive the call is she wants to enjoy a weekend camping in the mountains. Of course, our relationships are more complex than these examples because they involve combinations of activities, goals and values.

It is easy to say *YES* to relationship partners who share common interests and values. They satisfy our needs and are likely to say *YES* to our requests. We trust them because they consistently have said *YES* in the past. We learn not to depend on friends who repeatedly respond to our requests with dragon answers like: "I don't want to," "I don't like it," or "I don't feel like it.." Those *NO*s send a subtle message that "you are a low priority." Such *NO* people do not become close friends, and consistent *NO*s from old friends often can end relationships.

Saying *YES* creates and builds relationships. People who are my friends today are people who have generally said *YES* to the things I have asked from them, and have requested things to which I am willing to say *YES*. Sports, intellectual interests, cultural events, spiritual beliefs, hobbies, nature, etcetera, are activities in lasting relationships. Such activities are opportunities to share quality time and communicate openly and honestly with each other. Sometimes we may say *NO* when another need is a bigger *YES*. The bigger *YES*es demonstrate our values and our priorities, and they are easily accepted by those who trust us. It is important that we know our relationship partners' interests and values because, when we want what they stand for, we will know where to get it. Likewise, if our relationship partners understand our interests and values, they will know what they will receive from us when they are looking for a *YES*.

YES, *And...*

We achieve our biggest goals through teamwork, and teamwork always begins with **YES, and...**

YES, and... is more effective in building relationships than *NO, because...* Consider a team of stone masons building a cathedral. Big stones, little stones, round stones, square stones, brown stones, and red stones. Where will they be fit in the cathedral? The first mason places a stone in the wall. The second mason says: "NO, because *that stone is not the right color.*" He removes the stone and puts in a second stone. The third mason says: "NO, because *that stone doesn't fit right.*" Of course, "right" is a personal definition of "fit." He takes out the stone, and inserts a third stone to replace the first two. The next mason says: "NO, because *that stone is too small.*" He removes the stone from the wall and replaces it with a fourth.

Finally, after hours of lifting stones, the masons see that the *NO, because...* dragon does not work. There is no wall after hours of hard work. So they begin to use a *YES, and...* strategy. The first mason puts a stone in the wall. The second mason says "YES, and *here's a stone that blends nicely*" as he adds the second stone to the wall. The third mason says: "YES, and *this stone fits well with yours.*" The next mason says: "YES, and *this stone fills the tiny gap.*" It is easy to see that a *YES, and* approach will build a cathedral much more quickly than *NO, because*.

Building a relationship is like building a cathedral. *YES, and* is fun, while the *NO, because* dragon frequently produces frustration. The goal is to build a cathedral and to enjoy the creative experience, not any particular stone. The synergistic result of a relationship is important, not the merit or demerit of any specific idea a partner may suggest.

YES, and... is especially effective when people interact to share ideas and solve problems that seem to have no practical solution, like world peace. The synergy is awesome: *1 + 1 +...* solves the unsolvable. *YES, and...* fosters buy-in and inspires creativity. Everyone contributes to and feels part of the result. Individually and as a group, they help achieve the goal. Our world will become everything we want it to be when we work together with a *YES, and* attitude.

We Are Our YES*es*

YES*es and* NO*s determine who we are, what we have, and where we are headed. Fortunately, we can change them whenever we choose.*

You and I choose to be exactly where we are today, doing exactly what we are doing, and having exactly what we have by the *YES*es and *NO*s in our past. I am the sum of the *YES*es and *NO*s I have ever said: *YES* to change, *YES* to sports, *YES* to spirituality, *NO* to religion, *YES* to alcohol, *NO* to drugs, *NO* to smoking, *YES* to education, *YES* to marriage, *YES* to children, *NO* to divorce, *YES* to the Navy, then *NO* to the Navy, *YES* to starting a business, *YES* to technology, *NO* to politics, *YES* to government, and so forth. I have learned a lot about the subjects to which I have said *YES*, and I am mostly ignorant about the things to which I have said *NO*.

We paint a unique portrait of ourselves with our *YES*es and *NO*s. Each *YES* and *NO* puts a little dot in the picture of who we are. The more decisive the *YES*es and *NO*s, the clearer the picture is to others. Measured by material possessions, I have been successful because I said *YES* to education, technology, a dedicated work ethic, and starting a company. I am not Bill Gates-successful because I have said *NO* to investment risks that might have made huge fortunes. On the other hand, I still have what I have because I said *NO* to risks that could produce financial ruin. My life views lean toward safety, so I say *YES* to safety and *NO* to risk. *YES* to keeping what I have, and *NO* to having more (or less).

Our *YES*es and *NO*s shape the window through which we see the world. At this moment, we each look out our respective windows and say *YES* or *NO* to suggestions from those with whom we live, play and work. The *YES* and *NO* choices we make today will help us achieve our goals, or stop us from having what we want. There is no guarantee with any *YES* or *NO*. But each *YES* or *NO* changes the probabilities of what might happen. Even though we have said *YES* or *NO* to something all of our life, we have the awesome freedom to change the answer. Our lives change when *YES*es become *NO*s, or *NO*s become *YES*es.

Quality Time

YES *breathes fresh air into a relationship. It teaches us about ourselves and the person to whom we have said* YES.

Too many *NO*s wreck a relationship. *NO* to quality time, *NO* to shared activities, *NO* to pursuing a dream, and *NO* to self-improvement are dragons that slay relationships. My company paid for employees and their spouse or significant other to participate in a course designed to enrich relationships. The widely acclaimed course was held Friday night, and all day Saturday and Sunday. Eight of fifty-three eligible couples said *YES* to the offer. My wife and I were one of the eight couples. We believe an outside stimulus like a course, a retreat, or a shared book helps keep our relationship vigorous. The experiential course included exercises to compare personalities, to demonstrate how our communications styles conflict, to measure the trust we share, and to resolve anger and frustration.

That course taught me about synergy. Of the four possibilities to resolve a disagreement (your way, my way, compromise or synergy), three do not work very well. Compromise is often considered to be an effective way to resolve relationship issues. But compromise leaves both partners feeling that they have sacrificed something. Compromise can produce "married singles," with each partner going their separate way. Synergy is finding an alternative that combines the best of two ideas, an alternative that lets both partners say *YES* enthusiastically and feel they have gained something more.

The course was highly valuable, but saying *YES* to sharing the experience with my wife was even more important to our relationship. What priorities caused forty-five couples to say *NO*? What was a higher priority than their relationship? In some couples, one spouse said *YES* and the other *NO*. Several *NO* couples said: "Our relationship is perfect. It doesn't need improvement." Four of those couples are divorced today. Thirty-plus years of marriage convince me that *YES* is good way to sustain an exciting, zestful relationship. Even if our relationship is perfect today, we will have fun saying *YES* while we make it better tomorrow.

The Tooth Fairy

Children acquire knowledge and skills through activities to which their parents say YES or NO.

My youngest daughter lost her first tooth when she was six. She had seen her older sister receive money from the Tooth Fairy by putting teeth under her pillow, and she was determined to do the same thing. As the family watched TV before bedtime, our daughter wrote a note to the Tooth Fairy. Suddenly she jumped up, ripped the note into pieces, and threw it in the garbage. My wife asked: "What's wrong?" She answered: "I misspelled a word. I spelled tooth T-O-T-H. How would you like it if someone misspelled your name?" My wife responded: "YES. It's important to communicate with the Tooth Fairy and all of us clearly." Sure enough, the Tooth Fairy left a dollar under the pillow for her tooth, along with a return note in which all the words were spelled correctly. To this day, our daughter is meticulous in her writing and may become a published author one day.

Saying *YES* to children builds their confidence. When children form a plan or new idea and present it to their parents, the response should be *YES* if at all possible. *YES* produces ownership in the child for the results of the plan. Whether it succeeds or fails, the child learns. *NO* responses feed the dragons of self-doubt. The maxim "It's easier to build confident children than to repair adults" was never more true than today.

When a child asks "Play with me," they really are asking "Be with me." When my daughters were young I often said "NO, not now" and promised to play with them when I finished work or after the football game. The message in my *NO* responses was that work or a football game were more important than my daughters. Clearly, that is not true for any parent. Today, I would say *YES* and enjoy playing with them. I especially would look for opportunities to say *YES* to their unusual and demanding requests, even if the requests left me feeling a little bit uncomfortable.

Sounds Like YES

"I understand how you feel" *sounds like* YES,
even though it is empathy rather than agreement.
People feel appreciated when they feel heard.

I overheard a conversation between a male supervisor and female subordinate in my company. The woman said: "I feel I can't succeed in this company because I'm not a man, and I lack military background." The supervisor's response was: *"NO,* you're not right. Look at the other women who are successful here." The supervisor's intent, of course, was to encourage the employee, but the messages he sent were: "Your feelings are wrong" and "You're not as good as other women."

Too often in personal situations, I find myself invalidating the feelings of family and friends by saying "You shouldn't feel... (afraid, angry, sad, discouraged, etc.) because..." My intentions may be noble, but the message I send is: "Your feelings are wrong because..." A *YES* response using the Triple-F technique (feel-felt-found) can be highly effective in turning around difficult situations: "I understand how you feel. Others may have felt that way too. And they have found that..."

Unfortunately, we sometimes send negative messages to those we love (spouses, children and parents) when we really mean to say *YES*. For example, as Mr. FIXIT (a common male role) I dispense helpful advice even when I have not been asked for help. When my daughters were in school, I often jumped in to help with homework assignments. My noble intention was to say: *"YES.* You can count on Dad. He's always here to help."

But the ferocious, relationship-slaying dragon embedded in the Mr. FIXIT message was: *"NO.* I don't think you can succeed without my help." Looking back through twenty years of hindsight, my approach today would be to show interest in their projects, ask them about their ideas, and be available to help *if* they asked for it. Respect for the ability of others to succeed or fail on their own sounds like *YES,* even though it is more like understanding and compassion than it is agreement. People feel good when they are respected.

Climbing the Walls

Saying YES *to activities we think we will not enjoy often produces incredible learning experiences.*

My wife and I traveled to South Carolina to visit her sister for Thanksgiving. The weekend started much the same as Thanksgiving weekend for millions of families. We arrived Wednesday night after an endless drive, several hours longer than expected. On Thanksgiving Day, we had turkey with all the trimmings, ate too much, and watched football for most of the day. Friday morning at breakfast my teenaged niece asked her dad, brother and me to go climb an indoor mountain in a warehouse. My first reaction was *NO*. I never climbed a mountain before, outside or inside, and it did not sound like something I should start learning at age fifty. Even though I watched two football games on Thanksgiving, I was looking forward to more games that afternoon with a turkey sandwich and a cold beer. She persisted in the request, and finally we all reluctantly agreed to give it a try.

The result of conquering the resistance dragon and saying *YES* was a stimulating challenge, an exciting experience I will never forget. Strapped securely in a safety harness, I climbed three progressively more difficult indoor mountains. Each mountain was a forty-foot vertical wall with built-in handholds around large protruding obstacles. The first two mountains were physically challenging, but I reached the top easily. In addition to being the most difficult, the third mountain was a bigger challenge because I was tired physically and emotionally. About ten feet from the top, with both hands and arms aching, the thought that I might fall first entered my mind. Before that thought, falling was not a possibility. Less than thirty seconds after the thought, I fell and was caught with a jolt by the safety harness.

My niece remembers it as the day we said *YES* to her request. I remember the day as my first and last mountain-climbing experience. I also received a refresher lesson letting the fear dragon into my thoughts. When I focus on something in my thoughts, I cause it to happen in my reality. It is not unusual to have an exciting learning experience when we say *YES* to an uncomfortable new activity.

Saying *YES* to Myself

Saying YES *to ourselves is a joyful experience, while* NO *is painful. Begin the joy by saying* YES *to yourself.*

As I write this vignette during the holiday season, I am struggling with my diet and exercise habits. I know that healthy eating and regular exercise are things I should do. I want to reduce my weight, but I do not want to change my lifestyle. Exercise is forcing myself to do something that I hate. It hurts. If I ate only healthy meals, eliminated snacks, and skipped my glass of wine with dinner, I would feel like I was depriving myself of things I have worked hard for and deserve. Intellectually, I know what tames the dragon of lifestyle habits. If only I could embrace the goal of my own health, it would be easy to say *YES* to exercise and healthy eating. But by saying *YES* to my health, I would simultaneous be saying *NO* to unhealthy living habits I have had for decades. But I do not want to do it!

Too often we say *NO* to ourselves, and in doing so surrender a slice of happiness to the dragon of self-deprivation. But there is little joy in forcing ourselves to do what we do not like, or denying ourselves the things we want. Self-deprivation, a trait in which some people take pride, is painful and may lead to feelings of depression, emptiness and dissatisfaction. It just plain feels better to love ourselves by saying *YES* to things we want. Why resist change when the real joy lies in saying *YES* to change?

Since each *YES* is simultaneously a *NO* to something that is less important (hopefully), we can focus on positive *YES*es rather than painful *NO*s. By attaching the "want" label to things to which we say *YES*, we align our thoughts and actions, and eliminate crippling inner conflicts. By being clear about our choices, we avoid the indecision and stress of wavering between conflicting choices. By genuinely wanting physical fitness, for example, a healthy diet and exercise actually become fun. They become enjoyable when I embrace the *YES*es, instead of wrestling with the tormenting *NO* dragons that I seem to invite into my life so often.

Too Many YES*es*

Choose the best YES, *and have the courage to pleasantly say* NO *to other possibilities even if they also are good things.*

When I tell my wife: "Honey, I'll be home at 6:30 tonight" and arrive at 7:15, it is probably because I said *YES* to too many meetings, e-mails and phone calls. But none of them were as important as my wife and family. I may blame the traffic, but that is just a convenient excuse since it is the 2,000th consecutive week night there was heavy traffic on the Washington beltway at 6 p.m.

The good-guy dragon pushes us to say *YES* when *NO* is a better answer. However, we are afraid that *NO* will: (1) disappoint a friend, (2) take too long to explain, or (3) be politically incorrect. None of these are valid reasons to say *YES* when we mean *NO.* Saying *YES* may avoid a confrontation, but the people to whom we say *YES* expect us to do what we say. They plan on it. And when it does not get done, the misunderstanding is worse than if we had said *NO* in the first place.

Most of us feel compelled to meet commitments, to do what we say we will do. Unfortunately, we also make too many commitments. And while trying to meet the commitments, we steam with frustration about saying *YES* (at the time it looked like an easy way out) when we wanted to say *NO.* As company president, employees feel obligated to say *YES* to me. However, I am disappointed when someone says: "*YES*, I'll have it Monday" and the job is not finished Monday. I would rather they had said *NO* in the beginning. Of course, I do not like being told *NO.* But *NO* forces me to explore other alternatives and, in the long run, more gets done on time.

Too often we say *YES* to something that looks urgent, but there is something even more important to which we simultaneously say *NO.* Even when the urgent task is good, the good holds us back from doing what is best. Too many *YES*es is a disaste. Too many *YES*es produces stress, broken commitments, and weakened relationships. Sometimes it is vital for us to say *NO* to one good thing in order for us to say *YES* to the best possibilities for our health, our family and our career.

Too Many *NOs*

Unless you are incapacitated, "NO, I can't" *really means that something else is more important to you.*

During a trip to Italy my wife and I went to Fiesole, a town near Florence known for ruins that date before the time of Christ. We took an hour bus ride from Florence to reach the small hillside town. After a splendid day in town and tasty dinner at a local restaurant, our traveling companions returned to the hotel in Florence. I wanted to leave too, but my wife wanted to visit Villa San Michele, which was designed by Michelangelo. As we walked up the winding hill to the villa, we heard a piano on the balcony playing *Phantom of the Opera*. My wife wanted to go in. I was worried about missing the last bus to Florence. As we entered, the bellman offered a cordial welcome and directed us to the bar. After relaxing drinks and conversation, we had enough time to run down the hill and catch the last bus to Florence, laughing all the way.

NO can be a barrier to enjoying life. Several times on the trip to the villa, I felt like saying "NO, I don't want to" even though there was no good reason for *NO*. Such *NO*s erode relationships. Unless *NO* is to a bigger *YES*, *"NO,* I don't want to do…" can easily be interpreted as "I don't want to be with you." Too many *NO*s is just as ineffective as too many *YES*es. Frequent *NO*s cause separation and monotony. On the other hand, my reward for taming the *NO* dragon in Fiesole was a marvelous memory rather than a disagreement with my wife.

Similarly, the first reaction to a change or a new activity might be: *"NO,* I can't" even though such *NO*s lead to life in a small box. And the statements it is not true either. Unless we are a quadriplegic or are hospitalized in a full-body cast, *"NO,* I can't" really means something else is higher priority. Hopefully, the something else is a big *YES*. A more open and honest response than "I can't" might be "Sounds like fun, but something else is more important." That may seem harsh, but direct *NO*s make priorities clear to everyone. Too many *NO*s weaken relationships, while *NO*s that simultaneously say *YES* to our highest priorities and values are vital in joyous families and prosperous careers. Start saying *NO* to the *NO* dragon.

Bad Hair Day

Saying NO *can arouse the dragon of defensive responses.*
That dragon is much easier to tame with YESes *than* NOs.

A high-priority project at work taught me that progress follows *YES*es, not *NO*s. It was a complex, high-priority project whose success depended on full collaboration by three companies and two government agencies. The project manager from the lead company presented a fifteen-month project schedule to the team. I essentially said *NO* by pointing out where the schedule was weak and incomplete. It used the big-bang approach: like magic, the three critical paths finished on the same day at the end of the project. I argued for incremental implementation, and identified several intermediate steps that should be added to the plan. After a major showdown in an open meeting with our mutual customer, my ideas were rejected and the schedule was adopted.

I call it my "bad hair day" because anger at having my suggestions rejected damaged several valuable relationships. My ideas might have been embraced by the team if, instead, I had focused on strong points of the schedule. It would have been more effective to identify the strong points in the schedule, say *YES* to them, and then offer improvements. The fact that two years later, actual project results showed that my suggestions were correct is irrelevant. Several key relationships were forever damaged. In that painful experience, I missed the big *YES* (the project's success) and learned the importance of saying *YES*.

The dragon of defensive responses falls asleep when it hears *YES*. *NO*, on the other hand, wakes him up and fuels his fiery breath. We will achieve more of our goals by letting that dragon sleep. So just say *YES*. If one person says *YES*, others will say *YES* too. A few people saying *YES* encourages others to join, and that builds teamwork. With a harmonious atmosphere, new ideas can be inserted easily. Resources become available and the team's efforts are aimed coherently toward the goal. On the other hand, *NO* causes conflict, which diverts some energy to fight the conflict. That energy is more productive being used to build synergy among ideas. So let the defensiveness dragon sleep peacefully. Just say *YES*.

Right Doesn't Matter

Pick your battles. Ask yourself if the clash that damages today's relationships will really matter a month or a year from now.

A divorce was granted for "irreconcilable differences" when the wife cited example after example where the husband was a slob who refused to clean the house, and the husband testified that the wife was a neat-nik who cleaned the windows after a rain storm. Who was right? Does it matter? To the newly divorced couple, being right about a clean or messy house was more important than the marriage, children, decades of shared experiences, and financial stability. Was it?

Like marriage, politics is another arena where intelligent people often say *NO* to each other and are burned by the being-right dragon. It is sad to watch the President, the Republicans, and the Democrats in Congress argue about the annual budget. The issues are different every year, but the results are the same. By law, the budget should be passed by Congress and signed by the President by September 30th. I do not recall a year in the last ten when they met that statutory requirement. Nor do I recall an issue that was so crucial to the country's future that it was worth paralyzing the government for weeks and months. I do remember dreadful budget arguments, name-calling, and Continuing Resolutions (CRs) sometimes lasting into January.

Look at the results that the being-right dragon produces. Budget impasses that cause Federal agencies to limit operations for months while Congress argues over who is right. One-third of the fiscal year gone before the agencies know how much budget they will get (or not get) for their most important programs. The well-intentioned men and women in Congress have decades of experience in public service. They believe intensely in what they are doing. But apparently they fail to realize that being right does not produce the results they are committed to achieve. They appear to have lost sight of the bigger *YES* for which they were elected. Are you and I any different at the level at which we operate? Do we give in to the being-right dragon, and wonder why our relationships are strained? Maybe we could achieve more of what we want in our lives if we were not so right.

Sandblasting

A relationship changes forever when a request is made. Whether the response is YES *or* NO, *the relationship cannot remain the same as it was before the request.*

A friend invited me to a Saturday morning course in glass sandblasting. I had never done sandblasting before and, frankly, was not interested in learning. However, except for some routine chores I had nothing important to do. If I said *NO*, I would be saying that routine chores were more important than the relationship. *NO* might send the wrong message, since the request was more about companionship than sandblasting. On the other hand, an open and honest response like: "*YES,* I'll go. I'm not sure about sandblasting, but I'll enjoy being with you" would send a message that the relationship was a priority, even if sandblasting was not. Of course, my answer must be *NO* if there was a bigger *YES* for Saturday morning.

NO to a bigger *YES* can create opportunities to grow relationships by combining ideas. The bigger *YES* in this case might be Big Brother volunteer work with fatherless boys. I might have responded: "Thanks for the invitation to sandblasting, but I already committed to be a Big Brother to two boys." He might say: "Let's combine the two ideas and take the boys sandblasting." And I could say: "That's a super idea. I'll call the boys and you arrange for make the course." Combining our best ideas takes relationships to new highs.

Whenever a relationship partner makes a request, the relationship changes. It cannot be the same. When the answer is *YES*, our partners feel good. When we say *NO*, dragons play in their heads wondering why. Relationship partners risk rejection and judgement to make requests. The request is a search for more, and part of them is afraid to be rejected. When we reject a request (a *NO* response) and judge it to be boring or inappropriate, our relationship partners may apply that judgement to themselves. When we say *YES*, we endorse the value of their suggestion which, in turn, shows how highly we value them. In summary, since *YES* strengthens relationships and brings joy into our lives, why would we ever say *NO*?

How to Say YES

Understand the person to whom you say YES *or* NO,
since YES *and* NO *sound different to different people.*

Believe it or not, *YES* does not have the same effect on everyone, mostly because each *YES* is really a *NO* to something else. *YES* sounds different and has different meaning to people who make decisions quickly or slowly, who are very concerned with how others will feel, and who are obsessed with having all the information. Consider these four personality styles using a football metaphor.

• Cheerleaders are high-energy, *yea-rah-rah* people who are excited by new ideas and other people. They are stimulated by passionate *YES*es and utterly deflated by *NO*s. Be ready for immediate action when you say *YES* to a cheerleader since they will move into action quickly! If you know any of these people (and you probably do) and must say *NO* to them, offer another exciting choice (a bigger *YES*) with great fanfare and energy so they will not become depressed and will be willing to move to other ideas.

• Team chaplains are gentle, kind people who make decisions very slowly. They want to be sure that everyone will be happy with their *YES*es and *NO*s. They will be relieved if you are happy about saying *YES,* and uneasy with your *NO*s. When saying *NO* to the team chaplain, it is helpful to provide an alternative that most others will accept, and an explanation of why *NO* will be best for everyone.

• Fullbacks gather the available information, make decisions quickly, and charge forward into *YES* or *NO.* If you do not agree with their YESes or NOs, it may be best to stay out of their way until they run into a wall. These time-driven, assertive people have difficulty hearing your *NO*s, especially quiet or uncertain *NO*s. To be heard by a fullback, *YES*es must be firm and unequivocal, and *NO*s must be clear and confident. I know because I am a fullback.

• Statisticians are deliberate, well-organized people who research all of the facts before making a decision. They have a hard time saying *YES* or *NO* because they always want more data. Whether you say *YES* or *NO* to a statistician, they will want to know, in detail, the complete basis for your decision. Be ready to explain using clear, well-documented facts.

The interactions among these four personality styles are humorous and entertaining. A statistician is perplexed when a cheerleader says: "*YES*, it feels good!" because "feels good" cannot be verified using a desk calculator. Looking at it the other way, cheerleaders are frustrated by statisticians because they take so long to say *YES* or *NO*. And, when a statistician does respond, the answer is preceded by a frustratingly long analysis of the facts.

Interactions between fullbacks and team chaplains are equally amusing…and strange. It seems like they speak different languages or exist on different planets. Misunderstandings are commonplace when team chaplains make sure that everyone agrees, while the fullbacks lunge into decisions not concerned at all if anyone agrees.

Effective *YES*es and *NO*s differ among cultures too. For example, conversations among people from eastern cultures appear to be indirect and inefficient to westerners. A direct *NO* is rarely given, because *NO* is deemed to be rude. The eastern way of saying *NO* is to ask questions that identify probable adverse consequences of the *YES*. Similarly, *YES* emphasizes probable positive consequences. This method of saying *YES* or *NO* avoids conflict, but increases confusion and the chance of a misunderstanding.

The effectiveness of the *YES*es and *NO*s (always to a bigger *YES*) we deliver to our relationship partners depends on knowing their personality style, their tendency to make quick or slow decisions based on people or facts. Similarly, we must be aware of, and acknowledge, the cultural preferences of the people with whom we deal to build effective and satisfying relationships.

Closing Thoughts on Saying YES

Dictionary Definition of Serendipity: "The discovery of happy, agreeable and valuable things by accident."
YES *brings serendipity into our lives.*

Last night I walked through the office kitchen and was surprised to see an employee washing and putting away the coffee cups. He had made the kitchen spotless, much tidier than the cleaning crew leaves it at the end of the day. I said to him: "Nice job. Thanks for making the office look spiffy." His smile was immediate, and pride in a job well done beamed on his face. In the weeks and months that followed, I noted a sustained shift in the dedication he applied to the small details of his job, making them just right. Each time I observed his extraordinary attention to detail, I wondered if his new attitude had anything to do with the encouraging words I offered in the kitchen.

That experience caused me to trace the good things in my life to their origins. At first analysis, they seemed to happen by chance. I was in the right place at the right time, and things worked out for the best. Or a friend helped me when I would not have succeeded alone. Or I had a fortuitous past experience that enabled me to know exactly who to call or what to do. However, on closer examination, I saw that every good thing in my life came from saying *YES*: *YES* to meeting someone new, *YES* to a helping a friend, or *YES* to something new. The more *YES*es, the more success I experienced. The separation between the *YES*es and "accidental" success often was years, sometimes decades. But the accumulation of my *YES*es has brought happiness and success in serendipitous ways. Look at your life. What was the origin of the good things you are enjoying? They probably all started with a *YES*.

Each time we say *YES,* we lay a stone in the foundation of future success and happiness, with no conscious idea of what future success or happiness or success look like. *YES* is a dragon tamer. *YES* builds relationships. And relationships are what will bring us success and happiness in the twenty-first century. If you would like more serendipity to occur in your life, adopt the habit of saying *YES*. *YES* to change. *YES* to keeping old relationships and building new ones.

Part III

Our Actions
The Path to Happiness and Success

What we think, what we believe and what we know are in the end of little consequence. The only thing that matters is what we do.

Frozen in Indecision

Our lives will be what we say we want them to be, when we take actions consistent with our dreams.

We all know the story about the driver who sees a deer in the road while traveling through the forest. He blows his horn and slams on his brakes. The startled deer looks up, freezes in the car's headlights, and is killed when the driver cannot to avoid the collision. Like a deer, many of us freeze in indecision when we see the headlights of a major change in our lives.

Indecision is a dragon that causes us to resist the actions we know are needed to achieve our goals. In the time-space realm of our human existence, only actions produce results. Dreams may be enchanting fantasies, but they remain locked in our heads until we translate them into actions. Where we are at any moment in our lives is less important than the goals we set for our future, and the actions we take to achieve those goals. Our collective actions or inaction will have a larger and more immediate impact in the twenty-first century than ever before. Today's high-speed communications, coupled with increasing cooperation and self-awareness, are an ideal environment for us to transform our dreams into reality. Dreams are a vision of what is possible, the embryo of our future reality. Thoughts and words give birth to dreams, and actions breathe life into them.

Now is the time for us to produce what we want in our world, individually and collectively. This part of the book challenge us to take personal responsibility for taming our dragons, to make clear choices, to dream big dreams, and to realize our dreams by sharing them. We will start with vignettes about thought before action and transforming thoughts into actions. Your next action is to read the vignettes.

Like a Rocket

Actions can be carefully planned or spontaneous.
Either way, the consequences last a lifetime.

When *Apollo 13* traveled to the moon and back, a 500,000-mile round trip, it was powered for just a few minutes to escape the earth's gravitational pull and, in emergency conditions, just a few seconds to circle the moon and return the astronauts safely to earth. Similarly, actions that occur in an instant can have a huge impact on our lives. A wedding ceremony lasts roughly forty-five minutes, but no matter what happens to the future of the relationship, including death or divorce, those forty-five minutes affect every day. Some actions require a long-term investment, but pay lifetime dividends. Four years of college may seem like forever to a student about to graduate from high school, but statistics clearly show the four-year investment in college more than quadruples lifetime income on average.

Marriage and education are actions generally taken (or not taken) after considerable thought. Unfortunately, in other cases the dragon of immediate gratification sometimes entices us into actions that are not thought through as clearly but have just as large an impact. A flash of anger may injure someone, destroy property, or irreversibly damage a key relationship. A brief sexual encounter may produce a broken marriage, an unwanted pregnancy, or a life-threatening disease. A drunken celebration may rekindle an addiction, damage a reputation, or contribute to a deadly auto accident. Spontaneous actions like these are impulses of the moment. We may regret such actions for decades, even though they lasted just a few minutes or a few hours.

Life does not require us to be loving or angry, patient or rash, careful or spontaneous, frugal or extravagant, faithful or unreliable, empowered or helpless, open-minded or intolerant, thoughtful or insensitive, honest or devious, or generous or stingy. It does, however, require us to endure the consequences of our actions. Consistently basing our actions on dreams for the future propels our lives like a rocket in the direction we want it to go.

DO-DO Days

Choosing the right things to do is much more important to our future than doing things right.

If you let it, the DO-DO dragon of daily routines will push you ninety miles an hour (the safe speed limit is fifty-five) even if you are traveling on the wrong highway. Go, go, go. Do, do, do. More. More. More. Faster, faster, faster. But if you are not on the highway to your dreams, every mile you travel will take you further away from them. Periodically it might be helpful to relax for a moment in an imaginary hot air balloon floating over the highway to your dreams, looking down calmly at the things you do each day. You might find yourself yelling down from the balloon: "Dummy, you're on the wrong highway!" even as the *DO-DO* dragon encourages you to work harder, faster and longer.

Life is hectic when our actions are compulsive and repetitious, instead of being linked to a clear dream and well-thought-out plan to reach it. It is a sure sign that we have lost sight of our dream when our energy is spent in *DO-DO* days. A *DO-DO* day has so much to DO that we cannot DO it fast enough. I have DO-DO days all too frequently. I rush through the day DOing everything on my worklist. I have a list for weekends too. I use planning tools and read time-management books that help me DO things more efficiently. But efficiency is not a cure for the stress of having to much to do. Getting more done in less time just means that I will fill the free time with more things to DO.

Stop *DO-DO* days by looking what you DO each day. Eliminate things that do not make a real difference. For example, I have stopped compulsively checking and double-checking to ensure that tasks I have assigned get done. That was a disruptive behavior that consumed huge amounts of everyone's time, including mine. In today's helter-skelter world, it is incredibly easy to have DO-DO days. While efficiency is important, our dreams determine what we should be DOing. Efficiency may increase the speed of our imaginary cars, but our dreams should be showing us the highway on which we should be traveling.

Hoping, Wanting & Wishing

"I'll do it tomorrow" *is the first milepost on the highway to never.*

The actions we have taken so far in our lives are the reason why we have what we have today. We say we want more, but sometimes our actions do not align with our words. Like many people, we play games with the *I hope...*, the *I want...*, and the *I wish...* dragons and delay the actions necessary to transform our hopes, wants and wishes into reality. The truth is that, in our heart, the value of the prizes we *want, wish* and *hope* for is less than the price of the sacrifices and the actions needed to obtain them. We do not really want the prizes *that much.* In the dream-plan-act sequence, we are stuck in the dream step. Consider these stories, for examples:

• ***Hoping.*** The instructor in a self-empowerment seminar asked: "How many of you *hope* to win a lottery?" All fifty people raised their hands to say yes. Asked if they had purchased tickets in today's lottery, four said yes, and one claimed that he bought weekly tickets. Just ten percent of the students. The answers to "What would you do if you win?" were also vague. Most said it depended on the size of the prize. The instructor said to use today's jackpot of $40 million, $2,000,000 each year for twenty years. The students had no real answers for what they might do with $2,000,000 a year. Even those who purchased tickets did not have a clear plan for the money. Everyone *hopes* to win a lottery, but few buy tickets. Daydreaming about the things we *hope* to have may be an engaging dragon, but it is insufficient to achieve our dreams.

• ***Wanting.*** A young woman claims: "I really *want* a Corvette. I've *wanted* one for years." When asked what stops her from having the car, she says: "Money. It's more than I can afford." Asked if she had taken a test drive in a Corvette, she answered: "No. But I rode in one once when I was twelve." Queried about the color she liked, she said: "I'm not sure. White ones are slick, and the sapphire-blue convertibles are awesome too." Asked about price, she admitted: "I don't know how much a new Corvette would cost." Her commitment to *wanting* a Corvette beginning to waver, she guessed at the pricet. She figured: "More than $70,000. Five thousand dollars down and payments near $700 a month." She was told that a twenty-hour-a-week part-time job at just ten dollars per hour would give her the down payment in less than a year and cover the monthly payment. She thought for a brief moment and said: "I don't want a Corvette enough to get a part-time job. I enjoy my friends, and I don't have time for a second job." The evidence indicates that a Corvette was more a whim than a burning *want.*

• ***Wishing.*** Many men and women *wish* that they were more attractive. More attractive might mean attractive hair, flashy clothes, a healthy physique or shapely figure, and a pleasing personality. Relatively simple actions can be taken to improve each characteristic of "more attractive." Women and men who seriously *wish* they were more attractive take those actions. Stylists can provide a hair style that highlights special features. Trendy clothes for men and women are available in any mall. Healthy eating and regular exercise produce shapely figures and strong physiques. An inexpensive self-help course will help us master the quirks of our own personality. But those actions take too much time or are too expensive for men and women who only *wish* they were more attractive.

Hoping, wanting and wishing may feel good. But do not confuse the want-hope-wish dragons with action and results. When we delay action on our most pressing challenges, we push today's issues into tomorrow. The burden of yesterday's inaction is a heavy load to carry on top of today's new challenges. Achieving our cherished dreams for the future requires action today. Hoping, wanting and wishing will not get it done. Actions pave the road to our dreams.

Delaying action to the future pushes today's problems into tomorrow, making the burden of tomorrow's challenges that much heavier.

Analysis-Paralysis

Take a giant leap when it is needed. You can't cross a six-foot-wide chasm with two three-foot jumps.

When I was six, I drove with my grandmother in her green 1948 DeSoto from New York to Cleveland on the Pennsylvania Turnpike. Traveling on that new super highway seemed endless and boring to me. It was over ninety degrees and the car did not have air conditioning. I played at least twice with every toy in the back seat, and did not know what else to do. So I exercised the unbridled freedom of a child. I took off all of my clothes, and threw them out the window. Every last piece including my sneakers and underwear. My grandmother was shocked when she discovered me nude in the back seat and realized what I had done. But the trip no longer was boring for either of us.

Oh to enjoy the freedom of a child without having to battle the dragons of fear and doubt that freeze us in inaction. Too often when we are dissatisfied with our current situation, we analyze the possibilities over and over again. But the twin dragons of fear and doubt keep us from taking action. We are not sure which actions will work, and we are afraid to fail. But failure is like a skinned knee: it hurts for a brief minute but the pain is insignificant. Meanwhile, frustration grows as we think about the problem or opportunity, hoping a genie will jump from a magic lantern to make the decision that will solve all of our problems. *Analysis-paralysis* is frustrating. It consumes enormous energy. Analysis-paralysis is like Superman with amnesia: we forget our dreams and lose our power.

But our doubts and fears can be regulated like an emotional thermostat. Actors make a living doing it. They are confident, daring or enthusiastic on cue no matter how they feel in real life. By working through our doubts and fears, we discover what is possible in our lives. That discovery unleashes awesome personal power. It is a stimulating, almost instant feeling of relief. The obstacles in front of us do not disappear. They just are not overwhelming anymore. We know we can conquer them, and the solution is in our confidence. The obstacles that loom before us fall into three categories.

• ***Obstacles We Control.*** Least threatening are the obstacles that we directly control, such as spending the time and money that we already have. We generally feel empowered to make unilateral decisions over matters in this category.

• ***Obstacles We Influence***. Obstacles over which we have influence, but not control, are mini-dragons. We are frustrated by them because other people like parents, spouses, children and coworkers make the final decisions and they may, or may not, listen to our suggestions and requests.

• ***Uncontrollable Obstacles.*** The big dragons are obstacles over which we feel we have no control or influence. Many people put politics, laws, the weather and world events into this category, and feel powerless to wrestle with such monster dragons.

We often measure our personal power in terms of the first category and, to some extent, the second. However, our attitude toward the second and third categories is what empowers us to achieve our biggest dream. By changing how we influence others and proactively moving obstacles from the third to the second category, we grab the power in our hands to achieve our dreams regardless of how big they may be. The most powerful men and women we know deal effectively with obstacles in the third category.

The power to achieve our biggest dream lies in overcoming obstacles that we do not directly control.

Different Actions, Different Results

Our world is rich with fantastic possibilities. Our actions or inaction will determine which of them become reality.

One definition of insanity is taking the same action and expecting different results. The dragons of change must be insane, since they encourage us to repeat the same actions while expecting better results. Different actions are needed to produce different results in our lives. Repeating the actions of the past produces essentially the same results. So if our goal is to improve our careers and family life, our actions must change. Seem simple and obvious? Consider these areas where many of us want to change our results:

• ***Ideal Weight***. When my daughter visits our home and fixes a tasty chicken Parmesan with a bottle of Chianti, I want to stay on my diet. But just this once I give in (or is that just today's excuse?) and show how much I appreciate her thoughtfulness in cooking the dinner. I eat the meal and postpone exercise until tomorrow. With that attitude, my results on the scale are no surprise. We know that a healthy diet and regular exercise produce the ideal weight. The hunger we feel when we skip a meal, and the sweat on our foreheads when we exercise, are reassuring signs of progress. To change our weight, we must first change our attitudes about eating and exercise.

• ***Higher Income.*** If we seek improved living standards, we will enjoy learning new skills, finding a better job, working harder and longer, and taking risks in business, maybe even starting our own. Recreation will be take a back seat to study at night or paying for courses. Grades (even if they are not as high as we would like), job interviews (even if they are unsuccessful), hours on the job (even without extra pay), and other productive investments (even if they do not yield immediate returns) are clear indicators of progress. It may take a few years before the results show up in our paychecks and bank account. To change our living standards, we must first change our attitude toward the efforts that make such improvements possible.

• ***New Friends.*** Building new relationships is hard work. If we seek new friends, we will enjoy meeting new people even if such encounters are uncomfortable and lead nowhere. We will look for people who meet our intellectual, recreational or romantic needs. When we find a candidate, we will be open and honest in attempting to build a relationship with them. Most attempts will fail, but rejection will be a sign that we are taking the risks needed to discover and build new relationships. We may be disappointed in rejection, but not discouraged. We will keep looking for the ideal new friends because we know that if we give into fear and stop looking, it will be impossible to find him or her.

The fundamental change in these examples is taking new actions even though such actions are different and uncomfortable, and the initial results may take longer or be less than we want. We create our results in our attitudes and our actions. New results are nothing more than new attitudes in action. Therefore, to create new results, create new attitudes, and take new actions.

To achieve new results, we must become comfortable with the uncomfortable new actions that are necessary for us to take.

Make Your Own Weather

When you think you can, you are usually right.
When you think you can't, you are always right.

People with clear dreams make their own weather. Snow, rain or sunshine (and the other trials and tribulations that life sends our way) do not change their dreams. They do not allow the weather to become a dragon that gets in the way of the actions necessary to achieve their dreams. Even full-scale hurricanes do not make a difference for very long. They find a way to make the weather fit their dreams, rather than changing their dreams to suit the weather.

Proactive people are totally committed to achieving their dreams. Quitting is not an option. The possibility of failure does not enter their minds. They are excited by each milestone on the journey, eager for every possibility that tomorrow brings. Those who believe that they can achieve their dream usually do, because they will do whatever it takes. Those who doubt that they can achieve their dream usually do not achieve it, because they do not try everything.

Like Thomas Edison inventing the light bulb, people who are committed will make as many attempts as necessary, no matter how many previous attempts failed. It makes no difference how many people say *NO.* Each *NO* and each failure is a learning experience. They savor failure and transform it into an opportunity to grow, to try another way, or to approach someone else. Eventually, they find the highway that takes them to their dreams.

Traveling the highway is recreation, not a chore. The speed of travel is not important. Their actions focus on the dreams even when conditions do not support the dream. Nothing stands in their way. They take action to eliminate obstacles, rather than quitting because of bad weather or other obstacles. They see obstacles as interesting and exciting challenges, merely speed bumps on the highway to dreams. No matter what the weather conditions may be in their lives, they know the solutions to their problems never lies "out there." The solution lies entirely in our attitudes, our choices, and our actions.

Our Own TV Show

Write a script that embraces your biggest dream.
Then produce that script in your everyday actions.

Life is like having our own reality TV show. As the producer, director and leading actor or actress in each day's episode, you and I determine the content and quality of our shows. They can have any format we want: sports event, situation comedy, soap opera, talk show, musical, police story, news broadcast, or the evening business report. We survey the world that surrounds us and find materials to broadcast each day. We observe that the most highly rated shows have producers who focus on success and are passionate about the materials that they broadcast. Our shows will be about subjects we love too. They will be about our dreams, unique among all the TV programs that have ever appeared in prime time.

We can plan future episodes, or let them occur spontaneously. We can write the script our way, or let someone else write it their way. We can do reruns and show the same episodes over and over again, or write a new script every day. But each episode, each new day, starts where the previous one ended. Our shows will be on the air for our entire lives even if nobody watches.

Our shows are broadcast live, so they include frequent ad-libs. We can change the format or subject of the show any time we want to. Drop-in guests appear every day and often surprise us with what they do. During some shows, hilarious, sad or disappointing events happen that were not in the script that we wrote. Everyone we meet is on the Neilsson panel that rates our show. They may give us an award for the best directed, most successful, most imaginative, most exciting, most enjoyable, or most useful show. They may give us no awards at all. But their awards do not make much difference because inside we know if the show is really our dream. We give our show our best because we want it to be a top hit even when we are no longer here to produce new episodes.

Closing Thoughts on Actions

Success and happiness do not come by chance. We may be disappointed if we fail, but we're doomed if we don't take action.

The Hail Mary pass is an exciting play to watch at the end of a close football game. The team that is behind desperately throws the football as far down field as it can hoping for a miracle touchdown that will win the game. The play almost never works, but nothing else has any chance at all. While our lives seldom face a hard deadline like the end of the fourth quarter, maybe a few Hail Mary actions would be effective in achieving our dreams.

Our biggest dream can be realized if we identify it clearly, assume personal responsibility for making it real, and take the necessary action. The dragons of change will encourage us to analyze an opportunity or problem, talk about it endlessly, expect someone else to do something about it, or hope it will go away by itself. But only action will produce change when we are not experiencing the results we want in our lives. The vignettes in the following four sections will help you take effective and joyous actions:

Tip #7 - ***Exercise Personal Responsibility:*** Personal responsibility is personal power. When we embrace responsibility for how things are today, actions to change them come easily. We might not be able to change everything we face, but nothing will change until we face it. These vignettes confirm the futility of blaming others, describe how to commit to effective action, and provide tips on how to use personal responsibility as the pathway to dreams and the solution to problems. When we exercise personal responsibility, no person, event or thing can stop us from having our dreams come true.

Tip **#8** - ***Make Clear Choices:*** We have more choices available today than ever before. How do we choose from such a cornucopia of alternatives? How do we sort through the rainbow of inputs to make clear choices? How do we choose when we do not know what to choose? These vignettes show how our past choices have built the life we have today, describe ways to leap hurdles that block the choices we want to make, and provide techniques to make effective choices each day. Clear choices lead to enjoyable actions and tame the dragons of anxiety and indecision. Clear choices bring peace into our lives.

Tip **#9** - ***Dare To Dream:*** Pick a dream: travel into space, be a sports hero, build a business, nurture a family, develop a miracle cure, clean the environment, eliminate world hunger. The choice is yours. Enjoy it. Be passionate about it. Each of us makes a difference by what we do, and how we influence others. These vignettes explore the importance of dreams to our future happiness, provide ways to discover our dreams, and outline techniques to make our dreams come true.

Tip **#10** - ***Share Your Dream:*** We can achieve our biggest dream, but probably not alone. We are on planet Earth to help each other. We do not dream alone. The universe will provide all the help that we need if we just ask for it. So tell everyone about your dream. Soon you will meet others who share similar dreams. Work together. These vignettes describe the importance of individual action in realizing global dreams, ways to find others who share your dream, and how our collective dreams determine the future of our world.

Today is the day for us to begin producing what we want in our world, both individually and collectively by exercising personal responsibility, choosing what our lives will be, clarifying our dreams, and sharing those dreams. Now it is time for your to take action: read and enjoy the following vignettes.

-------Essential Tip #7-------
Exercise Personal Responsibility
~ Design Tomorrow

"Some men see things as they are and ask WHY? *I dream things that never were and ask* WHY NOT?"
— George Bernard Shaw

Your Responsibility

When I acknowledge I AM WHAT I AM TODAY because of the choices I made yesterday, I gain the power to say: I WILL BE DIFFERENT TOMORROW!

Two homeless men reviewed their lives as they shared a bottle of cheap wine. One said that he had a father who was a drunk, so he never got an education. The other sympathized: "You did well to survive. Imagine how successful you would be if you were born into another family." The first said: "You're right. I wouldn't be on this bench if I had been born in a different family." Stories of the past, especially from our childhood, can be relentless dragons that fuel a lifetime of depression, disappointment and mediocrity. On the other hand, accepting personal responsibility produces action and results. The power to determine your future is entirely in your hands. It is your personal responsibility.

We first learned about personal responsibility in childhood songs like "Row, Row, Row Your Boat." The lesson was you are the only one who can row your boat where you want it to go. The lessons continued in nursery rhymes like:

Humpty Dumpty sat on a wall.
Humpty Dumpty had a great fall.
All the King's horses and all the King's men
couldn't put Humpty together again.

Of course not. Only Humpty could put Humpty together the way he wanted to be. And just like Humpty Dumpty, we each have the power to achieve our dreams—if we exercise personal responsibility.

Personal responsibility is personal power. We gain substantial personal power when we take responsibility for: (1) how we are, how our family is, and the condition of the world today, and (2) how they will be tomorrow. We surrender our power to dragon of blame when we complain about how bad things are, whine that no one ever helps, or wait for someone else to change. The essential first step in improving ourselves, our family and career, and the world around us is to accept that we made them like they are.

Any time we believe that someone or something else keeps us where we are today, we are powerless to change because that someone or something has stolen our power. When we honestly acknowledge that: "I put myself where I am today with choices that I made yesterday," I seize the power to change my future circumstances.

==========================

The essential first step in changing the world around us is to accept that our choices made it like it is today.

==========================

When we embrace responsibility for the entire universe, every piece of it, we gain the power to change the parts that we care the most about. We exercise personal power when we see things as they could be, and take personal responsibility for making them that way.

Response Ability

Maybe we can't change everything we want to change. But nothing will change until we take personal responsibility *for it.*

The word *responsibility* is often associated with the dragon of blame. But it also means that we are *able* to *respond* in any way we choose. The *American Century Dictionary* defines *responsibility* as "being the primary cause." It also offers the common definition of "morally accountable." Many people avoid responsibility because they connect it with being held accountable for results, good or bad. They quickly say "I'm not responsible!" since *responsibility* is a source of fault or blame. However, we are powerless if we are not *able* to make a *response.* If someone or something else is responsible for what we have in our lives, that person or thing possesses our personal power!

For example, we all are *response able* for world hunger because we are *able* to *respond* to the hunger if we choose. Most of us choose to ignore it, but some make hunger a passionate cause and travel the world feeding hungry children. We also are *response able* for abortion and freedom of choice, since we can choose to support one cause or the other. No blame, no defense. Just choice. We also are *response able* for deteriorating family unity and a high divorce rate. I have chosen to act in that area by giving unconditional love to my wife and family, and by creating a family-friendly environment in my company.

Response ability is not given, it is taken by choice. As we learn more about ourselves, we see attitudes and actions that are incongruent with our values (*who we are*) and our dreams (*what we want).* We are individually *response able* to change ourselves. Nobody else can do it. Successful business and community leaders willingly choose *response ability* for how they will be in the future. They do not see a problem and hope that someone else will fix it. They take action. In the twenty-first century, we have unparalleled opportunities to lead our families, our jobs, and our communities by exercising personal *response ability.*

Twenty Minutes to Live

Blame doesn't solve problems. They can only be solved by taking responsibility for how things are, and taking action to make things like we want them to be.

Personal responsibility saved my life. I was scuba diving forty miles off the Delaware coast on the wreck of the *Washingtonian*, a 400-foot refrigerator ship that sunk in 1910. We were in ninety-five feet of water and visibility was poor, about fifteen feet. I was trailing my dive buddy, an experienced diver, by just a few feet as we searched the scattered wreckage for bugs (lobster). Even with the limited visibility, I was within sight of him when my regulator suddenly became caught in fishing line tangled on the wreck. Before I knew what had happened, my buddy was out of sight. The more I struggled to free myself, the more the line coiled around my arms, legs and equipment. The dragons of fear and anger grabbed and held me tightly. Seeing my air gage at 1500 pounds, my first thought was: "I have twenty minutes to live."

I felt sorry for myself as thought about my wife and daughters. I was angry at the fisherman who carelessly lost their tackle. They were to blame for my situation. I was furious at my buddy for leaving me. I tamed those dragons by telling myself: "Blame won't save you. Do what you're trained to do, and do it now!" I took off my diving gear and laid it on the wreck, keeping the mouthpiece just like I was taught in my certification course. Using the knife strapped to my left ankle, I cut the fishing lines one at a time. When my gear was free, I carried it away from the wreck to open sand and put it back on. When I finished, the air gage read 400 pounds (about five minutes of air). Just then my buddy, who had been looking frantically, found me. Safely back on the boat after the dive, we laughed as we described the exciting adventure to the other divers who were unaware of my near-death experience.

Personal responsibility saved my life that day. I almost wasted my air and my life blaming the entanglement on someone else. How often in our daily activities do we figuratively die wasting our air on self-pity, blame or guilt when personal responsibility would save the day and fix the problem?

Only Human

We exercise personal power when we use phrases that accept responsibility, and acknowledge the need for us to take action.

The newspaper reported that an Air Force officer had been court-martialed for having sex with enlisted men, which is blatantly against military regulations and traditions. She pleaded not guilty because the sex was consensual. Commenting on the case, a U.S. Senator said: "We're treating her unfairly. After all, she's only human." Are humans so weak that sex urges are stronger than our integrity, our commitment, and our personal responsibility?

The phrase "I'm only human" is a dragon that denies personal responsibility for our actions and results. It is an attempt to justify what we know to be self-indulgent choices. Choices that do not produce the results we want. I have used the phrase myself as an excuse for having four pieces of pizza for lunch when most people have two, or serving two bottles of wine with dinner when one would be quite sufficient.

The words we use reflect the personal responsibility we feel. Proactive individuals use words that portray their personal power and acknowledge their personal responsibility. Such individuals use their personal power to make the world like they want it to be. On the other hand, reactive people use words that deny personal responsibility and project themselves as being powerlessness. Reactive people may say things like:

• ***"That's me. It's just how I am"*** implies that our habits and personality are fixed and we cannot change them. But we are not our habits. We can change our habits if we really want to, eliminating those that stop us from reaching our goals. As humans, we have the ability to learn effective new habits, and to unlearn habits that no longer work in our lives.

• ***"I want to, but I don't have the time"*** suggests that something outside of us controls how we spend our time. Lack of time is a trumped-up excuse to justify not doing things that we do not want to do. Everybody gets exactly twenty-four hours every day. We can spend those hours on dreams, or on habits. I get choose how I will to spend my twenty-four hours today, and you get to choose how to spend yours. We do have time!

• ***"If only my spouse would…, then I could"*** means that action or inaction by someone else (a spouse in this case) stops us from realizing our goals. Waiting for another person to do something is frustrating. Waiting gives power to the person or thing we wait for. Like lack of time, waiting is often an excuse to avoid doing things that we really do not want to do anyway.

• ***"I'm too tired."*** Tired is a mental choice, rather than a physical condition. Saying "I'm tired" when someone asks us to do something implies that we want to do it, but we are physically unable to. It is just not true! If we really wanted to do the something, the tiredness would disappear instantaneously.

Phrases such as these are dragons of powerlessness. Their purpose is to transfer responsibility to something or someone else by saying *I can't do it* or *I won't try*. They convey a belief that our lives are decided by external factors that we cannot change. But we are *able* to choose our *response*. No circumstance, event or person forces us to do what we do each day.

The language of personal power is a language of commitment and positive choices: *I take responsibility for doing it!* I prefer using the "only human" label to describe heros like Martin Luther King, Abraham Lincoln, Sister Theresa and others who have contributed so much to the quality of our world. They took personal responsibility for the world as it was today, and how it could be tomorrow. They were able to exercise personal power because they are *human*. Unlike animals, they had the power of choice just like you and I do. They make me be proud to be "only human."

No circumstance or person forced us to do what we did today. We chose to do it. What will we choose for tomorrow?

Pass the Course

Life's experiences are training courses. We pass the course and move to the next lesson only when we have learned the lesson.

An employee from my company received an exciting six-month overseas assignment under a subcontract with another company. The project manager from the prime contractor apparently was a poor leader and the project failed. The employee, surrendering to the dragon of blame, said: "There was no way we could have succeeded with him in charge." More accurately, he could have said: "I didn't know how to make the project succeed with him as manager." Or he might have said: "I didn't find a way to make the project succeed because I didn't look for it. Instead I spent my time discussing the project manager's weaknesses with other team members."

Alternatively, the team could have focused its time and energy looking for a solution. Maybe they would have found a way to make the project successful. Or maybe not. Either way the employee would have learned a lesson in how to succeed in spite of a weak manager. The course began the day he judged the manager to be ineffective, and did not know how to fix the problem. When asked if he had worked for other poor managers in the past, he responded: "Of course, several times." When asked if he expected to see other ineffective managers on future projects in his career, he answered: "For sure." Unfortunately, he had not learned the lesson from previous experiences in the "Weak Managers 101" course, and had to take the course over again. If he had passed the course the first time, he would have known what would work in such situations.

Most of life's experiences are much the same: first job, first home, first marriage, first investment, first child. When we tame the blame dragon and learn our lessons the first time, we avoid having to repeat the course. Personal responsibility enables us to complete each course because we take ownership for the part of the problem we can change, instead of blaming it on someone or something else. We repeat the same lessons in life until we learn them, and go on to the next course.

Missing the Plane

My wife and I celebrated our thirtieth wedding anniversary with a Caribbean vacation. We bought first-class seats six months in advance, and looked forward to leaving the snow behind. The tickets showed departure as 8:18, so we planned to arrive at the airport about 7:15. We left home twenty minutes later than planned, but were just five minutes late at the airport. I parked the car and my wife checked the luggage. A cup of coffee and croissant were waiting for me when I returned from the parking lot. Enjoying the coffee, we noticed that the flight board listed departure as 8:00. We ran to the gate and arrived at 7:54. The plane had not left, but the doors were closed. The attendant said spitefully: "I gave your seats away."

At first, the blame dragon bit me hard. We were at the gate six minutes before the flight time. The airline moved the flight eighteen minutes earlier without telling us. Who was "to blame" for our missing the plane? Who could have prevented it? If either the airline or we had responded differently, we would have been on the plane. My anger at the attendant and the airline did not replace our *response ability*. It did not prevent us from missing the plane, and it made the first few hours of our vacation painful. Re-routed through Dallas, we arrived in St. Maarten six hours later than expected. After regaining our *response ability*, we enjoyed our first-class seats on the extended flight and tamed the blame dragon with champagne.

Airline Response Ability	***Our Response Ability***
• Mail new tickets in advance • Tell us the new time at check-in • Hold our seats at the gate • Cooperate at the gate	• Call to confirm the flight time • Leave home on time • Skip the coffee • Go to the gate early

The airline, my wife and I were response able for missing the plane. Each of us had opportunities to change the outcome.

It is easy to blame somebody if something goes wrong. But blame does not change things. Each participant contributes to the outcome. We all have the *ability* to *respond* in a way that could change the outcome. Do not miss your chance to be *response able.*

Thin Air

Leaders make things happen through determination and personal responsibility. Are you a leader?

Leaders create dreams from thin air and then make them happen. Thomas Edison imagined an electric light bulb long before he invented one. Albert Einstein set out to define new physical laws to describe the universe. President Kennedy said: "Let's put a man on the moon!" Martin Luther King shouted: "I have a dream!" Where do such dreams come from? Leaders make them up with little concern for how, how much, when or who. Those are details that can be worked out later.

Leaders cause things to happen through sheer determination and personal responsibility. On the other hand, some people are victims of events. They suffer pain, disappointment and frustration—the *effect*s of unfortunate events that seem to be caused by someone or something else. Leaders use their personal power to change what is, while victims feel powerless. The table at the top of the next page describes three levels of leaders who cause positive change (Champions, Players and Cheerleaders) and three levels of victims who feel powerless to change events (Destroyers, Pessimists and Wimps).

Champions have the personal power and confidence necessary to change anything. They are know for choosing big dreams and pursuing them with great passion. Being the champion for a big dream is a lifelong task. Edison worked for years to perfect a light bulb design that worked. Failure after failure did not discourage him. Einstein was notorious for working several consecutive days without sleep. Martin Luther King gave his life spreading his dream in cities across our country. Champions exude such passion and such commitment that other people willingly support their dreams and goals. Players provide the workforce that helps leaders accomplish their goals. They offer their skills and resources to achieve the big dream that a champion visualizes. Players can contribute to several big dreams concurrently. Cheerleaders are at-cause people too. They encourage the champions and players to press on toward the goal even in the face of setbacks and intermediate failures.

LEADERS *take personal responsibility for their actions and their results*	**Champions** create dreams and goals, enroll others to pursue them, and are passionate about achieving them. Champions pick a few concepts or goals to accomplish with passion!
	Players commit to achieving goals set by others, choose to participate, and are lead willingly. They prefer to help others achieve their goals rather than be champions themselves.
	Cheerleaders embrace goals and want them to be achieved. They offer encouragement so others can achieve their goals, and choose not to participate actively in the battles.
VICTIMS *believe their actions and results are determined by others*	**Destroyers** actively make new ideas fail and are the nature opponents of leaders. They enroll others to ensure failure and can destroy the morale of an entire team.
	Pessimists are adept at recognizing weak points in an idea. Often heard saying: "*That won't work because......*" or "*Yes, but......*" Rarely suggest way to achieve important goals.
	Wimps frequently complain about how our world is messed up. Blame others for what is wrong. Reluctant to take action to implement meaningful change either alone or with others.

Champions have natural opponents: the destroyers. History records the names of only a few destroyers because such dragons literally leave *nothing* behind. As surely as a leader can stimulate a team of players and cheerleaders to achieve a worthwhile goal, a destroyer can derail the whole team. Wimps and pessimists are a destroyer's allies. Wimps complain about everything and do little. Pessimists do nothing because they see thousands of reasons why every possibility will fail.

People who oppose us are not necessarily destroyers. They may be leaders for another goal. When someone opposes our goals and has a positive goal of their own, it is an opportunity to listen and change. We may want to be a player on their team or our teams can merge to pursue a larger joint goal. Leaders (champions, players and cheerleaders) work together. They share life's challenges. Victims (wimps, pessimists and destroyers) share gloom, sadness, pain and depression. We each choose to be either a leader or a victim when we answer the question: *Am I responsible for the universe, or is the universe responsible for me?*

Set a Big One

The goals we set for ourselves are measures of our personal power, the height to which we are willing to reach.

An article in the business section of Sunday's newspaper described a company whose annual revenue five years ago was $51 billion with six percent net profit ($3.1 billion). The company set a five-year goal to grow to $177 billion revenue, and its leaders worked six months to devise a strategy to achieve that goal. At the end of last year, the final year in the five-year plan, revenue was only $103 billion with a 7.1 percent net profit ($7.3 billion). Because of the unexpected downturn in the economy in 2002 and 2003, they reached *only* fifty-eight percent of their goal. Did they fail? The shareholders did not think so because the stock price had skyrocketed.

Goals quantify our perception of our personal power. Do we set them high enough to succeed, or do we give into the *It can't be done* dragon? A goal actually becomes a ceiling, the highest we can go, because we aim at the goal and reality limits what we actually achieve. For example, if an $90,000/year job is our goal, we prepare and execute a plan to reach $90,000/year. We do our best and, when the unexpected happens, as it always does, we settle for $75,000/year. However, that is not a failure. The plan just was not big enough to accommodate the unexpected. The goal was not big enough to produce what we really wanted, unless what we *really* wanted was a $75,000/year job.

The same applies to career goals, relationship goals and health goals (want to lose fifty pounds, plan to lose seventy-five). Fear of failure is a subtle dragon that limits our success. We are so afraid of failing that we set a reachable goal, and then miss it when reality happens. Some set a floor, the least they will accept, and are content to just get by.

When we are afraid to set a big goal (a high ceiling) or are afraid to risk everything (going below the floor), we live in a tight crawl space. Personal responsibility tames the dragon of fear. It does not make any difference, really, if we do not reach a goal because striving to reach it adds zest to our lives. Win or lose, we are happier trying than being afraid. Set your goal *BIG* and go for it with everything you have for as long as it takes.

Dad's Board Meetings

Personal responsibility may mean going it alone. Being committed looks unreasonable to those who are not committed.

As the treasurer, my dad was an *ex officio* member of our church's board of directors. One summer, he took me to the church and let me play on the swings while the meeting was held inside. There was no air conditioning then, so the windows were open. When the issues got hot, I eavesdropped on the heated discussions from my seat on the swings. When the vote was six to one, my dad was usually the single dissenting vote. As a successful businessman, he knew how to plan a project, prepare a budget, and manage money. He said *NO* to unrealistic ideas and altruistic do-good schemes. To me it seemed like the other board members thought their projects would succeed by divine intervention. In the end, the board members usually saw things his way because of the clear choices that he offered.

Leaders often find themselves facing their dragons alone. The courage of their convictions and clarity of their thinking sustains them until others join the team. Being alone does not seem to deter leaders. Most great leaders of history stood alone in their beliefs for a long time. Copernicus said the earth was not the center of the universe. Abraham Lincoln sought to abolish slavery. Jesus taught lessons about love and forgiveness. These men are considered heroes today.

But in their times they were misunderstood and rejected. When they spread messages of knowledge, acceptance and love, people refused to listen. Even when rejection turned to anger and hate, these courageous men continued steadfastly to spread their beliefs widely. When verbal opposition was unsuccessful in tearing them from their beliefs, they were treated brutally and murdered. But even death was not enough to deter them from clear beliefs and lofty dreams. It has been said: "We haven't lived until we believe in something enough to die for it." That is the personal power and commitment is often required to achieve big dreams!

Great Strength or Great Weakness?

Our greatest strength simultaneously may be our greatest weakness.

I am often complimented as a *confident, disciplined leader*. Just as often, I am called *arrogant, inflexible* and *controlling*. I am not usually called *irrational*, but I am never considered to be *spontaneous* either. We treat ourselves unfairly if consider worry about our weaknesses, but ignore our corollary strengths. Our greatest weakness often is simultaneously our greatest strength. What appears as a favorable trait in one circumstance may be a weakness in others.

The left-hand column in the table lists personality traits that are generally thought to be favorable. The right-hand column lists the same traits using words generally judged to be unfavorable traits. For example, *courageous* is a favorable trait, while *foolish* is considered to be weak. We are responsible to use our strengths wisely, otherwise they might grow into weaknesses. When we change a personality trait because someone calls it weak, we may be giving away our most valuable strength. Balance is critical. Taken to the extreme, any strength can become a weakness. When traits grow into obsessions, they become dragons in our family lives and careers.

We have different points of view regarding when a personality trait transitions from a strength to a weakness. Each of us is responsible for choosing our personality traits independent of anyone else's likes or dislikes. No matter what others may think, we choose the personal power traits most suited to the goals we have chosen for ourselves.

Favorable TRAIT	Unfavorable TRAIT
Accepting	Gullible
Ambitious	Greedy
Attractive	Vain
Charming	Manipulative
Committed	Obstinate
Confident	Arrogant
Courageous	Foolish
Creative	Unrealistic
Decisive	Hasty
Dedicated	Workaholic
Disciplined	Inflexible
Determined	Stubborn
Eloquent	Verbose
Firm	Insensitive
Focused	Narrow-minded
Helpful	Meddlesome
Leadership	Controlling
Methodical	Slow
Precise	Tedious
Sharp-Witted	Sarcastic
Spontaneous	Irrational
Thrifty	Miserly
Trusting	Sucker
Understanding	Weak

Time Limits

The question is not how much we are capable of accomplishing.
The real question is how long are we willing to keep trying.

Only time separates champions from also-rans. Joe Torre was in professional baseball for thirty years as a player, coach and manager before he won his first World Series with the New York Yankees. Great accomplishments take years to complete: four years to paint Sistine Chapel ceiling, nine years to put a man on the moon, ten years to dig the Panama Canal, fourteen years to chisel four faces on Mount Rushmore, over fifty years to erect a pyramid. The men and women who completed these feats fully understood that commitment conquers time.

GOAL	TIME REQUIRED
Go to the store	30-60 minutes
Paint the house	3-5 days
Lose 25 pounds	3-6 months
Buy a new house	5-9 months
Write a book	15-24 months
Prepare for a better job	1-3 years
Earn college degree (part time)	4-8 years
Become a doctor	8-10 years
Compete as Olympic gymnast	12-15 years
Discover cure for a disease	15-25 years
Create peace in the world	A lifetime plus

Many of us surrender our personal power to the time dragon. Time limits our success more often than lack of ability or resources. Not that we do not have enough time. Rather that we are unwilling to spend the time to achieve our big goals. We like instant gratification, so we may tackle short goals like going to the store (minutes) or cleaning the house (hours). But we may not be willing to allot sufficient time to achieve big goals like preparing for a better job or saving for a new house.

Few people have the determination to achieve goals that take many years of effort like competing in the Olympics, or finding the cure for a major disease. It is a rare individual who will dedicate his or her life to human rights or peace on earth knowing such a lofty dream probably cannot be realized in one lifetime. We create wonderful dreams in our minds. The rest is just time. The more time we are willing to commit, the bigger the dream we will be able to achieve.

Honey, I Shrank the Couch

Tasks are completed easily when we have clear intent to get the job done. Lacking clear intent, a pebble in our shoe may be enough to make us quit.

My wife and I bought two new couches for our basement recreation room, and donated our old furniture to charity. The new furniture was scheduled for delivery on Monday, so it was urgent to remove the old furniture from the basement. The charity's truck arrived to pick up the furniture at 4 p.m on a Friday. The two experienced furniture movers on the moving truck were well-equipped physically to move couches. They tried for an hour and could not get either couch through the narrow door at the top of the basement stairs. They asked my wife if the door had been built after the couches were installed. She assured them the couches were delivered after the basement was finished, and joked that we had inflated them. The moving men made one final but unsuccessful attempt before quitting for the weekend at 5 p.m.

My wife told me the story when I got home from work. I did not understand why there was a problem. The couches were placed in the basement just a few years earlier. It should be easy to get them out. With help from my neighbor, the two couches were gone thirty minutes later. We removed the door at the top of the stairs, turned the couches on their side so the legs went out first, and inched the legs around the door frame and the corner.

It has taken longer to write this story than it took the two of us to move the couches. Moving the couches demonstrates how easy it is to abandon our personal power to the dragon of frustration. Too often we quit even when, as in moving the couches, there obviously is a simple answer somewhere. It seems that when we lose commitment to solve a problem, our attempts at finding a solution are half-hearted. We quit mentally first, then physically. Clear intent, a little bit of logic, and a some manly strength moved the couches that night. You might say that our personal power shrank the couches.

Cod Liver Oil

Personal power enables us to ignore the minor pains we inevitably encounter on the road to our biggest dream.

As a young boy, I was underweight and sickly even though I had a healthy appetite and exercised vigorously. Sickliness may have been a way for me to get the sympathy and attention that I never got as a baby. I had pneumonia six times before I was thirteen, including double pneumonia twice. Each winter I would get sick around Christmas, and miss a week or two of school. My mother and the doctors tried several different cures. Finally, I got sick of being sick, and was willing to try anything. I took every vitamin known to mankind in the 1950s. For two winters I wore an adhesive patch on my chest. It was painful, uncomfortable and did not help. I still got sick every winter.

Then a doctor suggested that I take a full tablespoon of cod liver oil every morning and every night. I did not think that would work either. And the taste of the cod liver oil was horrible. It tasted like dragon oil. I threw up the first time I tried to swallow a spoonful. I would have quit taking the horrible stuff, except that I did not want to be sick anymore. I took personal responsibility for being healthy, and was willing to do what was necessary. Gradually, I began to tolerate and even like the flavor of cod liver oil. It was not long before I was drinking it straight from the bottle. There was no chance anyone else in the family would drink from the same bottle.

I took a tablespoonful cod liver oil twice a day for five years, and have not had pneumonia in almost forty-five years. Was it from taking the cod liver oil? Maybe it was just the natural process of growing older? Or maybe it was because I was sick of being sick, and I was willing to do anything, including something as obnoxious as cod liver oil. Taking cod liver oil illustrates the importance of personal power that comes from conquering little annoyances in order to make steady progress on the path to achieving our dreams.

Free $20 Bills

The big triumphs in life happen when we take personal responsibility, ignore the fear of failing, and pursue a significant goal without any self-doubt.

The pastor of our church delivered an inspirational sermon about the talents that God gave to each of us. He explained that a talent was a valuable coin in Roman times. Some people had many talents, others only a few. Yet we each are held responsible to use our talents wisely. After the sermon, collection plates were passed from row to row in the congregation, but not to collect money. These plates were filled with crisp new $20 bills, and the pastor invited us to take as many of them as we would like. No receipts required. We were told to invest the talents (the $20 bills) any way we wanted, and return the proceeds within sixty days to reduce the church's mortgage.

At the tender age of ten, the self-doubt dragon told me that the pastor did not mean me. Then my dad whispered in my ear: "Take one and do the best you can with it." I was scared as I took the money from the plate. I had never had a $20 bill of my own, and did not have a clue what to do with it. That $20 bill was an awesome *I-can-do-it* lesson in personal power. After a week of indecision, I purchased 200 magazines wholesale for a dime each, and sold them door to door for a quarter.

I could not pronounce the word *magazine,* so I called them "books" when someone answered the door. Some people laughed at my mispronunciation. But I ignored my embarrassment, sold all of the magazines and earned $50. More than doubling the $20 talent given to me. The overall result was even more amazing. The church distributed $10,000 in $20 bills and received nearly $50,000 back, enough to pay off the $40,000 mortgage and make other improvements.

I learned personal power from that $20 bill. The self-doubt dragon is often the only obstacle in the way of our personal and professional success. It may seem easy to accept mediocrity, and avoid the embarrassment of failing. But exhilaration and joy lie in conquering the obstacles on the road to our success.

Double Blip

Personal responsibility does not mean doing it alone. Rather it means taking responsibility for getting it done, and asking for help when help is needed.

I learned the power of acknowledging that *I don't know* during the experiments for my PhD thesis. The experiments involved complex equipment and a finicky linear accelerator that operated continuously from 5 p.m. Monday to Sunday at noon. Monday was used to set up the next experiment. Since accelerator time was very expensive, we were required to verify proper operation of the data collection system by taking oscilloscope readings at each cable connection. One Monday my experiment was scheduled to run, and the setup took longer than I had expected. At 4:55 p.m., I signed the log to certify my setup as ready to go even though I had not completed the verifications. I surrendered to the dragons of "rushing," rather than admitting to my coworkers in the laboratory that I need help to finish setting up the experiment.

After three full days of data taking, the result was "double blips" (twin peaks on the CRT display of the data). The second blip echoed the primary signal because I had not installed an attenuator on a cable connection, and verified the signal with an oscilloscope. The data were worthless. Seventy-two hours of accelerator time at roughly $2,000 per hour was wasted. My error was obvious to everyone. When the lab assistants heard the story, they laughed and gave me the nickname "double blip." Never before or since have I been so professionally humiliated as I was that day. I lacked the courage to acknowledge that I did not know if my experiment was ready to go. I lacked the courage to ask for help.

I don't know is a clear statement of personal responsibility, a sincere request for help. Almost universally, *I don't know* will elicit instant support because people experience a sense of giving and self-worth when they help someone who says *I don't know*. There is nothing weak or ignorant about *I don't know*. As a matter of fact, *I don't know* can be the most powerful and most intelligent thing we can say. It opens new possibilities and allows others to help us succeed.

Captain of My Ship

Blame is useless because it doesn't solve problems. Taking personal responsibility for "what is" is the most reliable way to achieve goals and eliminate problems.

As a former naval officer, I admire the personal power of a ship's captain. But his power is directly related to his enormous personal responsibility. He is responsible for the ship no matter what. If the ship runs aground in the middle of the night, the captain will be court-martialed for the accident. Even if he was not on the bridge directing operations at the time of the accident, he is responsible because he should have: (1) commanded the ship personally through dangerous waters, (2) provided more effective training for the crew; or (3) issued clear, specific orders regarding the dangers ahead.

Similarly, each of us is the captain of our life, and it will go only in the direction and at the speed we tell it to. We are responsible when it goes aground, even if we were oblivious to the potential danger around us. Instead of blaming people and things for the accidents in our lives, we can look further ahead to avoid tomorrow's rock piles.

The coming days of our life must start where we are today, but we choose the direction of those days. We cannot command our lives from the stern because we cannot see where we are headed. From the stern, all we see is yesterday's garbage. And where we go in the future is not determined by yesterday's garbage. Where our lives head next is not determined by where we have been in the past. We each choose where our lives will travel next. We can stand on the stern paralyzed by the garbage of past failures, and pretend to be disappointed and surprised when each new day brings more failures. Or we can go to the bow, choose our next goal, set the course in that direction, and navigate our lives through the difficult waters and hurricanes that surely lie ahead. Like a ship's captain, our personal power comes from taking responsibility for our lives *no matter what happens*.

Closing Perspectives on Exercising Personal Responsibility

"The longer I play, the more certain I become that a man's performance is the outward manifestation of who, in his heart, he really thinks he is."
— Hale Irwin, three-time U.S. Open Golf Champion

Who we think we are is our personal power. Personal power is not force or intimidation. It is taking responsibility for what we have and what we want in our lives, and helping others to find what they want. The dragon of blame, the opposite of personal responsibility, does not work because it is a thinly veiled attempt to change others. Personal responsibility is the power to change ourselves, the only person whom we can really change.

Personal power is born in the images we create in our minds. We create the future by imagining what is possible. When emotions control our actions, we have surrendered our personal power to those emotions. Our thoughts determine the actions we will take. We think it first, choose action next, and then make it happen. Even simple things like eating lunch are first created in our minds. We feel an urge to eat. We choose the food we want. Then we shift into action to get the food and eat it. If we never thought about food, we would never eat lunch.

Similarly, we have the power every day to imagine great things. Since we create our lives in our minds, why not choose a *BIG* life? Let others lead small lives, and yield to the dragons of fear and blame. But not you and me. Let others worry about what people will think. But not you and me. Let others argue over small things and wonder if the world has enough for everyone. But not you and me. Let others anguish over small hurts and hold grudges. But not you and me. Let others surrender their future by blaming others. But not you and me. Let others have small dreams and wonder why they do not come true. But not you and me. Choice is our power as human beings. Let us choose a *BIG* life with big dreams, big risks and big joys. The few who exercise *personal power* are the envy of the many who watch others, wait for others, and blame others.

-----------Essential Tip #8----------
Make Clear Choices
~ Pick from the Smorgasbord

"The truth of the matter is we always know the right thing to do. The hard part is doing it."
— General Norman Schwarzkopf

A Smorgasbord of Choices

Choice is the knife that whittles a universe of possibilities into your future. Use it wisely to shape your personal and professional lives.

Late one Christmas morning, our family gathered at an aristocratic hotel in downtown Richmond to enjoy the grand buffet. We walked down the palatial staircase into the midst of a sprawling smorgasbord. Waffles, omelets and fixings on one wall; twenty appetizers on the second wall; an assortment of meats, seafood and vegetables on the third wall; and a dozen pies, chocolate mousse and sundaes in the middle of the room. My first thought was: *"Wow, what a great spread! What will I choose to eat?"* I took samplings from each table and added the toppings. I ate so much I got sick.

Others in our family reacted differently. One admired the decorations and splendid presentation of the food. Another thought the spread was excessive and wasteful. A third ate almost nothing in the three hours we were in the hotel. Most sampled selections from a few tables. Some ate just seafood, while others focused on desserts. One voiced a fear that she would eat too much, and proceeded to do exactly that. Amid such a rich smorgasbord of choices, which was best? Of course, the answer is: "It depends."

Life seems complex as we begin the twenty-first century. Very much like a smorgasbord, life offers many choices and each choice has multiple variations. Would it be simpler to have fewer choices? Simpler maybe, but not as challenging or exciting. Simpler really means having clear criteria for making choices. Goals for the future and personal values become the criteria for simple, uncluttered choices. Too often we give into the dragon of instant gratification by forgetting our values, losing sight of our goals, neglecting our closest relationships, and sometimes even damaging our health.

Making clear choices forces us to prioritize our desires: *Which is most important*? In a world where we cannot do or have everything we would like, our desires compete with each other. However, our core values and goals show through in the choices we make each day. For example, when we value family over work, we take that extra day off to be with the family. When we value health over pleasure, we choose exercise instead of a snack. When faced with conflicting possibilities, *Masters of the Universe* steadfastly focus on what they really want. They choose the high road that embraces their goals and values.

Tomorrow's results are determined by today's choices. Tomorrow will be as big as the goals we set today. We are reaping karmic rewards or paying karmic debts today for the choices we made yesterday. For example, my weight (which is more than I want it to be) is a karmic debt for my past eating and exercise choices. The good news is that we make new choices every minute of our lives. To the extent that my choices are different today than they were yesterday, my life tomorrow will be different than it is today.

========================

Following our values will not reduce the pressures we feel today, but it will reduce the problems we face tomorrow.

========================

Sometimes we rush through our days acting from habit instead of conscious choice. Habits are predictable and automatic. But they are not conscious choices. Three things come together in conscious choice:

(1) *Consideration* of the alternatives, the range of available choices,

(2) *Willingness* to risk making a different choice, and

(3) *Ability* to execute the choice and perform the actions we choose.

Our choices may be conscious or unconscious. That is our first choice. We can put our life in autopilot and fly wherever the wind carries us. Or take control, choose to change course, and fly where we want to go. The vignettes in this section show how our choices created the life we have today, describe ways to leap the hurdles that block the choices we really want to make, and describe techniques for making more effective choices. Choose to read these vignettes with an expectation that some of them might be helpful in your life.

The Cancer Ward

As we get older, our gene pool and childhood become less important, and our choices become more important in determining our success and happiness.

Outside my building, a group of men and women gather each day to smoke. They have a sign on the wall that reads: *Welcome to the Cancer Ward*. One day the group seemed sad as they smoked. I approached a person I knew and asked: "What's wrong?" She answered: "Herb died of cancer over the weekend. We're all going to his funeral later today." I sadly thought to myself that Herb chose cancer, and his friends were choosing to follow in his footsteps. We all know the statistics that say people who smoke significantly increase their chance of contracting lung or throat cancer, heart disease or emphysema. Similarly, drivers with blood-alcohol levels above 0.1 percent are seven times more likely to have an auto accident than sober drivers, and the accident is twice as likely to be fatal. Consciously or unconsciously, we choose to increase the probability of those disasters when we smoke or drink and drive.

The lives we lead today are a mix of family genes and the choices we have made in all of our yesterdays. The life we will have tomorrow is who we are today, *plus* the choices we make today. As we get older, our gene pool becomes less important and our choices more important in shaping our future. When we made yesterday's choices, we either: (1) carefully evaluated what could happen today and consciously accepted it; or (2) ignored what might happen today and unconsciously accepted it. Either way, today is the result of yesterday's choices.

As human beings, we have the freedom of choice, but the laws of society and the Universe impose the consequences. We can choose to live any way we want. If we defy nature's laws by jumping off a ledge, we may break a leg. The good news is when we resume abiding by the laws, no further damage. Instant forgiveness. But there still are consequences today for yesterday's choices (like the broken leg). Your choices have brought you to this point in your life. Your choices today are what you want tomorrow. Your choices will make it happen, or not happen.

Multiple Choice

The choices we made in our yesterdays shaped our life today.
If we make new choices today, we will have a new life tomorrow.

You have chosen your life and I have chosen mine. We each have already taken the multiple-choice quiz shown below and made a choice in response to each of the ten questions. If we have satisfying careers and families, it is because we chose them. Whether we like where we live or not, we chose to live there. Even if we have less than we want, it is because we chose to have what we have. Sometimes, a choice in one area influenced results in another area. But we chose which area was most important, and accepted the results that a choice produced in other areas. Circle the things you currently have in your life, the results of choices you have made before today. If your answer is not among the choices, just write it into the box. These are your answers today.

Area	The Options	Area	The Options
Relationships	a. Open & honest b. Trust must be earned c. Joyous & caring d. Distant, arms length e. I avoid relationships	***Type of Job***	a. Self-employed b. Small company c. Large company d. Government e. None
Personal Appearance	a. Neat & clean b. Unusual, unique c. Fashion buff d. Casual & relaxed e. Over or under weight	***Home Location***	a. City b. Suburbs c. Seashore d. Farm e. Mountains
Marriage	a. Happily married b. Unhappily married c. Divorced/separated d. Same sex partner e. I like being alone	***Income Level***	a. Poverty b. Just scraping by c. Middle class d. Affluent e. Wealthy
Primary Goals	a. Fame & fortune b. Power & influence c. Peace & quiet d. Self-gratification e. Being accepted	***Favorite Music***	a. Country-western b. Classical c. Golden oldies d. Reggae e. Rock-n-roll
Personality Style	a. Quiet & unassuming b. Outgoing & busy c. Conservative d. Aggressive e. Analytical	***Level of Education***	a. Not very much b. High school c. Vocational d. College degree e. Masters degree

However, where you are today does not determine where you will be tomorrow. It only determines where you must start. Now circle how you want your life to be several years from now. Differences in your answers, if any, point to new choices you must make starting today. You will probably think of several reasons why you cannot make new choices. Those "reasons" are the higher-priority choices you have been making either consciously or unconsciously. Those "reasons" may be insidious dragons that stop you from having what you really want in your life. If you continue to surrender to those dragons, they will make your tomorrows be just like today.

How your life is today does not determine how it will be tomorrow. It only dictates where you must start when you make your new choices.

For example, you may prefer living in the mountains, but the job you have today is in the city working for a large company at a good salary. That means the choice you are making today is to put income level ahead of home location. You could reverse your choices at any time and put home location ahead of income level. If so, you would actively look for job openings in the mountains. You might visit the several mountain areas and spend a few days looking at available jobs, living standards and amenities, and the cost of new homes. You may have to learn a new skill that is valued in mountain country. Maybe become a forest ranger. At the end of the visit, you may choose to stay with your current career. The point is that each of us has the power to make different choices today than we have ever made in the past. Life is a multiple-choice quiz. On any day you can change your answers to the important questions.

Free Choices

The highest level is free choice: we make a choice only after we consciously evaluate all of the alternatives.

We choose everything in our lives, even the weather. Not that I can change the blizzard that has dropped twenty-eight inches of snow on Washington in the last two days. Rather, I choose to live here and snow is normal in Washington. In a very real sense, free choice brought the snow into my life. I could have chosen to live in Florida, Arizona or St. Maarten where it never snows.

Free choice means that tomorrow can be different than today. For example, predicting that you will have dinner at home tonight will be correct for over eighty percent of those who read this book. But the accuracy of my prediction does not reduce your free choice to have, or not have, dinner at home. It just means that having dinner at home is likely. But simple habits can become dragons that cause us to choose today the same things that we chose yesterday, even when we do not like what happened yesterday! As humans, we exercise choice at several levels, including free choice, habits and compulsions.

Free Choice is the highest level of choice: we consciously analyze alternatives and pick one for identifiable reasons. Free choice does not know the outcome in advance. It is like going into a new restaurant and ordering dinner from the menu. You imagine the taste of each choice, feel its texture on your tongue, inhale its imaginary aroma, and swallow as if a bite of the meal was on your mouth. After you taste several of these no-calorie meals in your mind, you choose the best one. Even if you do not like the meal, you have enjoyed the freedom of choice. We exercise free choice when we consider choices beyond the convenient, comfortable choices that we have made many times before.

Habit involves less choice because we know the answer in advance. It is a mental automatic pilot that acts without thinking to repeat past choices. In a restaurant, habit is looking at the menu and ordering the same meal you ordered on your last visit. Presumably, the past choice was a good one so you order the same meal again, and again, and again. Sometimes habit works well and sometimes it produces repetitive poor results. My morning ritual is an example of a habit that works. I wake up, turn off the radio after a five-minute snooze alarm, walk into the bathroom, turn on the shower, take my vitamins while the shower water warms, put a towel on the sink, take a shower, etc. The ritual eliminates the need for me to make hundreds of choices every morning, and frees me to consider the day's important decisions. The nice thing about habits is we can change them when we want. For example, the morning ritual is very different when I am late. By taking back the power of free choice, I complete the ritual in about half the time by choosing to leave out the unimportant steps.

By breaking habits, we get more of what we really want for tomorrow, instead of more of what we already had yesterday.

Compulsion is having no real choice, even though we feel like we are choosing. Consciously, we choose one action but unconsciously do something else. Drugs, alcoholism, smoking and eating addictions are compulsions. They are difficult to change and can be life threatening. Addicts often promise one behavior, but compulsively do another. The compulsive behavior is often a coverup for hidden pain. It is easier for an addict to lose themselves in the addiction than to face their painful dragons. While most of us do not suffer from addictions, we tolerate in ourselves behavioral compulsions like lethargy, procrastination or anger, which are usually coverups for pain or fear. To regain the power of choice, we must identify and tame the pain or fear.

Habits and compulsions are behavioral obstacles that stop us from freely choosing our tomorrows. But they can be changed if we choose to change them. Habits can be overcome with individual effort, while compulsions often require outside intervention and consistent help for a long time. We regain our power to choose by making the free choice to conquer habits and compulsions with consciousness and commitment.

Sometimes, the most important choice we make is to choose NOT TO DO something.

The Winning Bet

If we enjoy happiness and success today, it's because we made a series of well-reasoned "bets" in the past. Make your bet and take your chances.

When I was a college student, my future father-in-law took me to Aqueduct Race Track near New York City. Kelso was the favorite in the featured race, running at one-to-four odds (paying $2.50 to win and $2.10 to show on a $2.00 bet) after winning the Kentucky Derby. Everyone knew that Kelso would win the race. I did too. But it seemed boring to bet on such a sure thing. So I bet a $15 win-place-show wheel on a horse named Mischievous, who had never beaten Kelso. In a photo finish, Mischievous won by a head. Kelso finished fourth, the only out-of-the money finish of his career to that point. I was ecstatic at wining $200. A well-dressed man standing next to me quietly dropped a fist full of tickets and walked away. I looked at the tickets: twenty $100 tickets on Kelso to show. He had bet $2,000 with the expectation of winning $100 and lost it all. There are no sure things in this world. Not even odds-on favorites like Kelso. But what are the odds on the choices we make every day? None of them are a sure thing either.

Some choices require us to risk today's fun on tomorrow's dreams. Do we bet tomorrow's happiness for a moment of desire, or gamble the possibility of long-term suffering for short-term pleasure? Consider the odds on the following bets (choices) that many of us have faced:

• ***Tomorrow's Dreams or Today's Fun?*** There are so many fun things to do today, and earning a college degree takes so long. We know that, on average, a college degree will quadruple our lifetime income over a high school degree, and graduate degrees add another fifty percent. But some of the richest people in the world, Bill Gates for example, never finished college. So even if we do not get a college degree, it is possible to be among the richest people in the world. And we all know some college graduates who are failures in economic terms. Make your choice and take your chances.

• ***Tomorrow's Happiness or Today's Desire?*** We all know that unprotected sex is risky. But there are so many handsome men and pretty women. If we are discreet, our spouse will never find out. Of course we know intercourse could result in pregnancy. But the odds of pregnancy are one in ten for unprotected sex, and one in ten thousand for protected sex. Even if the worst happens, there is always abortion. And statistically only a few people get AIDS. Make your choice and take your chances.

• ***What You Want Tomorrow or What You Have Today?*** Start your own business? Take a pay cut and risk my savings? Over fifty percent of new businesses fail within five years. Only a few pay off big, and startup businesses require twelve-hour workdays and weekends too. Why not keep today's job? If you work until sixty-five, the retirement package will pay seventy-five percent of what you earn today. First save for a new house and the kids' college. After those are done, maybe then start your own business. Make your choice and take your chances.

• ***Today's Pleasure or Tomorrow's Pain?*** Some of us choose pleasure today and accept a possibility of pain tomorrow. There is only a sixty percent chance of getting cancer, emphysema or heart disease if we smoke two packs of cigarettes a day. We all know heavy smokers who lived past seventy in good health. Maybe we will be like them. And we know smokers who died in their fifties, and some who were okay into their late sixties before suffering a smoking-related disease. In the United States, over 400,000 people die each year of illnesses aggravated by or linked to smoking. Make your choice and take your chances.

The choices we make today spawn tomorrow's karma. The *Law of Karma* says that what we give today will be multiplied and returned to us tomorrow. We are paying karmic debts or reaping karmic rewards today for the choices we made yesterday. But what if we have already made a bad choice? Then make a new choice today while paying the karmic debt. If we cover up yesterday's choices, we usually continue making the same choices, which yields negative karma. That is like doubling your bet on the instant replay after seeing your horse lose the race. Make your choice and take your chances.

Flooded with Messages

Clear goals give us the power to sort through a cacophony of physical, emotional and intellectual messages.

Last Sunday my wife and I participated in an autocross event with our Porsche Boxster. In an autocross, a single car races on the track to negotiate an intricate pattern of cones that defines the course. Fastest time wins, except that two seconds are added to the driver's time for each cone that he or she knocks over. In my three trips through the course, I did not knock over a cone. My wife knocked over several, but her time was faster than mine in all three races even after penalty seconds were added. Before and during the race, my mind and body were flooded with physical, emotional and intellectual messages. *What are the dangers? When should I brake? How fast should I take the corners?* I responded to those messages by running a conservative race without pushing the car's performance or my abilities. My wife, responding to the same messages, made a different choice and had different results.

Physical, emotional and intellectual messages bombard our consciousness every minute of every day. They come at us like dragons from all angles. Sometimes they flood our working memory, and it is hard to think straight. We can ignore, but not escape the messages. Sooner or later we must make choices.

• ***Physical Messages.*** Physical messages spray from the faucets of hearing, sight, touch, smell and taste. They range from soothing music to piercing thunder, breathtaking panoramas to horrifying tragedy, orgasmic delights to painful sensations, savory aromas to sickening odors, and gourmet delights to foul flavors. Messages of pleasure point us toward happiness, while feelings of pain protect us from physical damage. Hedonists are driven by physical messages to the exclusion of other sources.

• ***Emotional Messages.*** Emotions are a strong second source of messages. Emotions reveal our intentions, what we really want. Messages of love tell us we are wanted and accepted. Messages of fear warn of danger. Messages of joy and peace encourage us to continue what we are doing, while messages of sadness suggest we have lost something. Messages of excitement tell us good things are about to happen. Temperamental people follow emotional messages and ignore other sources.

• ***Intellectual Messages.*** As if physical and emotional messages were not enough, intellectual messages cause us to evaluate and judge people and things. Intellectual messages are produced by a high-speed mental computer that accesses a huge database of our prior experiences, education, and judgements of good and bad. Analysts often make choices solely based on intellectual messages without considering their physical and emotional messages on an equal basis.

Physical, emotional and intellectual messages often conflict with each other. For example, if I entered the kitchen while my wife was baking fresh bread, my nose would sense the appetizing aroma of the bread and I would be hungry (a physical message). Concurrently, my intellectual messages might scream: "Don't eat the bread. You're dieting!" while my emotional messages appreciate my wife for making the bread. What choice do I make? Do I eat the bread or not? With or without margerine?

These messages are *not* me. The real *ME* is above them. A higher *ME* who processes the messages and makes the choices. It is a spiritual being that applies values and goals as the criteria for making one choice or another. When we ignore either our physical, our intellectual or our emotional messages to make our choices seem easier, we risk out-of-balance, disappointing results.

As a result of challenging childhood experiences, I disregarded for most of my life a stream of emotional messages that were too painful to acknowledge. Only recently have I begun to treat emotional messages as equal partners with my intellectual and physical messages. A more effective *ME* has learned to integrate my physical, emotional and intellectual messages into choices—choices that are consistent with my values and my dreams. Values and dreams are the criteria that enable us to make effective choices after processing the millions of physical, emotional and intellectual messages that we receive every day.

Boiling a Frog

Choice is the time gap between receiving and responding to a stimuli. When we respond habitually to stimuli, we abandon the power that choice gives us to change our lives.

I am told that if a frog is dropped into a pot of boiling water, it will jump out of the pot. However, if the frog is placed into comfortable water that is gradually heated to the boiling point, it adjusts to the increasing temperature and eventually is boiled to death. But humans are different than frogs. We are not subject to the creeping compromise that the frog feels as the water temperature rises. We have the power of choice because we sense and process many stimuli (like the increasing water temperature), and respond to them with our choice of action. We are conscious of the time gap between receiving an external stimuli and our response to that stimuli, and we use that time gap to make reasoned choices.

Scientist-philosophers suggest the possibility of higher beings who exist in dimensions where *thought is instantaneous reality*. Such beings do not have the power of choice, at least not as we know choice. Neurologists estimate that our brain receives several million stimuli each second from various parts of our bodies. However, our brains can process only about a hundred thousand stimuli per second. How do we choose which stimuli to process and which to ignore? Clearly, something inside us serves as a filter that passes some stimuli and ignores others.

The filter is learned behaviors. For example, the big toe on your right foot has been sending stimuli to your brain as you read this book. Most likely, the stimuli say that everything is okay with your toe, and those feelings are being filtered out of your consciousness. You are not continuously spending mind share on the thought: *"My toe feels okay. My toe feels okay."* However, if a heavy object dropped on your toe, the pain stimuli probably would get through the filter. The toe would hurt in your conscious thoughts.

The filtering appears to occur in our spinal cord and the lower part of our brain. After years of training, we have taught those portions of our nervous system what we want to filter, and what we want to pass through the filter to our consciousness. Hypochondriacs have taught their nervous system to pass low levels of pain stimuli. Their learned behavior is to feel it all. At the other extreme there are men and women with broken legs who run into burning houses to rescue children. They have filtered out even the severe pain stimuli of a broken leg.

After choosing which physical stimuli to let through the filter, we also choose how to combine them with emotional stimuli (sad, mad, glad, etc.) and intellectual data to make choices. Consider a novice running a marathon against a seasoned runner. They both experience about the same levels of pain. But the pain motivates the experienced runner to run with increasing determination, while pain causes a novice to contemplate dropping out of the race. Simultaneously, intellectual stimuli tell the novice to continue running the race because the pain is temporary, and emotional stimuli say that he/she will be embarrassed by quitting the race. After combining these stimuli in the frontal lobe of the brain, the novice runner makes his/her choice.

Who creates the criteria for choices? Each of us does individually, of course. We can be reactive and let our choices follow the strongest stimuli, or we be proactive and use our values and goals as the criteria for our choices. Choices based on values (*who we are*) and goals (*what we want*) are more effective than knee-jerk reactions to the strongest physical, emotional or intellectual stimuli. We choose the quality of our lives by how we use the time gap between stimuli and response. We can choose to remain in the pot as the water temperature increases, or choose to jump out!

Drop that Banana!

To have what we really want tomorrow, we may have to let go of a few things that we have today.

One way to catch a wild monkey is to put a cage in the jungle with a banana inside and narrow spaces between the bars. Monkeys instinctively want bananas. They grab every banana they can get, and stubbornly will not let go. So the wild monkey reaches its hand into the cage, grabs the banana, and cannot remove its hand. The monkey wants to escape from the cage, but it is not willing to let go of the banana. The banana is more important than freedom.

Like monkeys, we may use our power of choice to *not* to make a choice. We would rather hold on to the life we have, than reach for the life we want. Consider, for example, a mother with young children who is in an abusive relationship with an alcoholic or drug-addicted husband or live-in partner. She wants to leave to be free of the abuse and protect her children. But she is unwilling to give up the house, the financial support, and the fading memories of good times long past. Those are her bananas. She chooses to remain caught in the relationship (the cage) as life goes by one day at a time. To this woman, the appearance of family life and financial support are more important than freedom and safety for her children. I call such situations the aroma phenomena: *We know it stinks, but we get accustomed to the smell.*

Too often we spend considerable time solving problems that never should have occurred in the first place. Each of us chooses how we will use, or not use, our power of choice. Maybe we should take a really close look at the value of the bananas that we are holding on to. Those bananas may be dragons that are destroying our happiness and success. What bananas stop you from making the choices that you otherwise would like to make in your life?

Go Ahead, Make Me Change

Waiting for someone or something to change, or manipulating them into change doesn't work. We can only change ourselves.

How many psychiatrists does it take to change a light bulb? Just one, but the bulb must choose to change. No one can force us to change. Mostly, the dragon of fear stops us from changing. It makes us afraid that we will lose something, or afraid that things will be worse if we change. Despite the dragon, we choose to change *when, where* and *how* we want. The door to change has one doorknob, and it is on the inside. I am the only one who can open my door. And no matter how much I may entice, cajole or coerce you, only you can open your door.

What causes us to choose change? Just two things: (1) self-motivation to improve our lives, or (2) an external stimuli that pushes us toward a better or safer way to live. Self-motivation distinguishes humans from other creatures in the animal kingdom. They only change in response to external stimuli like danger, or lack of food and water. Humans also are above animals with respect to our ability to deal with external stimuli. Given the same external stimuli, you and I might make different choices. And given the same external stimuli twice, I might make two different choices. Most people stop smoking after a lung cancer operation. But, even after such a strong external stimuli, some still smoke. They may make a new choice after a second operation or the onset of emphysema.

The twenty-first century presents virtually unlimited opportunities for us to change. We each individually choose to change or not. Furthermore, if we choose change we also get to choose how we would like to change. For example, the Internet is changing world communications. Some people choose to keep up with the technology and others do not. Both choices may be fear-based. Some feel that success requires knowledge of the Internet. Others are afraid of the difficulty of learning a new technology like the Internet. Nobody and nothing can force us to make a specific choice, but each of us will experience life tomorrow based on the choices we make today.

A River in Egypt

Denial ("da Nile" *- a the river in Egypt) inhibits choice.*
It allows us to trade tomorrow's new possibilities
for a tenuous feeling of security today.

One day I found a puddle of water on the floor under the kitchen sink in our home. I removed the cleaning fluids and powders that were under the sink, and mopped up the water. There was no visible leak, so I concluded the sink overflowed while we were washing dishes. The cleanup took thirty minutes. Three days later, another puddle, another cleanup, another thirty minutes. Still no sign of a leak. But there was no evidence that the sink had overflowed either.

I was puzzled. The cleanup was wasting time, and the water was leaking into the basement. I could continue mopping up the puddles or acknowledge that there was a problem bigger than the puddle. The third time I found a puddle with no evidence the sink had overflowed, I looked for another source of the problem. Minutes later, I found that the drain pipe from the sink vibrated and leaked when the garbage disposal was turned on. It did not leak when the disposal was off. I tightened the joint on the disposal and it has not leaked since. No more puddles. No more cleanups.

Many of us deny problems with much more significant in our lives than a puddle under the sink. The denial dragon lives on even as people who care for us try to help us to see the problem. But if we refuse to acknowledge that our experiences today are not what we want them to be, or if we do not see that a problem exists, then we will not look for a solution. We deny the reality of our experience saying: "Things really aren't so bad." As soon as our denial ends, we seek new possibilities and new choices, and usually find them relatively quickly.

We each have the power to choose whatever we want in every moment of the day. No one can take away our power of choice. But we can throw it away. When we do that, we repeat the same negative experiences over and over. But we cannot ignore our experiences as long as we choose to. But sooner or later we gets the message. Why not sooner? Someday may be too late. End your denial today and have the life you really want tomorrow.

Fuzzy Thinking

The courage to risk being ourselves, to venture into the emotional unknown, can propel us to the happiness we seek.

People sometimes say: "I'm confused and don't know what to do." But when they explain the confusion, it is clear they are not confused at all, but instead lack the courage to do what they know they should do. You may have seen this phenomenon, for example, while comforting a friend who is having marital difficulties, or is contemplating separation or divorce. When asked: "What do you want?" the friend's responds:

> *I want to stay together, but this is not a healthy environment for our children. I love him (or her), but I don't know what to do.*

> *Our relationship has been dying for a long time. I'm not sure if she (or he) wants to be with me. How can we revitalize our marriage?*

These statements are the fuzzy-thinking dragon. They are not missing clarity. They are missing the courage to make a decisive choice, take action and risk rejection.

Often, the separated individual wants to reconcile with his or her spouse but is afraid to express their needs, or is unwilling to forgive. They fear rejection by a spouse who might say: "But I don't want you." It is a real fear. So what! The desire to reconcile is not altered by that response. The lack of courage to face rejection may be the reason why the relationship has been dying for a long time. Maybe the partners have been afraid to express their needs and fears. In my experience with separation (twice), once my wife was clear about her choice for us to be together, and once it was me who was clear that I wanted us to be together. Fortunately, in both cases the fuzzy thinker overcame his or her indecision because of the clarity and courage of the other partner.

The fuzzy-thinking dragon touches all parts of our lives: changing jobs, making major purchases, or changing old habits for example. When we think we are confused and do not know what to do, it may be just a lack of courage to make the choice that we know is "right." The confusion disappears when we accept that choice, and act on it.

My History Book

To have tomorrows better than our yesterdays, we must shake free of the events that happened in our past and shape the events that will be in our future.

As I write this vignette, I am finishing the sixtieth chapter in the history book of my life. Each chapter has been a unique story about success, pain, triumph, tears, adventure, failure, disappointment, joys, old and new relationships, and growth. Some chapters are relatively boring, and others could form the plot of a soapbox opera or dime-store novel. Some are *WOW!* As I review my history book today, it is hard to believe that it all happened to me. I ask myself:

- *Who could know that is what would happen?*
- *Why did I choose that? It was a dumb choice.*
- *I'm glad I made that choice, it worked out better than expected.*
- *How did I get so lucky? I really dodged a bullet there!*

But none of the sixty chapters determines what will happen in future chapters, however many there may be.

The first sixty chapters, some more than others, affect where I must begin to write my sixty-first chapter. However, while experience is a big factor in decision-making processes, my experiences do not determine my choices. J. Paul Getty said that in times of major change, our experience and past successes may be our worst enemy. Our past becomes a dragon if we let it determine our future.

None of our past experiences determine what the next chapter in our lives will be. Our history is not our future. We can make new choices at any instant of time. Some choices we many not want to change because we like the results we are having. Most of us have a few choices that we definitely want to change. Our tomorrows will be what we choose today for them to be, regardless of all the good and bad events in our yesterdays. What do you choose tomorrow to be? And are you taking action to implement your choice?

A Golf Story

Today's good life may be a barrier to experiencing a great life. Too many times, the success we enjoy today is the biggest obstacle to our future success.

A popular bumper sticker says: "A bad day on the golf course is better than a good day at work." A successful salesman I know who had a sixteen handicap considered that sticker and asked himself: "If that's true, why work when I could choose to be on a golf course?" He quit an $90,000-a-year computer sales job, invested all of his retirement savings and more to buy farmland, and opened a driving range.

Family and friends thought he was insane to risk everything on such a crazy idea. "Mid-life crisis," they scorned, "he'll get over it soon and go back to a real job." Today, he goes to work at the driving range. Over time he has added a putt-putt course, a practice sand trap, and an eighteen-hole executive golf course. The amazing thing is, besides enjoying each day doing what he wants to do, his golf business is fabulously successful. His income is way more than his best year selling computers.

Hopefully, you enjoy your job. I enjoy mine most of the time. The point is that if we do not enjoy our jobs, why do we choose to continue doing them? And concurrently choose not to do what we really want to do? Why would we make such choices and be miserable going to work every day? Today's success may be the dragon that is holding us back from what we really want. This is our one and only life. It is not a dress rehearsal for some bigger event that comes later.

You might say: "That's a great story, Dick, but let's get real. I have to work to pay the mortgage, make car payments, have food to eat, and buy books like this." My response is that we may be asking ourselves the wrong question. Maybe the real question should be: "Do I really want my house and car so much that I'm willing work every day in a job that I hate?" Or "Is my job so boring, so… (fill in your own words) that I'm adversely affecting my health and my family's lives?" Each of us individually chooses what we will do today. And today's choices can be different than yesterday's choices.

What We Really Want

The picture of what we want can get out of focus, especially when we attach high importance to things that aren't directly related to our happiness and success.

As a fraternity pledge during Hell Week, I learned that *what I think I want* may not be *what I really want*. Throughout the week, pledges received black marks if they offended a brother. Over forty years later, I still remember the definition of a black mark: *One swift stroke well laid on at the time of reckoning.* On the other hand, white marks were given for helping a brother. We were never told the definition of a white mark, but I assumed it was something I would want like erasing a black mark. I did things I ordinarily would not do, just to earn white marks. At the "time of reckoning," I learned that a white mark was two black marks. And I had spent the entire week trying to get white marks and avoid black marks!

We lose sight of what we really want when we pursue dragons that, at best, are second cousins to what we really want. For example, many people think that money is what they really want. They equate more money to more joy, happiness and peace. They make choices to get more money, even though the choices do not bring joy, happiness or peace. At best, money is a second cousin to happiness. It is a mixed bag of blessings and curses. It does not buy the love, health, successful relationships, or respect that are so important to most of us.

Unfortunately, the pursuit of money sometimes produces pain and unhappiness. For example, the choice to work long hours has been a big issue in relationships with my wife and daughters. *Why* do I work hard and long to earn more money? *Why* do I need more money (these are the "cousins"): to buy a big house, to take more vacations, to have more fun. *Why*: to have joy, happiness and love. Workaholics, no matter how much they earn, often get divorces and create dysfunctional families. It makes more sense to skip excessively hard work and go directly to what we really want: quality time with our families. When what we really want is clear, our choices give top importance to those things.

The Shooting Gallery

Each day gives us a twenty-four-hour stream of creativity, love and energy. We can spray it toward many different targets, or focus it on what we really want.

My grandson was fascinated by the water-pistol shooting gallery in the penny arcade. For a quarter, he shot a one-minute stream of water at his choice of many colorful targets, but only a few of the targets scored points. As I watched him spraying water randomly at the targets, I was stuck by the idea that life is much like a shooting gallery. We can spray a target for a long time or a short time within the twenty-four hours of each day, but we can only spray one target at a time.

We enjoy spraying creativity, energy and love on our families, friends and hobbies. Most of us enjoy spraying our jobs. Our health needs some spray too. And it is important that intellectual and spiritual growth get sprayed. Our detractors and need for instant gratification will take big portions of the spray if we let them. Some areas need at least a little spray every day, so we cannot waste our spray on low-value targets. If we focus the whole spray on one target, say our job, then nothing will be left for other people and activities. When we are angry with difficult people or harbor resentments, we spray targets that do not score points in terms of peace and happiness.

Some of us spray part of our twenty-four-hour stream being angry about past events. That seems like wasting of a very limited resource. On the other hand, if we do not spray a target at all, like health, it may disappear. When we get older, it may be too late to direct part of the spray to healthy living. The spray may be needed for survival and recovery. Effective choices put high-value targets first in line for a significant share of our spray. We may allocate the spray differently at different times in our lives. Personally, I gave too much of my spray to work when I was young. Now my new choice is to redirect the spray to my family. Clear dreams and values help identify the high-value targets in our lives for us to spray.

The Choice for Growth

Pleasures are easy to choose. Our challenge is to choose more personal, intellectual and spiritual growth.

Immediate gratification draws us like a flame draws a moth, while actions that produce future happiness and success seem like mountain climbing. We say to ourselves: *I'll stop smoking on New Year's Day. I'll exercise and diet after my birthday. I'll enroll in college courses in the spring.* Of course, when New Year's Day and the birthday pass, and the spring term begins, we find new reasons to delay those actions, to delay the promises we made to ourselves. Those reasons are dragons that destroy our future success and happiness.

I have consistently encouraged family, friends and coworkers to participate in personal-growth seminars. I have taken several myself. The responses are revealing lessons in human nature. Some said: "Life is good enough just like it is," only to complain in the very next sentence about someone or something that was going poorly. Any time we say something is good enough, we discard the possibility of it being better. Some friends claimed to be "very interested in growth" but declined to take a seminar for thirteen consecutive courses over two years. The weather is bad (January's excuse). I have gardening and house repairs to do (April's excuse). We are planning a vacation that weekend (July's excuse). And the Redskins are playing the Cowboys that weekend (October's excuse).

It is so easy to procrastinate the growth choices that move us toward our goals. Unfortunately, before we realize it, a month, a year, a decade, a lifetime have passed and the actions we knew were needed to achieve our biggest goals never got started. Each day offers a new set of choices. Most will have little or no effect on the future, but a few will be significant growth opportunities that build a strong foundation for future success and happiness. The choice for growth is crucial in enhancing our relationships and extending our capabilities. Growth is the priority choice if our goals are real, and not just daydreams.

New Choices

Choice occurs in an instant. We may agonize over possibilities for years. But when clear choice occurs, actions follow immediately and results start changing.

A friend who was a drug and alcohol abuser has been in recovery over six years. For thirty years prior to that he was a street bum living in boxes on hot-air gratings, begging or stealing food, in and out of jail frequently, working odd jobs long enough to earn money to feed his habits. One day I asked what caused him to change so dramatically and suddenly. He answered instantly: "When I was sixteen years old in high school, I was already on drugs. My mother told me that when I got tired of living that way, there were other choices I could make. I lived in the streets for years. Every time I saw her, she reminded me that I could make new choices. One morning when I woke up with a broken arm and an terrible hangover, I remembered what she has told me for so many years and decided I didn't want to live that way anymore. That morning I chose to change my life."

And he has acted decisively on his new choice. Today, he has a job that requires a Certified Driving License (CDL). One requirement to maintain the license is a random drug test at least once every six months. He said the other drivers hate the test, but he enjoys it. When the test is over and he gets the results, he jumps with joy and shouts: "Yes, I did it! Clean and sober again!"

He is discovering life's joys like a child, having experiences that most of us had as teenagers even though he is over fifty years old. Things that are old to me, things that I take for granted, are exciting and new for him. He has taught me two valuable and lasting lessons. First, the little things in life are really the biggest joys; and second, no matter what we have done in the past or how long we persisted in doing it, we can make a brand-new choice today. Those new choices give us the awesome power to change the fundamental direction of our lives.

Closing Thoughts on Making Clear Choices

We recreate ourselves (or not) every day in the choices we make. Are the choices that you're making today moving you closer to your goals for tomorrow?

What if hell is not a horrible place that we might go when we die? What if instead it is a place that we put ourselves in today by choice? The only power we have is the power of choice. Any other power that we think we have today is the result of choices we made in the past. The success and happiness we will have, or not have, tomorrow depend on what we choose today. When the primary criteria for our choices is immediate gratification or being accepted by others, we do so at the risk of losing our self-esteem and our dreams. We do so at the risk that we may live in hell today and remain there tomorrow.

The social mirror of other people's opinions reflects our true inner self about as accurately as fun-house mirrors at a county fair accurately reflect our physical being. Those fun-house mirrors make us look thin, fat, short or tall depending on which mirror we look into. Similarly, the feedback we are receive from those around us, even close family members and trusted friends, is a mixture of:

(1) *Their perceptions.* But they may not see things as they really are,
(2) *Their desires* for how they want us to be to satisfy their needs,
(3) *Their opinion* of what we should be, and
(4) Our actions and the results they produce.

So what we choose to do is only one part in four of their evaluation of us. The other three parts are things we do not understand and may not even agree with. We are wrestling with insatiable dragons when the criteria for our choices is strongly influenced by what others think.

Making clear choices also means nobody forces us to do anything. Not our employers, spouses, parents, children, nor friends. Society, the government or the United Nations cannot force us either. They may create a culture where it is easy to make the choices they want us to make. But they cannot force us to do anything. For example, the Internal Revenue Service (IRS) says that we will go to jail if we do not pay income taxes every year. But the choice is ours:

pay taxes or go to jail. The government hopes we will not choose to go to jail, but it is our choice. If we choose to protest objectionable government actions, jail may be a better choice than paying taxes. However, if we prefer being free, then paying taxes would be the most effective choice.

Similarly, when a client asks me to finish a job by an unreasonable deadline, the choices I have are to: (1) say *YES* and turn my life upside-down (consequences: please the client, but anger my wife), (2) say *NO* (consequences: please my wife, but possibly lose the client), or (3) negotiate a more realistic deadline by explaining why the deadline is unreasonable and being flexible to meet the client's priority needs (consequences: unknown at the start). Each choice has favorable and unfavorable consequences. So I am not really choosing my actions, I am choosing my consequences.

In every situation we face, the choice of actions (or inaction) is ours to make and, after we make the choice, the consequences are ours too because we chose them. But consequences are not really a big deal either because, after we taste the consequences of one choice, most of the time we have the power to make a new choice that will yield different consequences. The power of choice is the most powerful tool we have to shape our lives. Let us use it wisely.

---------Tip #9---------

Dare to Dream

~ Imagine Your Future

"What one man can do is dream. What one man can do is love. What one man can do is change the world, and make it work again!"
— John Denver

Dreams of the Future

A dream is a powerful tool that focuses our intellectual, physical and spiritual skills, and aligns our actions with our purpose.

Even though his record has been broken several times, Babe Ruth is still remembered as the greatest home run hitter of all time. His most celebrated home run was in the 1932 World Series against the Chicago Cubs when the Babe stood at home plate, looked up at the fans, and pointed to the right center field stands. Everyone in the stadium knew what he meant, and they cheered wildly when he hit the next pitch into the spot where he had pointed. Did the Babe dream that home run, or was it a prediction of the future based on self-confidence? Is there a difference? The dreams we have for the future are our prediction of life's coming attractions. We create the future by imagining what our lives could be like, and then taking action to make it so.

You and I are stars in the exciting adventure called life. The adventure offers a wide choice of roles, some big and some small. We get to choose our role, and work to make it real. Unfortunately, if we do not choose a dream for our life, we risk becoming merely a pawn in someone else's dream. If we let them, the twin dragons of fear and embarrassment will stop us from dreaming. They will frighten us into believing that dreams never come true, or delude us into thinking that we will be criticized for an unrealistic dream. Those dragons also may try to have us be embarrassed to declare that our dream is to help and support others.

It may seem easier not to dream at all. But we need a dream to keep from being frustrated by the little failures that happen almost every day. Dreams are our ticket out of the boredom of everyday activities and recurring problems. Lack of a dream leaves us depressed, wondering why we are alive. Dreams are a visualization, a mental image of *who we are* and *what we want*. Dreams become the criteria for making choices as we play our chosen role in the adventure of life. What better time to dare new dreams then at the start of the twenty-first century and a new millennium?

Most things in our world were created twice. First in someone's mind, in his or her dreams; and second in physical reality. Material-based dreams of wealth, self-indulgence and domination have created a world with poverty, pain, crime and war. When we see our lives as possessions and good times, our dreams become an insatiable quest for more. We can never get enough.

On the other hand, we create synergy when our dreams are based on the contributions we can make. Dreams that are bigger than we are. As the master plan for our lives, our dream is what we really want. Building a dream is not a once-in-a-lifetime task. Actually, we reshape and refine our dreams continuously as we travel through life gaining knowledge, having more experiences, and seeing the results of the dreams of others. When we conquer the dragon of blaming others for our lives, we gain the power to dream what our future will be and the power to make it so.

The reason we fail to achieve many of our dreams is that we do not define them clearly enough, research them thoroughly, or even seriously consider them to be achievable. Those around us who are living their dreams can tell you exactly where they are headed, and how they plan to get there. Simply stated, a goal is dream with a plan and a schedule.

Dreaming the future is important because the future is where we will spend the rest of our lives. There are no impossible dreams. This tip on *Daring to Dream* includes vignettes that:

- Illustrate the importance of having a dream,
- Outline ways to identify your unique personal dream, and
- Describe the experience of taking acting to achieve our dream.

Daring to dream is more about discovering who you are than about having what you want. Do not rush the process of finding a dream. Enjoy exploring each of the possibilities. For now, it is sufficient if your dream is to find a dream.

The Super Bowl

Whichever Super Bowl you choose in life,
take full control over your personal game plan.

Professional football, like life, has three types of participants. First are the observers. Millions of fans who buy tickets to games and watch them on television. They do not scrape their knees, bump their heads, or break their bones. But neither do they score touchdowns or make interceptions. They do not feel the awesome joy of victory, or taste the bittersweet agony of defeat. They watch while others play, choosing not to play themselves. There are no fans in the Football Hall of Fame.

Second are the teams. Ninety players on the field for each game playing through heat, cold, rain, wind or snow. They dare to dream of the Super Bowl. They execute the game plan (or not), and make split-second choices that ultimately determine the final score. They run with the ball, catch passes, kick field goals, make tackles, and sometimes they fumble. When the game is over, goats and heroes are interviewed on TV, and their triumphs and miscues are reported in Monday's newspaper for the fans to read. Some wear a special ring because they played on a team that won a previous Super Bowl. Many achieve fame and fortune, but most players end their careers with pleasant memories of just playing.

Third are the owners and coaches who conceive the game. They make rules, build stadiums, select players, and prepare game plans. They invest in the game to create the opportunity for players to earn mega-salaries and fans to indulge their fantasies.

Everyday life has observers, players and owners too. It is said that: (1) one percent of us conceive big dreams, (2) nineteen percent help make the dreams of others happen, and (3) eighty percent observe daily events without a personal dream. I have no idea how those numbers were measured, or if they are accurate. But it does seem like too few people are pursuing a dream. We each have the chance to play in the Super Bowl of our choice: the Super Bowl of families, the Super Bowl of public service, the Super Bowl of business, etcetera. Whichever Super Bowl you choose, dream about being in the big game.

Personal Balance Sheet

Our contribution to the world is measured on a Balance Sheet just like the net worth of a corporation.

Whether a company is in communications, pharmaceuticals, autos, computers, or another sector of the economy, the stock market uses the difference between assets and liabilities to determine net worth. Like a company's business plan, a personal dream is a strategy to use assets to build net worth. We can choose any dream we want, even no dream at all. Our net worth will be the difference we make.

Whether our assets are few or many, our contribution is measured by how well we use them. Many of today's heroes have personal assets in large quantities. Mother Theresa may not have had as many, but used them effectively to make a difference. Rosa Parks also appears to have had few assets, yet she made a major contribution to our civil rights by courageously taking a seat on a bus.

Liabilities are damage we do to ourselves, others and the environment by using assets inappropriately. Each act of carelessness, selfishness, dishonesty or greed increases our karmic debts. Just like business loans, karmic debts must be repaid in the future. People who pursue dreams earn high returns by investing their personal assets to build net worth. Each of us has a unique blend of assets and liabilities which, when invested in our personal dream, yield opportunities to make a difference. How are you investing yours?

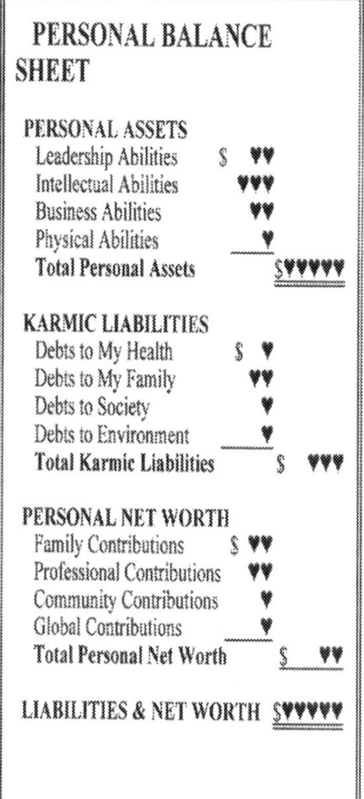
PERSONAL BALANCE SHEET

PERSONAL ASSETS		
Leadership Abilities	$ ♥♥	
Intellectual Abilities	♥♥♥	
Business Abilities	♥♥	
Physical Abilities	♥	
Total Personal Assets		$♥♥♥♥♥
KARMIC LIABILITIES		
Debts to My Health	$ ♥	
Debts to My Family	♥♥	
Debts to Society	♥	
Debts to Environment	♥	
Total Karmic Liabilities		$ ♥♥♥
PERSONAL NET WORTH		
Family Contributions	$ ♥♥	
Professional Contributions	♥♥	
Community Contributions	♥	
Global Contributions	♥	
Total Personal Net Worth		$ ♥♥
LIABILITIES & NET WORTH		$♥♥♥♥♥

Karmic Alchemy

By finding new dreams in sad experiences, we transform events that appear to be tragedies into opportunities to help others.

Like the mythical alchemists of medieval times who changed base metals into gold, we can transform our karmic liabilities into valuable assets. For example, I complained for decades about a sad childhood before I converted it into the basis for my dream. Events that appear at first to be tragedies can be the start of new dreams, dreams that provide life-changing benefit to thousands of people.

Consider a businessman who failed in business several times trying wild ideas, a mayor caught in a sting and convicted of drug possession, a football player accused of murdering his wife, and an actor crippled in a freak accident. These bigger-than-life heros earned prestige, wealth and power in good times before unfortunate events changed the course of their lives. The events seemed tragic when they happened. But were they rally?

Among these four examples, two men gave into the dragon of missed opportunity regarding their unfortunate events, while the other two men tamed the dragon and used karmic alchemy to transform an unfortunate event into a precious opportunity. Looking at the unfortunate events through the eyes of an alchemist, these men where given a golden opportunity to make a difference:

• The businessman (Walt Disney) built on business failures by trying one more wild idea, which became the foundation of an entertainment empire. Long after his death, he is remembered, not as someone who went bankrupt multiple times, but as a creative man who brought joy and laughter to millions.

• The mayor (Marion Barry of Washington, D.C.) might have used his questionable drug conviction to lead young men and women away from their drug habits. He is remembered as a mayor who angrily won reelection despite his drug conviction. He also could have been remembered as an inspirational leader against drug abuse in his city and the world.

• The football player (O. J. Simpson) might have used his unfortunate experience and the publicity of a notorious trial to begin a bold campaign against spousal abuse. Instead, he is remembered as a record-breaking football player who was found "not guilty" of murder. He also could have been remembered as a champion in the fight against family violence.

• The actor (Christopher Reeves) fought his quadriplegic disability and told thousands about the importance of enjoying each moment of their lives. While some remember him as the actor who played Superman and was paralyzed in a tragic accident, most think of him as a courageous leader and an inspirational speaker on the quality and importance of life.

Denying unfortunate events will not fulfill our dreams. Our challenge is to fit such events into our dreams. Karmic alchemy aks us to bravely and openly say: "I learned from my experience, and I have the unique opportunity to help others who struggle with similar experiences."

Life sometimes takes us down a highway that we never intended to travel. But if we look carefully, the scenery on that highway may be more attractive than the scenery on the highway we thought we wanted. The need to transform seemingly adverse events from liabilities into assets is not because the events are embarrassing or bad. Rather the events must be changed because they do not accurately portray *Who I Am.* They do not reflect our dream for ourselves.

Everything we do and say is a statement to the universe of *Who I Am*. If, after a tragedy or setback, we want to re-present ourselves to demonstrate *Who I Am*, then events that do not fit into how we want to be remembered must be transformed. Karmic alchemy enables us to transform the ugliest events into the foundation of an exciting new direction in our lives, a new dream. What seems like a failure today very well could be the cornerstone of tomorrow's dream.

Afraid to Dream

Where we are at any moment in time is much less important than the dreams we have for our future, and the actions we are taking to achieve them.

In the mid-1960s, my brother and I played a game called Pro Quarterback on Sunday afternoons as we watched the NFL games on TV. We got bored playing on a table, so we programmed the game in Fortran on an IBM 1130 computer. We displayed the players as *X*s and *O*s huddling in circles on the IBM 1130's six-inch control monitor while we selected our offensive and defensive plays. After we both had pressed *Enter*, random numbers determined the play's result, and the *X*s and *O*s would move on the monitor in patterns that loosely represented the action in an NFL football game. Very loosely.

The *X*-quarterback dropped back while the *X*-linemen blocked the rushing *O*s. The *X*-wide receivers ran pass patterns. The pass would be complete, incomplete or intercepted, and the *X*s and *O*s would run back into the huddle to await the next play. My brother and I were fascinated by the displays, and we played the game for hours. We saw business potential in the idea, but we were reluctant to dream success on a grand scale because the action displays were so ugly. This was years before the first Ataris and Nintendos. Pong, a game with primitive displays when first sold to the public, was not available yet. If my brother and I had looked past the simplistic displays to dream big possibilities, today your kids might be playing Stieglitz instead of X-boxes.

Dreams define possibilities, and action determines results. More of us need to dream big dreams, set high goals, and make big promises to ourselves and others. However, the dragons of past experience tell us that we often cannot keep promises, that goals are rarely met, and that dreams rarely come true. The dragons of fear tell us that people will judge us adversely if we do not keep our promises or reach our goals. Yielding to these experiences and fears, it is easier to not make promises, not set goals, and not to dream dreams. If we have dreams at all, we keep them as secrets locked deep in our heart.

Unfortunately, without promises, goals and dreams, life is like a rudderless ship adrift in a tide of daily events. We do not know which way to turn, what choice to make, or which actions are best. We can regain confidence and direction by: (1) making promises and do our best to keep them, (2) setting goals and working hard to reach them, and (3) dreaming big dreams and asking others to help make them come true. When we make small promises to ourselves and keep them, our self-esteem and sense of integrity grow. Little by little, personal integrity becomes a stronger influence on our decisions and actions than fear. We are no longer obsessed with reaching a goal after we have set it. Rather, we enjoy the events that occur on the road toward the goal.

Goals and dreams create a challenging game that we play every day. Quantitative goals are especially stimulating, since they provide a built-in scorecard to measure our progress during the game. Dreams generate the courage to accept responsibility for the world around us, the willingness to set goals for ourselves, and the power to make our lives like we want them to be. The surprise is that positive attitudes about goals, promises and dreams also enable us to accomplish more than we ever have before, and have fun doing it!

Top of the Chain

A dream is a destination and a map to get there. Dreams provide criteria for choices and a ruler to measure the effectiveness of our actions.

As humans, we are the top of the food chain. We perform all the functions of lower-order life forms but, of all living creatures, we alone possess the ability to imagine the future and make it happen. Fish do not swim from the Atlantic Ocean to the Pacific to find a better home. Birds do not build a bigger nest with a pool to accommodate a bigger family. Dogs do not learn to meow because they admire cats.

Unfortunately, the dragons of immediate gratification and daily survival make it easy to abandon our unique power to dream. When we continuously choose actions that have little purpose beyond collecting possessions and enjoying oneself, we may feel empty. Tired at the end of a long day, we ask: "Why did I do what I did today?" Too often the answer is: "I don't know, but it's what I do every day." I "feel like it" or "don't feel like it" are weak criteria for the big decisions in our lives.

To help me make choices when chaos and disappointment seem to be everywhere, my dream is written on the top of my daily work list. When things get hectic and there is not enough time for everything, my dream is the tie-breaker. I look at the alternatives, and choose the one that most clearly is on the path to my dream. The results are rewarding. The agony of indecision evaporates, and progress toward my dream becomes measurable.

By regularly exercising our ability to dream, little by little we achieve our dreams and broaden the horizon of possibilities. Those who do not have a dream will, of course, not achieve it. Even more damaging, their ability to dream may atrophy. The little voices inside our head that constantly whisper our dreams do not go away when we anesthetize ourselves with work, play, food, drugs, alcohol or other diversions. The top-of-the-chain voices are always there reminding us of *Who we are* and *What we want*. We can find our dreams by listening to those voices.

The Little Voices

Little voices whisper our dreams to us. They propose new possibilities that help us see our dreams more clearly.

My wife and I met over forty years ago in a most unusual way. She was fifteen and I was seventeen, and we were in high school. She saw me in the local park playing stickball when a little voice whispered to her: "Get him. This is the one." I had never seen her before when she walked up to me, sat in my lap, put her arms around me, and kissed me. She says her sorority sisters made her do it. While that may be true, she also acknowledges that she was listening to the little voices too. In either case, I was stunned and the rest is history.

Little voices inside our heads whisper our dreams to us. They suggest new ideas, and lead us to the answers we need to find our dream. Everyone has these voices. Some of us listen to them, and others do not. We are ignoring our voices and giving into the dragons of doubt when we say to ourselves: "This one time won't matter," "Nobody really cares," "I'll mind my own business," or "Let someone else do it." These self-limiting attitudes stop us from having *What we really want* and being *Who we really are*.

After being ignored consistently, the little voices may diminish into uneasy feelings, vague desires, or weak intuitions. But we know unconsciously that the voices are still there because we are not satisfied with *What is.* The voices keep whispering: "This isn't good enough." When we listen to the little voices, a dream begins to form in our imagination, and we are aroused by new possibilities. The dragons of fear and doubt are tamed, and the voices grow in clarity and passion. Our dream is taking shape.

The little voices speak to each of us with a different messages and intensity. Your voices are different than mine. That is why people hold different dreams of equality, family values, world peace, environmental protection, etcetera. In the words of the Platters' 1950s hit song "The Great Pretender," listening to the voices is "feeling what my heart can't conceal." Listen to your little voices and you will hear your dream!

Leading

Leaders create new realities when the current reality isn't good enough. To make things better they invent new concepts, new tools, and new relationships.

Many people do not want to dream, they do not want to lead. They would rather elect status-quo government officials, work for a big company, and hold popular beliefs. They ask: "What is my job? How do I fit in? What are the rules?" They request: "Make it easy. Tell me what to do. Tell me how and when." Then they become disenchanted or angry when they have less than they want. They followed the rules and did what they were told. What went wrong? When did their lives get off track? Maybe the train left the tracks when they made the choice not to have a personal dream, when they surrendered their creativity and independence to the dragons of complacency and compromise.

As a young boy, my dad encouraged me: "Be a leader. Do what nobody else wants to do, and your dreams will come true beyond your wildest imagination." Leaders are never satisfied with the way things are. Sometimes they are alone because they see new possibilities that others do not recognize. Leaders find things that need changing, and problems that need solving. Leaders do not limit themselves to what is known. They do not care if it has never been done before. They enjoy the challenge of being the first one to do it.

Leaders are not wrapped up in themselves or their possessions. Rather they wholeheartedly pursue their dream. The dream becomes a driving purpose. Leaders do not chase fame and fortune. Instead, they seek a better place for everyone, and fortune often just comes to them. Leaders do not find joy in power or intimidation. Their happiness lies in helping others and making a difference in the world. Leaders often are uncomfortable with praise and personal recognition. But they will endure being the center of attention if it is vital to the dream. Leaders create new possibilities when the current way does not work anymore. They create new ideas, new methods, and new technologies that make things better. Leaders are not limited by what they see today. They dream about that which does not exist--*YET*.

Infectious Dreams

Declaring our dreams openly enhances clarity, increases our commitment, and attracts others who have compatible dreams

At some point, most of us feel insignificant in this big world and wonder if we really make a difference. When we ask *Why am I here?*, we would like the answer will be a major discovery, an exciting career, or a calling that changes the tide of human affairs. When the dragon of self-doubt stop us from answering the question, we return to our daily routine still wondering *Why am I doing this?*

After looking in many places for a long time, it may be that our dream is right where we are, doing what we are doing. We might find we are living our dream and did not know it. We may be in the perfect spot to make a difference in our families, our community, or our workplace. A well-known story about making a difference goes like this:

> *An old man and a boy walk on the beach at low tide. Starfish by the thousands lie on the beach dying in the sun. The boy kneels down, picks one up, and throws it in the water. Then he throws another, and another, and another. After he has thrown several starfish into the water, the old man says: "You can't make a difference. There are thousands of starfish and only one of you." The boy reaches down, picks up a starfish, throws it in the water, and says: "Made a difference to that one." So the old man joins in and begins throwing starfish into the ocean. Other people also join in and soon all the starfish are saved. Just because one boy made a difference.*

Feelings of helplessness are everywhere in our world. What can we do about war, poverty and crime? Those are huge problems. Much bigger than you and I. We cannot stop the war in the Middle East, feed children who die from starvation in Africa, end crime in our cities, or save victims of floods and tsunamis. We cannot solve these problems by ourselves any more than the little boy could save all of the starfish. But our new mantra could be: "Made a difference to that one." Every dream is significant, no contribution is too small. Collectively, we can eliminate those problems together. Pick a problem you feel passionate about and start a solution. Throw the first starfish back into the water. You may be surprised by how many helpers you find. Dreams are infectious.

I Care, But What Can I Do?

"Climb every mountain, ford every stream, follow every rainbow till you find your dream. A dream that will need all the love you can give every day of your life for as long as you live."
— The Sound of Music

Dreams are personal. Sometimes we go through a day without a dream, wondering why we even got up that morning. It would be great to have a dream, but where can we find one? The dragons scare us into thinking that a dream must change our whole life, and make us doubt that our dream will make a difference. Or we are afraid that having a dream will force us to give up the friends, possessions, hobbies and other things we enjoy so much.

My experience was different. Having a dream did change my life, but the doubts and fears were unfounded. When I made a commitment to make a difference, building family togetherness became my dream. As a boy, I experienced the pain and low self-esteem that weak family unity produces. When families fight among themselves and ignore each other's needs, how can we expect countries to behave differently?

To find my dream, I considered radical ideas like quitting my job to start an orphanage, or working with charities that help families. Then I realized, as the leader of a company, I already was in the perfect place to unify my family and help others build theirs. You may find your dream and a way to achieve it using the same approach. It is a comfort to know that no one is expected to change the entire world, but each of us can change the part that is most important to us.

Your dream lies in your personal answers to the questions: *What do I love? What do I believe in passionately?* Maybe your dream is healing the sick, ending abortions, teaching children, building trust in relationships, protecting the environment, etcetera. If you know what you stand for and your belief is passionate, the choice does not matter because our world urgently needs all of our dreams, nearly eight billion of them. Each one is important.

The Fundamental Questions

The fundamental question WHY AM I HERE? *was not answered very clearly when we were young. But even when we achieve success, that question still does not go away.*

Sooner or later, every child asks his or her parents the fundamental questions: *Where did I come from? Why am I here? And where am I going?* Most parents cannot give meaningful answers. Their parents could not answer the questions either. I asked my parents the questions, never got adequate answers, and gave up. For most of my adult life, I ignored those haunting questions because I felt that real answers did not exist. Instead, I focused on gaining possessions in the material world of the 1970s and 1980s. Wealth and pleasure were why I was here.

However, even as I collected many prized possessions, enjoyed my work, and experienced the wonderful pleasures this world offers, those persistent questions would not go away. And more and more, my happiness seemed to depend on me finding the answers. My little voice continued to whisper to me: *There is* a Power greater than you. *There is* a reason for your existence. Periodically, I would ask the fundamental questions to myself and others. But nowhere could I find answers that were convincing and made sense in my life.

Then, in the twisting kaleidoscope of life's events, I found a clear dream for myself, a worthwhile reason for being alive on the earth. The discovery did not happen in an instant. Rather it evolved over time as I looked inside and asked myself:

- *What really excites me and what makes me angry?*
- *What do I believe in passionately?*
- *What unique experiences and gifts do I have?*
- *How can the world use my beliefs, experience and gifts?*

These questions had answers. They were simpler than the fundamental questions I had been asking myself for fifty years. My imagination translated the answers into possibilities, and the possibilities became the dreams that now guide my life's purpose and my daily decisions. A Higher Power led me to find these questions, answer them, and take action on the answers.

Declaring My Dream

Dreams gain clarity when they are declared openly. Let me declare mine. My dream is based on the belief that the most valuable legacy we create is our children and their values. They pass the values to their children and the future is secure. It is exciting to see youngsters grow, to see them pioneer breakthrough concepts and achievements beyond my imagination. Helping them find the breakthroughs is a joy for me. I am disappointed by a high divorce rate that forces children to live in environments of interrupted love, divided loyalties, and frequent conflict. I am angry that men and women abandon their families by physically leaving them, having affairs, or getting lost in addictions like drugs, alcohol, work, hobbies, gambling, etcetera.

My life includes a unique set of experiences: (1) my mother died when I was young, (2) I was abandoned by my biological father, (3) I was raised in a family divided by a divorce caused by an affair, and (4) I lost myself in an obsession with work. Based on these experiences, I believe that most problems in our world would be healed instantly, *they would disappear,* if we had strong family bonds and values. As I look back on my life, I am not surprised by my dream. Instead, I wonder why it took me fifty years to find that my core dream is:

To create a loving and trusting environment where families grow and prosper, starting with my own family.

My dream became clear when I declared it. It also resolved bothersome questions I had about my career. I was troubled that as a naval officer I helped produce weapon systems with awesome destructive power. The destructive power was not the bothersome part. I believe that power helped resolve international conflicts and avoid war. But avoiding evil was not enough. I want to create good. After examining my dream from a career perspective, I saw that trust also was a core issue in the relationships among governments, companies and people. Therefore, my dream translated into career activities is:

To create a trusting environment where government, industry and the people work together efficiently.

Trust begins in the family. Trust or mistrust is taught to children as a family value. Why have my wife and I been married over thirty-five years? What is the purpose of our relationship? We came from different kinds of families, each with notable dysfunctionalities and strengths. Discipline, reliability, control and aloofness are traits of my family. While celebrations, simple pleasures, broken promises and long feuds are attributes of my wife's family. These characteristics are not bad or good, they just were the environment where my wife and I learned about love and trust as children.

Coming from such backgrounds, family stability and trust became important to me, and *joie de vivre* and reliability are important to my wife. At times, my control addiction stifles my wife's enthusiasm and zest. At my best, I provide an environment of confidence and stability that allows her to be free. At times, her carefree attitude awakens the dragon of rejection inside me. During the best times, her zest lifts me to levels of joy that I never could have experienced by myself. We are a great team even though our backgrounds and our dreams are very different. Therefore, the joint dream for our marriage is:

To demonstrate that a family can recover from addictions, live every day to the fullest, and build family values based on unconditional love.

Dreams, and their integration into our careers and relationships, help us ask the right questions. They are criteria for making choices, yardsticks to measure success, and guideposts to tell us when we are off-track.

It is crucial that we declare our dreams and discuss them freely. Our dragons may breathe doubt and scorn into our minds when we talk about our dreams. But such reactions must not deter us from stretching to achieve them. Our dreams may change in the future. But declaring them today will sharpen our dreams and, if necessary, lead us to make any needed refinements. The physical things we leave behind in the world when we die will make a difference for only a short time. Our dreams make a difference for a long, long time.

A Rose's Dream

We can complain about the thorns on our life's rose bush, or enjoy the roses that bloom on the bush.

In writing about *daring to dream*, I was inspired by trimming the rose bushes that grew in my backyard. At first I discounted roses as being incapable of dreaming. Then I realized that a rose's dream is to bloom, and it is incapable of *not* realizing its dream. A rose blooms the best it can under any circumstances. It does not judge its own shape or beauty against other roses, not even those that grow on the same bush. It is not disappointed when no one admires its rich and vibrant colors and texture. It has no doubts about its importance. It does not blame aphids or Japanese beetles for any imperfections it may have. It is not angry about a lack of rain when it was young. It is not afraid of a hot sun that makes growing difficult. No matter what its color, a rose does not wish it were yellow, red, white or some other exotic color. Its total energy goes into its dream: to bloom.

Humans are not limited like a rose. We have a delightfully broad range of options in the dreams that we can choose for ourselves. One choice is not having a dream at all. Even when we have a dream, we might lose sight of it by giving in to the dragons of judgement, doubt, fear, blame, disappointment, blame or anger. Our actions can be determined by how we feel instead of by our dreams.

We forfeit the valuable intellectual, physical and emotional assets we have as human beings by not having dreams. Or we realize only a small portion of our full potential by quitting before we achieve them. People who have clear dreams and pursue them passionately experience joy, peace and fulfillment on a scale that cannot be known without having a passionate dream. Like a rose, we can bloom in any color we choose by having a dream and acting on it.

Visualize Victory

World-class performers dream victory before it occurs. They savor its taste long before the celebration dinner.

World-class athletes and peak performers in business and other areas dream the results they want. They conquer the dragon of potential failure by visualizing victory long before it occurs. They see details of the finish in their mind's eye. They feel the excitement of competition, and the exhilaration of each passing milestone. They experience the contest many times before living it. They taste victory long before the celebration dinner.

To be world-class performers in our own lives, we must see the desired outcome in our minds. Before each new experience, each big event, each key meeting, each volatile confrontation, and each night on the town, visualize the possibilities and mentally select the desired result. Imagine the events clearly, vividly, repeatedly. For example, visualize holding the winning ticket in a multimillion-dollar lottery as you walk to the counter to buy a ticket. Feel the rush of knowing it has really happened. Call your spouse to tell her or him of your good fortune. Know where to cash the ticket, and the safety precautions you will take. When you actually get into the situation (*it will happen*), you will not be unprepared because you will know exactly what to do.

A winning attitude affects everything we do positively. Winners are committed to finding solutions, while losers spend their time and energy complaining. Winners offer several possible solutions for each problem, while losers find the problems with every possible solution. Winners have a plan to succeed, while losers offer excuses. Winners say: "Let me do it," while losers say: "It's not my job. Find somebody else." Winners say: "It will be tough, but I'll give it a try," while losers say: "It may be possible, but it's too hard to try." Winners develop new answers when the old ones do not work, while losers quit and think that nothing will work. Dream with a winning attitude, enjoy the exciting experience, and results will take care of themselves.

Nothing Can Stop a Dream

The dream you set or don't set today will determine the success you will have tomorrow. Are you dreaming big enough?

The only thing that stops a dream is quitting. Some abandon their dream at the first significant obstacle, while others continue pursuing a big dream even in the face of a string of major setbacks. Consider Dr. Stephen Hawking, the Nobel Prize winner and best-selling author born in 1942. At twenty-one, he contracted motor neuron disease, also called Lou Gehrig's disease, and was confined to a wheelchair for life. Doctors said that he had just a few years to live, so he used those years to finish college and earn a doctorate in theoretical physics.

Believing his life would be short, he filled each day with a march toward his dream. A few years later, he lost his voice following an emergency tracheotomy. That did not stop him from teaching college-level physics. He designed, built and installed a computerized voice synthesizer on his wheelchair that enabled him to "speak" twenty words a minute. His dreamed of finding the "General Unified Theory of Everything." He postulated a new dimension in time to explain ambiguities in Einstein's Theory of Special Relativity. His best-selling book, *A Brief History of Time*, was written from a wheelchair by a man who could not talk.

As I write this book under significantly better circumstances, Dr. Hawking is very much alive. It seems nothing can stop him from pursuing his dreams in the world of physics. He accepts challenges as delightful, exciting experiences. The bigger the challenge, the better. I have never met Dr. Hawking, but I bet he says to himself something like: "I'm lucky because I have more challenges than anyone else. They have it too easy." A burning desire to pursue a dream no matter what the obstacles is a unique and fulfilling way to look at life's challenges.

Course Corrections

Being off course is not a problem, rather it is normal. However, failure to recognize that we are off-course and make course corrections is a real problem.

As a Navy midshipman in the early 1960s, my training included a ten-week deployment aboard the USS *Intrepid* (CVS-11) to the Mediterranean Sea. My first assignment was to work with the ship's navigator and quartermasters to plot our course from Norfolk, Virginia, through the Straits of Gibraltar to Naples, Italy. The proposed course across the Atlantic Ocean was planned meticulously day by day in every detail, including time allowances for flight operations and other training exercises.

One bright, sunny June morning we sailed out of Norfolk and followed the preset course. Each day at sea, I eagerly went topside to the navigation shack near the ship's bridge to monitor our progress across the ocean toward Gibraltar. I was shocked to find that we were off course every day. We never were where we should be according to plan that we had worked so hard to develop. We would be north of the planned track one day and south the next, miles ahead in the morning and miles behind at night.

While crossing the Atlantic, several unexpected events occurred, including a main engine failure, circumnavigation of a fishing fleet, and a helicopter rescue of a downed pilot. Those events never seemed to upset the navigator. Several times a day, he and the quartermasters would measure the ship's current position using star sights and radio signal triangulation. There was no Global Positioning System (GPS) in those days. With our current location, destination and targeted time-of-arrival clearly in mind, the navigator plotted our actual position and then recommended course and speed adjustments to the captain. Eight days later, as scheduled, we steamed through Gibraltar and entered the Mediterranean Sea safely despite being off course most of the trip.

Our daily lives are much like that ocean crossing. I often find myself off course relative to pursuing my dreams. Too often, I say and do things that do not build trusting relationships. I become controlling and domineering under pressure. I give love conditionally in an effort to manipulate those who are closest to me. I blame others when things go wrong. I get angry when I feel that I am not heard.

The dragon of failure tries to breathe his fire and scorch me with an attitude of failure. He tries to make me disappointed in myself for being angry, and make feel like I have failed. I should do better. The wonderful difference is that, by keeping my dreams in focus, I do not get off course as far or stay off course as long as once did in the past. I make the course adjustments I need in my life. My dreams bring me back on course quickly to realize *who I really am.*

Even though we may be off course almost every day, we still can achieve our goals by keeping our dreams in focus and making the appropriate course corrections. No anger, no self-deprecation, no depression. Getting off course is not the problem. Rather not recognizing that we are off course and making course corrections is at the root of life's biggest disappointments and saddest tragedies.

Closing Thoughts on Daring to Dream

Our world is like it is today because we are reluctant to dream the impossible dream. If world peace seems impossible, it is only because too many of us say that it is impossible.

In the luxurious condominium of life, some of us are stuck in the entrance hoping a seeing-eye dog will lead us to our dreams. It will never happen. Each of us must get in the elevator, and push the button that will take us to the penthouse of our dreams. Or take the stairs if the elevator is broken. Tune into your imagination, the womb of your dreams. Imagine *what life would be like if....* Create the embryo of thoughts that will grow into exciting dreams. And there is a way to make every dream come true. The path may include risk, hard work and sacrifice, but there is always a way.

Dreams give us a source of stability and consistency in an ever-changing world. They focus our actions and give them meaning. We are motivated to live our dreams when we see that they really make a difference. We are always making a difference, positive or negative. Just look around. Everything you see, hear and touch is evidence that someone has made a difference. The highways and bridges we drive on every day are someone making a difference. Cigarette butts thrown on the grass are someone making a difference. The music we enjoy on the radio is someone making a difference. Artwork and sculptures in a museum are someone making a difference.

Despite centuries of experience and exhaustive research by the most learned men in history, there are many fundamental questions of life that mankind has yet to answer satisfactorily. Living in the early twenty-first century, for me these questions include:

How do we educate the world's children and prepare them for life?
How do we preserve the earth's treasures for future generations?
How do we distribute the wealth of the world more fairly?
How do we eliminate war and have peace throughout the world?

If you have read this far into this book, these questions probably are important to you too. You may have other questions that should be added to my brief list. But where do we begin to tackle challenges as large as the those listed above? The answer is that each of us starts with whichever challenge we feel the most passionate toward and do something, anything, about it.

Whether we choose them consciously or unconsciously, every facet of our lives is created in our individual and collective dreams, or lack of dreams. The world around us is a combination of the physical creation of our dreams, and the random result of our habits and fears. The world is like it is today because many of us are afraid to dream the impossible dream. The dragons of doubt tell us that impossible dreams cannot come true, so why dream them? World peace and unconditional love may seem like impossible dreams. But there is no fundamental reason why these dreams are not already reality. They are impossible only because collectively we continue to say and act as though such dreams are impossible. When we dare to believe that they are possible and live as though they are coming true, impossible dreams become reality. Let there be peace on earth, and let it begin in your dreams and mine. And our actions too.

We create every facet of our lives through our dreams and the actions we take to achieve them.

-----------Tip #10-----------

Share Your Dreams

~ Engage the Power of the Universe

"Never doubt that a small group of thoughtful, committed citizens can change the world. Indeed, it is the only thing that ever has."
— Margaret Meade

Shared Joy and Shared Pain

Individually we choose* WHO I AM. *Collectively, our choices and our actionsor inaction co-create how the world is today and how it will be tomorrow.

Clinical studies show that newborn infants living in a nursery feel sympathetic joy and pain for each other. When one infant giggles with glee or cries in pain, it is likely that other infants will giggle or cry too. However, by the age of two we have met the dragon of independence. We discover that we exist as separate beings, and the joys and pains of others are not our joy and pain. Or are they?

You may say that conditions exist in our world today that no one wants or causes. However, those conditions were created and are sustained by our collective actions or inaction. Violence, crime, war and hunger are byproducts of our collective dreams, or lack of dreams. Individually, we may ignore such conditions because we are not affected directly by them, or feel powerless to change them. We may decide that such problems mean little, and do nothing other than to protect ourselves. However, by doing nothing along with billions of others who also do nothing, we enable such conditions to continue and expand. Eventually, when one of the conditions shakes our lives, we deny responsibility and say that the government failed us. We choose individually *who we are* in relation to world we live in today. Our collective choices co-create how the world will be tomorrow.

The twenty-first century shows signs of a collective awakening that will change the world for the better. Action by small groups of thoughtful, committed people have begun the changes. The groups are growing in number and influence. They do not have a specific name and, for the most part, they do not know each other. Rather they have many names, operate in many places, speak many languages, and solve many issues. Some have a dream to preserve Planet Earth, while others dream of eradicating a disease. Still others teach children, or focus on other causes. The groups are ordinary people in your family, at your workplace, and in your community who share a dream and take action. You may already be a member of one or more of these groups.

Acting together, our world will be what we say we want it to be. If you and I do not do it, who will? Who else is there? Each of us has an opportunity to be a leader. Leaders share dreams that are bigger than one person. Throughout history, the leaders of small groups have made a huge difference:

• Jesus Christ taught twelve disciples about love and salvation. The message is still spreading across the globe 2,000 years later.

• Clara Barton founded the Red Cross over 100 years ago to help needy people. Today it is helping victims of tsunamis and hurricanes, and is widely recognized as the primary source of humanitarian aid in times of disaster.

• Martin Luther King declared *I have a dream!* for human rights and equality regardless of race, color or creed. We celebrate his words and his message decades after his death.

• Mother Theresa set a new standard in compassion for the poor and helpless around the world by helping one person at a time.

These men and women created dreams from nothing. They did not know *how* to achieve the desired result. They just dreamed, shared the dream with others, and were passionate in its pursuit.

Leaders live their dream every day. They are clear in expressing their dream, committed to achieving it, consistent in sharing it, and courageous in erasing obstacles. The vignettes in this chapter show the importance of individuals (you and me) in building their dream, ways to find others who share our dream, and the effect of our collective dreams on the world. Our biggest dreams will come true when we help each other. We can be the candle which creates the light of our dream and the mirror that reflects the dream broadly.

A Jigsaw Puzzle

Dreams are pieces of life's puzzle. Since we each have a unique dream, let's share our pieces and solve the puzzle together.

As a young boy, I attended a church service where everyone was given a numbered puzzle piece as they entered the church. No one knew what the puzzle was, and no one could solve it from the single piece they were given. Friends and families shared their pieces, but could not figure it out. After a sermon about working together, we each went to the front of the church and inserted our piece into a numbered spot in the four-by-six-foot puzzle. In just minutes, the puzzle picture showed the people of the world sitting at Christ's feet embracing each other.

Fifty years later, the sermon grows in relevance as I see a parallel between the jigsaw puzzle piece and the unique dreams we each have. Our dreams are pieces of life's puzzle. Each of us has value, a unique piece of the puzzle. We cannot figure it out alone. We can ignore our piece, keep it a secret, throw it away, or share it. By cooperating to assemble the puzzle, we build a world that works for everyone. To assemble the puzzle, we must trust each other, share our pieces, and accept unusual pieces that do not seem to fit with ours.

To find clues about our respective puzzle piece, it is vital that we appreciate the differences in our beliefs and dreams. Surprising things happen when we:

(1) Understand others before insisting that we be understood,

(2) Express our feelings and needs openly, and

(3) Are honest about our dreams and fears.

When we share dreams we learn about ourselves, and the inaccurate perceptions that we have about others disappear. The tips in this book are my small piece of the puzzle. Let us trust each other and share our pieces to put life's puzzle together in the twenty-first century.

Four Motivations

"I" is a small word. "WE" is much bigger. Acting together, the world will be what we want it to be. If we don't do it who will? Who else is there?

Each minute of the day, we concurrently experience four types of motivation. Either consciously or unconsciously, we choose one type in preference to the others. When we live unconsciously, the choice is by habit. However, when we are living our lives consciously, the choice reflects our dream for ourselves and the world around us. Our personal satisfaction, and the duration and impact of the results we produce vary enormously depending on the motivation that governs our actions. The four types of motivation are:

• **Sensual.** Touch, sight, hearing, smell and taste are the realm of sensual motivation. Some sensations are pleasurable, some exciting, and some painful. Actions motivated by a desire to experience sensations are inward-directed toward ourselves. Hedonists are driven by a continuous need to feel pleasure and experience thrills. However, the most pleasing sensual experiences we will ever experience will be satisfying for a fleeting instant, and the memories will dissipate almost as quickly.

• **Material.** Material objects seem to be unchanging but, in fact, they are changing continuously. Even though we look about the same as we did on our last birthday, science says that ninety-eight percent of the molecules in our body are different today than a year ago. Individuals motivated by material things want more and varied possessions. They often are afraid of losing what they already have. Material achievements are satisfying, but also short-lived. The Seven Manmade Wonders of the World were awesome material achievements, but none exist today in a functional way. This book is the most substantial material thing I have created, but the ink on this page will not last long. History's best material achievements are stored in museums. The average ones have ben cast aside in junk yards.

• **Intellectual.** Intellectual ego motivates us to express our memories, beliefs, thoughts and expectations to others. For example, this book is a product of my intellectual motivation, rather than my material motivation. My mind transformed intellectual concepts into the physical action of operating a word processor. Intellectual creations are intensely satisfying (a sensational response), and can produce wealth and material possessions. But most intellectual works have a life span shorter than their creator. The creations of the world's greatest intellectuals (e.g. Plato, Aristotle, Einstein and Shakespeare, for example) outlived the best material achievements of the same eras. Some of the greatest intellectual achievements in history, like the works of Newton and Ptolemy, lasted just a few hundred years before being superseded by more complete and accurate intellectual theories.

• **Universal.** The motivation for universal benefit is an outward dream, a bigger-than-me dream. Individual motivation for universal good has produced the world's most significant and lasting physical and intellectual achievements. These achievements are manifestations of an individual's dream. Effective collaborative action on a worldwide basis will occur when we unite our individual dreams. So far, our world has avoided collaborative action by rewarding individual achievement. However, world peace, universal education for all children, the elimination of poverty and hunger, and the eradication of crime will require us to operate collaboratively for the common good. Such conscious motivation will happen in the twenty-first century, if we want it to. Otherwise, it will not.

Each type of motivation produces the results expected at all preceding types. Unfortunately, each type of motivation is oblivious to the results at the higher types. When driven by sensations alone, the possibility of physical, intellectual or universal achievement is ignored. A focus on physical possessions like houses, cars and wealth probably will provide joyful sensations, but will miss the opportunities for intellectual and universal achievement. At the upper level of universal motivation, we help others by transforming ideas into physical and intellectual achievements, while still enjoying the full sensation of success.

A Struggling Planet

Each of us is a vital contributor among the billions of "dots" on Earth. No dream is too small, every dream makes a difference.

Planet Earth is like a bit-mapped image. At six hundred dots per inch (600 DPI), a ten-foot by twelve-foot map of the earth would have about seven billion dots, roughly one for each of earth's inhabitants. No single dot dominates the map. But collectively, when each colored dot performs its simple purpose, the map has clear shapes. Countries, cities, oceans and islands are distinct in their fit with others. Similarly, the planet works for everyone when each of us contributes a simple dream without worrying what the other "dots" do. Unfortunately, Planet Earth is struggling today because too many of its seven billion "dots" are not contributing. *Struggling* means our world does not work nearly as well as it could. And *Contribute* means living a dream that provides value to others.

Many "dots" on our planet are apathetic, they do not care if they make a difference. The dragon of apathy is not destructive in itself, it just does not contribute. When twenty-five percent of the dots that make up our bit-mapped world are apathetic, the picture becomes cloudy. Interactions of the oceans, regions and countries are not clear. Collectively, the missing "dots" make a big difference. The world does not work well when just one in four people choose not to contribute.

Unfortunately, Planet Earth also has a relatively small number of destructive "dots." Terrorists, drug dealers, felons, corrupt government officials, and white-collar criminals who not only do not contribute, they destroy the contributions of others. Less than five percent among the seven billion people, but what a negative difference the dragons of greed and selfishness make. In the bit-mapped image of the world, they are like five percent of the dots having the wrong color. Even though no single "dot" destroys the image, the combined effect of twenty-five percent who do not make contribute plus five percent who make negative contributions has caused the world to struggle to survive. We each make a vital contribution among the seven billion "dots" on earth. Your dream is significant. Your dream makes a difference.

It All Comes Back

Acts of love and kindness radiate on the lake of life. When we perform such acts, they ripple out and return to us multiplied.

During a vacation at Deep Creek Lake in Maryland, I was sitting on the dock enjoying a beautiful fall afternoon when a speedboat rushed by, clearly exceeding the posted speed limit of five miles per hour. The boat's wake was only two feet tall, but it radiated widely across the narrow lake. Long after the speedboat was out of sight, other boats slammed against the dock where they were moored. I did not see any boats that were damaged that day, but the driver of the speedboat was oblivious to the possibility of the damage he might cause. Similarly, our actions and emotional outbursts ripple across the people that are around us each day. Why does today's world have so much pain, anger, sadness, hatred and conflict? What stops it from being all love, peace, kindness, sharing and joy? When we take a close look at ourselves, we realize it may be the things I do every day coupled with the things that you do.

I am a good person by most standards. I love my family, support several charities, care about my coworkers and others, and obey the law. But some days I am selfish. Maybe I am angry now and then. I brush people off occasionally if I am busy. Unfortunately, when I am angry with my wife, my daughters, my grandsons, my friends or my coworkers, they feel the anger and hurt, and they often pass it on to others. I spoil paradise on earth when I allow the dragons of arrogance, anger and selfishness to take hold of me even if it is infrequently and only for a few minutes.

We all do things that we know are not right, or fail to take the actions that we know we should take. Eventually, like the speedboat's waves on Deep Creek Lake, those negative actions come back to us. When we hurt people or we are angry, they may transmit similar hurts and angers to others. The chain of pain spreads like the damaging waves on the lake, until the hurts return to us multiplied by the hurts that others initiated, their waves on the lake. We may not recognize the specific pains that return, but the chain of pain is clear.

Any one of us can break the chain of pain. Fortunately, acts of love and compassion radiate just as quickly. The acts of kindness we perform also ripple out and return to us multiplied many times. The friend to whom we are kind and understanding is, in turn, kind and understanding to others. All it takes is a single thoughtful act to begin a chain of love. The chain propagates itself and everyone benefits.

===========================

Each act of kindness we perform travels into the Universe and starts it own chain of love.

===========================

Let us help and encourage each other to break the chain of pain. I will be kind when you are angry, and ask that you be kind when I am angry. Our world will become a beautiful, peaceful and joyful lake if we ripple kindness when we receive anger, understanding when we feel frustration, and sharing when our first thought is to be selfishness. How about you and I starting that today?

Ask the Universe

The power to have anything we want and achieve anything we dream is not entirely inside ourselves, and it is not entirely in the world around us. It's in joining the two!

Despite her affliction with rheumatoid arthritis, a longtime friend has been a consistent source of inspiration and motivation for me. She undergoes an extensive physical each year to determine how much the disease may have caused her physical ability to atrophy. During one physical, the doctor asked her: "Can you open a jar?" To which she responded: "Of course." The doctor, doubting her reply, handed her a jar of peanut butter and said: "Here. Open this." She took the jar, rolled it in her debilitated hands, and pondered the doctor's challenge. After a few seconds, she walked to the waiting room and gave the jar to the receptionist asking: "Please help me by opening this jar." The receptionist, eager to assist a patient, opened the jar and handed it back to my friend. She returned to the doctor's office, delivered the opened jar of peanut butter, and said: "Here, I told you I could open a jar." The point is that we can do anything we need to do and accomplish any goal we set for ourselves, but many times we cannot do it alone and must ask the Universe for help.

As Masters of the Universe, each of us has the power of the Universe at the tip of our tongue. We can have everything we want, everything we dream. All we need to do is to ask for it. The President of the United States is a Master of the Universe. But what does he really accomplish himself? Almost nothing. He just knows who to ask for help achieve his dreams. He does not ask the Secretary of Defense for labor statistics and recommendations to reduce unemployment. He asks the Secretary of Labor and keeps asking until he gets answers that work.

Franklin D. Roosevelt, a cripple who served almost four terms as President, was elected to lead a discouraged country that had suffered through the most severe depression in American history. In an attitude of abundance, he used his personal influence to create the "New Deal." He asked his advisors to design new, innovative programs that would put people back to work, expand our country's infrastructure, and restore an attitude of prosperity. Even though he died before most of us were born, we still see and feel the effects of his programs today, over seventy years later.

We must learn how to ask the Universe for the things we want. It may take a while for the Universe to respond, so we also must learn patience and trust. This may sound like gibberish. But what if we ask the Universe for world peace? What if you and I believed that world peace is possible, and we convinced just one other person? We could have world peace instantaneously, and have it last forever if everyone demonstrated that we really wanted it by giving love and trust.

Maybe we could ask the Internet for world peace. Let us try. Does the dragon of futility tell you it will not work? That dragon is why we do not have world peace today. But how much would be lost if we asked and the asking did not work? All we need is help and support from some of earth's seven billion inhabitants, just a few million people who genuinely believe in the dream of world peace. How many are out there? Are there enough? If not today, maybe tomorrow. So let us keep asking every day. It might be as simple as a person afflicted with rheumatoid arthritis opening a jar of peanut butter.

Tell-a-Vision

Tell-a-vision is an effective tool to find people who share your dream. You tell-a-vision to me, and I'll tell-a-vision (my dreams) to you.

The most effective way to find others who share your dream is tell-a-vision. Not the fifty-four-inch big-screen GE or Magnavox with remote control that you watch at home. Rather you tell-a-vision to me, and I will tell-a-vision to you. Our dreams are the visions that we share. Your picture and mine of what we want our world to be like. Everyone has their own channel on tell-a-vision. Billions of channels broadcasting together. Billions of dreams working in unison.

The shows do not give our power away to *Father Knows Best* or *Leave It to Beaver*. These are personal responsibility shows with names like *Happy Days* or *One Life to Live*. The *Odd Couple*, *Flintstones* and *Munsters* are welcome too. No reruns of yesterday's misadventures. Each day is a new episode. Live broadcasts of the *Days of Our Lives*. First we plug in and turn on the power of the Universe. Channel-surf if your dream is cloudy. Study tell-a-vision shows from people who have dreams you admire. Use their theme on your show. At first it may feel uncomfortable. You may flub a line or two. But when you tune into the shows you like, you will soon find a unique picture for your show.

When the theme of your show gets clear, get on the air! Ignore Nielsen ratings. It is not a failure if no one listens. Keep broadcasting. You are the only one who can take your show off the air. Your dream will become more clear with each broadcast. If you are turned on and passionate, people will tune into your tell-a-vision show. Viewers who enjoy your show may adopt your theme in their show. A dream shared is a dream doubled and tripled! They may even broadcast your dream more eloquently than you can, and get higher ratings. Who cares? Success on this network is seeing the dream become reality. Each show is different because we each believe in different things. That is not conflict. The differences are our joint power to change the world, all of it. I will broadcast my dream on my tell-a-vision show, and look for your dream on your show.

Support Is Everywhere

Support groups exist everywhere today, which indicates we are sharing more dreams in the twenty-first century than ever before.

A friend of mine ran for *Man-of-the-Year*, a title awarded by the National Leukemia & Lymphoma Society in a charitable event that raises over $250,000 each year. He felt he had little chance to win, but fighting leukemia was an important cause to him. His strategy was to request support from his business associates. Before he asked me, however, he did not know that my mother died from leukemia and my brother-in-law recently battled lymphoma into remission. My wife and I attended the awards ceremony because we wanted to be there. He was surprised to finish as the first runner-up among the twelve candidates. Unexpected support during the silent auctions (they offered an splendid collection of scotches) put him second in total donations. The event was a celebration of giving to a worthy cause and a fun party. He won because leukemia had touched many of his friends. Which he learned only after he asked for support.

Support groups exist on almost every subject. The broad range and growing number of support groups indicates that we are sharing our dreams more closely in the twenty-first century than ever before. Such groups allow us to validate and spread our beliefs. There are support groups for political views, drug abuse, dieters, recovering alcoholics, family relations, environmental protection, pro- or anti-abortion, exercise, doll collectors, and endless other subjects. The groups meet in every corner of the world, including the Internet. During a Caribbean cruise, I noticed that daily "Friends of Bill" (Alcoholics Anonymous) meetings were held. Support groups have the collective power to accomplish miracles.

The Bible tells us Jesus fed thousands of people with two fishes and five loafs of bread. What if it really was a support group meeting with thousands of people? Jesus described his dream for a world that shares, and the support group made the dream a reality by sharing lunch. Which would be a greater miracle: feeding thousands of people with several loaves of bread and a few fishes, or inspiring an environment where thousands of people willingly shared their food until everyone was fed?

Unfortunately, negative support groups for terrorism and crime also are impacting our world. A minuscule portion of the world's population engages in violent crime. Yet international, national, state and local governments are forced to spend trillions of dollars every year on law enforcement to control criminals and discourage others from choosing crime.

My wife participated in a business support group called a Leads Network. Twenty-five people, each offering a different product or service, meet once a week for lunch to exchange sales leads. Each person comes with one or more leads for the other members of the group. The group creates win-win relationships where each member has twenty-four sales representatives.

More and more the workplace is a support group for personal values and dreams. In the past, the dragon of fear forced us to separate values and dreams from our work because we did not want to be seen as idealistic. However, connecting with others and serving others are increasingly important today. Employees are unwilling to turn off their values and dreams to work like robots. Little by little, they are speaking out and finding work environments where personal dreams and values are supported by the company, its senior executives, and their coworkers. Interviewees often share their values and dreams with me, and we discuss my company's mission and values. Such employees are highly committed to the work they do, and the clients they support.

More and more, we are unwilling to turn off our dreams during daily activities. We search for support groups and work places where our dreams are supported.

We each choose to lead, participate in, or passively embrace the goals of the support groups related to our dreams. Support groups are an effective way to pursue our dreams in a caring environment. They often are an effective way to achieve those dreams. Do you participate in support groups that are consistent with your dreams for the world?

Dreams in the Workplace

Industry is finding that higher revenue and profits can be obtained through superior customer service, employee rewards, and preserving the environment.

The nature of the work place we choose as employees, and the relationship we are willing to have with our employers is changing in the twenty-first century. As government and industry move from industrial-age attitudes of the 1900s to the information age of today, corporate values of cooperation and shared purpose are replacing cutthroat competition for scarce opportunities. During the twentieth century, too many businesses behaved like greedy profit-takers with no conscience and little concern for employees, customers or the environment. Government seemed to be an ally of these businesses, rather than the people's friend.

Today, businesses and government agencies are adopting explicit values and ethics. Oppressive regulations and employee exploitation are out. Successful twenty-first-century businesses are no longer obsessed with competition to increase market share. Rather they focus on innovation and improving the quality as the primary growth strategy. Executives are finding productivity and profits grow fast in an atmosphere that fosters employee creativity and passion. And Wall Street is rewarding such changes with higher stock prices. The perspective of many businesses is shifting from products and services that yield the highest profit, to products and services that satisfy the mutual needs of owners and employees. Consider the following examples:

• "Save the Seas" is the motto of the Royal Caribbean Cruise Lines. At the Welcome Aboard cocktail party, half of the captain's speech addresses ways that we can preserve the purity and beauty of our oceans.

• The state of Maryland requires high school students to spend seventy-five hours in community service as a criteria for graduation. The program increases the awareness of students about the unique needs of their local communities.

• EuroMotors, which sells luxury automobiles like Mercedes Benz and Rolls Royce, aggressively supports the U.S. Marine Corps' annual Toys For Tots program. In advertising to their customer base, they point out: "The toys you donate probably won't go to kids in your neighborhood, but they will go to kids in your world."

• Thoms of Maine donates ten percent of its earnings to environmental causes and requests that its employees spend five percent of their working hours (paid by the company) performing volunteer work for an environmental cause.

• The Service Corps of Retired Executives (SCORE) is 10,000-plus volunteer executives sponsored by the U.S. Small Business Administration to help small businesses succeed. The SCORE volunteers have enjoyed successful careers and return value to their communities by sharing their time and expertise with inexperienced entrepreneurs.

• "Moderation in all things" is the theme of Bacardi, the world-famous rum manufacturer. As visitors tour their picturesque facility in San Juan, Puerto Rico, signs everywhere encourage moderation in all that we do, including alcoholic beverages.

These businesses and governmental agencies, and many others, are giving back to their communities. Industry has discovered that growing their business base, developing new technologies, and increasing profits are entirely congruous with superior customer service, sharing profits with employees, and preserving the environment.

The leaders in my company encourage mentoring relationships at all levels. Their primary job is to empower employees to grow, to be creative, and to take risks. We value employee viewpoints, solicit their ideas, and seek to satisfy their needs along with the needs of our clients and shareholders. It appears that the current trend toward increased importance on corporate values and the quality of products and services will accelerate in the twenty-first century. Today, everyone has the option to choose a workplace that is consistent with their values and dreams.

The Naysayers

No matter how worthwhile a dream, someone will be against it or say it can't be done. The bigger the dream, the more people will be against it. Ignore such naysayers.

External disapproval does not measure of the value of our dreams. The bigger our dream, the more *naysayers* will be against it or say it cannot be done. There were naysayers among Jesus' twelve disciples. One betrayed him for thirty pieces of silver, and another denied Him three times. President Lincoln declared freedom for the slaves even though many people were against the idea. He stood by his belief in freedom when the Confederate states seceded from the Union and war started.

Imagine President Lincoln's interaction with the naysayers among his trusted advisors. They had good arguments too: "Abe, is this what you really want? Brother killing brother, son killing father? Freedom for slaves can't be worth this." The war lasted over four long, bitter years to prove "whether that nation, or any other nation, so conceived and so dedicated could long endure." The naysayers may have almost swayed him, almost talked him into abandoning the war without ending slavery. Throughout the bloody war he focused on his dream and ignored the naysayers. If we let them, naysayers will be the dragons that squash our dreams. Do not let them!

As for me, I tell everyone my dream of *a trusting environment where government, industry and the public work together efficiently*. The naysayers respond: "That would be great. But it is a utopia that will never happen." It is painful to be with naysayers. They try to sway us from our dreams by telling us how hard it will be, how small our chance of success is, or how little difference it will make even if we do succeed.

Of course we enjoy being with people who support our dreams. But our influence with the naysayers determines the difference we make with our dreams. We make a huge step forward when just one naysayer becomes a supporter. Unfortunately, naysayers who could not build an outhouse will campaign to destroy the Taj Mahal. But in the end, the only ones who fail are those who quit on their dreams.

Global Dreams

The Berlin Wall came down even though many said it would never happen. Former enemies collaborate to create prosperity in ways that were unthinkable just a few short years ago.

Global dreams and global cooperation are required to solve global problems. The pursuit of wealth and physical pleasure has spread our most challenging problems to remote corners of the world. The World Health Organization's *World Health Report* says diseases of the rich (i.e. heart disease, stroke and cancer) have become commonplace in third-world countries where "the people are acquiring the unhealthy lifestyles of the industrialized world including eating poorly, not exercising enough, and the use of tobacco, alcohol and drugs."

Fortunately, we are sharing dreams and solutions on a global basis too. Government programs are fading as the primary way to increase living standards, educate children, provide jobs, and establish stronger families. Rather, industry is investing in underdeveloped economies by educating the population with the goal of transforming them into productive employees. People everywhere are breaking the unhealthy dependence on governmental safety nets and welfare programs, and are taking personal responsibility for overcoming self-perpetuating poverty dragons. Support is appearing from private sources. And effective, lasting personal relationships and corporate liaisons are forming based on shared dreams and goals.

To accelerate the trend, it is crucial that each of us participates in the area of our dream. Today, former competitors and international enemies are collaborating for prosperity and freedom on a level that was unthinkable only a few years ago. As of this writing, the "Partnerships for Peace" coalition has twenty-six member nations of all sizes, cultures and demographics working together to build a world that works for everyone. Membership is increasing steadily. The leaders come from rich countries and poor countries, from small farms and big cities, from diverse races and religions. By sharing our dreams, you and I join the leadership group. The Universe needs our leadership today more than ever before.

A Living Dream

Leaders broadcast their dream as the first step in gathering needed resources. Hearing the leader's commitment, others who have similar dreams often step forward to help.

When President John F. Kennedy committed the United States in 1961 to land men on the moon and bring them home safely before the end of the 1960s, there was no rational basis for the dream. That did not stop him. He told his cabinet. He told the country. And he told his dream to the world consistently, clearly and courageously. His closest advisors warned that the country did not have the materials, the fuels, the scientists, the engineers, or the budget for such an enormous undertaking. His response was: "Now you have a list of things to do. Let's get started. What do you need from me?" Men walked on the moon in 1969 despite President Kennedy's death in 1963. The passion, tenacity and leadership he provided for three years was sufficient to motivate the team to achieve the dream six years after his death.

Leaders are not "reasonable" in their dreams, and they are not discouraged by *NO*s from important people. They have the confidence to withstand the unpopularity of their dream until others recognize the possibilities. When Christopher Columbus said he would sail west to find the Indies, several kings laughed at him. Patrick Henry was unreasonable when he said: "Give me liberty or give me death." Martin Luther's ninety-five theses were an unreasonable challenge to the Catholic Church of the late 1500s. Many consider Gloria Steinem to be unreasonable about women's rights. But such men and women lead exciting and rewarding lives even if we do not share a passion for their particular dreams.

Leaders do not have a dream, they *live* a dream. A leader does not see a dream as something outside him or herself. Every fibre and sinew of their body lives and breathes the dream. They pursue the dream with passion and will *be, do* or *give* whatever is necessary to achieve it. Leaders enjoy being out on a limb with their dreams. They listen to and join with other leaders whose dreams are compatible. Collectively, leaders change the world in which we live.

Christmas Every Day

We could have Christmas every day. Instead of asking for presents in pretty red and green bows, ask the Universal Santa for support in our dreams.

Christmas is a joyous time of year. We ask for our favorite things and receive them as presents from family and friends who collectively create a loving, giving environment. The recent Christmas holidays illustrate what it means for the Universe to provide. After opening presents with my wife, daughter and grandson, and visiting with family and friends, I surveyed the bountiful gifts under the Christmas tree. My wife had received butterfly larvae to grow and set free, two butterfly books, and a large papier-mâché butterfly to decorate her office. She did not ask Santa for butterflies. She did not even know butterfly larvae could be bought. However, she did send a message to the Universe that she liked butterflies. Butterflies were part of her public dream, and the Universe responded with gifts. I received a Covey calendar and a family plaque. I did not ask for these things either, but the Universe heard and responded to my dreams about values and family unity.

We could have Christmas every day by elevating the gifts we request from *things* to *dreams*. And it would not be expensive either. Instead of asking for presents wrapped in paper and bows, we could ask the Universal Santa to support our dreams. First, we would clarify our dreams and broadcast them consistently to the Universe, especially to our family, friends and business associates.

What if we sent a clear, consistent message that our dream was peace and abundance for everyone? For the Universe to believe and respond, it is essential that our actions be aligned with our dreams. Therefore, our actions must reflect peace and abundance. In just a short time, we would meet others who, prior to hearing our message, had silently dreamed of peace and abundance. People who stood for conflict and selfishness would avoid us. If enough people dreamed in this way about peace and abundance, the people who once preferred selfishness and conflict might switch. Christmas every day would be a joyous life.

Lego Blocks

Big dreams are built easily and quickly when the building blocks are provided by people with no concern for who gets credit.

2003 was the 100th anniversary of the Wright Brothers' first flight. While waiting patiently for a flight to San Francisco in the Monday morning chaos of Baltimore-Washington International (BWI) Airport, I thought about Wilbur and Orville Wright. I wondered if they understood what they began by flying just over 100 feet in Kitty Hawk. When they worked in the bicycle shop in Dayton, did they imagine the jobs and industries they were creating? Or was their dream just to fly?

Did they envision mega-airports and jumbo planes carrying cargo and passengers to the far reaches of the world every day? Probably not. Today, nearly one thousand people work at BWI, and over twenty thousand people travel through the airport each day. The Boeing-747 has a wingspan longer than their first flight, and it carries more people than lived in Kitty Hawk when the first flight occurred. The Wright Brothers did not build jet planes and huge airports, nor do they deserve credit for them. But they started it and may have suspected they were starting something really big. They placed the first Lego block and others built on it.

Too often the dragons of secrecy and selfishness stop us from collaborating on our biggest dreams. Some people are reluctant to work with others because they are afraid that their ideas will be stolen. They may feel it takes too much time to work together, or believe they can do it better alone. Such fears, feelings and beliefs may even be true sometimes, but they severely limit the number and size of the dreams we can achieve collectively.

Paradoxically, by working together with others, one person can change the world. Recognition and physical rewards are not the goal, it is the dream that counts. A dream is more fun and is more easily achieved working with people who share it. When others fit their Lego blocks with ours, we achieve dreams together that are bigger than any one of us could imagine alone.

Eliminate Welfare Today

Welfare would be eliminated if we stopped categorizing some human beings as less-than, and started treating everyone like full partners on Planet Earth.

For the last eighty years, every session of the U.S. Congress has debated the moral and financial implications of welfare programs. No matter what they decide to do this year, collectively we could eliminate government welfare if we chose to. Poverty is a natural companion to the accumulation of wealth. Most wealth is built through competitive transactions where some parties win and others lose. A relatively small fraction of the world's population has been extraordinarily successful in accumulating great wealth. Most people compete well enough to exist comfortably. But some groups, because of circumstances or their own choices, depend on welfare just to survive. Would welfare programs be needed if we practiced abundance and generosity instead of scarcity and competition?

Abundance and generosity do not mean giving away the precious possessions we have earned to the poor. Rather, each of us must make a difference. Statistics show the number of families on welfare is about twice the number of tax-exempt churches in the United States. What if each church adopted two welfare families? What if the congregation (that is you and me) provided abundant food, housing and clothing, helped educate parents and children, advised them in acquiring skills for a rewarding job, and counseled them on family values and helping others? Welfare would disappear as we became the safety net under each family and child in need.

No matter how sad and difficult a welfare case may be, or how rampant substance abuse and other self-defeating behaviors are, we can encourage today's welfare recipients to take the first step toward having a dream. This approach to breaking the poverty cycle does not require the government to intervene with another new educational, employment or rehabilitation program. However, it does require you and I to be role models by courageously sharing our resources and time. It requires each of us to participate personally in the new campaign.

The Information Age

Our world is changing rapidly. You and I can either cause the changes we want, or react to the changes that others cause.

The instantaneous availability of information through the Internet is fueling cultural change and shrinking our world to a small fraction of its former size. For thousands of years, knowledge was limited to what people could remember or write by hand. Cultural change was slow. Mass information dissemination began when Gutenberg invented the printing press. He started the information explosion by creating a media that enabled people to know more than what they saw and heard personally. Printed ideas lasted longer than buildings that people built. Still, information dissemination in those days was limited to the speed at which people moved, although it could travel in several directions simultaneously. For example, the American Revolution was over almost two months before most people in Europe knew.

My grandmother, born over hundred years ago in 1896, lived to be ninety-two. Her perspectives on cultural changes caused by airplanes, autos, telephones, TV, computers, and space travel were fascinating. As a young girl such technologies were beyond imagination. The rate of cultural change increased substantially during her lifetime as the speed of information dissemination increased. Unfortunately, she died in 1988 and never saw the culture change fueled by the Internet.

Today's computer industry, a change agent in almost every facet of our lives, demonstrates that by working together we can achieve more than any individual person could imagine. Millions of software, hardware, communications and application experts do a little bit each day to create huge advances. The Internet is a source of unlimited possibilities for everyone to share their dream. Now we read about dreams in books, see them on television, and retrieve information about them on the Internet. The Internet is like the Oracle of Delphi. We can ask any question and the answer returns. We may not know where the answer is, but we can find it almost instantly. By harnessing the power of the Information Age to achieve our dreams, we can make larger contributions in the twenty-first century than we ever could before.

Plug Into the Flow

Plug into the flow of the changes around you.
That flow will carry you to the goals you want to achieve.

I joined my wife in New Orleans for the quarterly managers' meeting of the women's fashion company for which she works. During a motivational lecture to the husbands who had accompanied their wives, the owner of the company described himself as a person who "plugged into the flow." He explained that meant his objective was to flow as much of the profits from clothing sales through to the wives as he possibly could. He believed that was the most effective way to attract people to join the company, to continue its growth and success, and to expand his own wealth.

He added that some people act as reservoirs. They attempt to accumulate as much wealth as possible. In doing so, they disrupt the flow and impede everyone's success, including their own. To illustrate the disastrous effects of being a reservoir, he cited the recession that began after the September 11th terrorist attack. The Universe (all of us acting collectively) surrendered to the dragon of fear, and decided that we would conserve resources and stop spending.

In effect, we became reservoirs that stored, instead of flowed economic resources. The result was a recession for everyone. What would have happened, on the other hand, if we had decided to spend our life's savings? The dragon of fear scares us into thinking that we would be left destitute and unemployed. However, with all of us plugged into the flow, the likely result would have been an economic boom that flowed vast economic resources to the Universe (all of us). All of our financial conditions would have improved!

Several times each day we have a choice to plug into the flow, to be a reservoir that disrupts the flow, or to separate ourselves from the flow. In addition to the economic flow we just discussed, there is also a love flow, an e-flow of connectedness on the Internet, and the flow of change. Are you plugged into them? Plugging into the flow of changes around you will carry you to the goals you want to achieve.

Closing Thoughts on Sharing Our Dreams

By having an open adventuresome spirit, we tap the enormous potential of the Universe to help us achieve our dreams.

The surest way to have your dream come true is to believe in it passionately, share it with the Universe (everyone around you), and take action. We share our dreams in every action we take, or do not take. There is virtually no chance to realize our dreams without action, since inaction is a message to the Universe that we are not sure about our dreams. When our actions are weak, we had better hope a miracle will occur because the Universe will respond weakly to help us. When we demonstrate full commitment to our dreams, the Universe rises to the occasion and helps make them real.

Since the Universe may not cooperate according to our desired timetable, it is essential that we be patient with the progress we make toward reaching our dreams. Disappointments and setbacks are just temporary detours on the road to our dreams. They are actions that did not work the way we intended. We can try something new, or do the same thing again. In the end, the only people who fail are those who quit and take no action at all. Dreams are not impossible until we stop believing that they are possible. When we quit believing in our dreams, we stop taking meaningful actions to make them come true. Inaction sends a message to the Universe that we do not want help.

The superhighway to achieving our dreams is sharing them with others. That is how we find people with similar dreams, people who will achieve their dream by helping us achieve ours. It is important for us to listen to the dreams of others, as we share our dreams with them. When we meet people who have a big dream that encompasses or supports our dream, listen carefully because they may offer new ways for us to work together. Support groups are vital because people share their dreams in such environments. Let us go to places and be with people who share dreams similar to ours. I will be there to help you, and I know you will be there to help me too.

More Dragons Ahead...

"You may say that I'm a dreamer. But I'm not the only one.
I hope someday you'll join us, and the world will live as one."
— John Lennon

The dragons of change are immortal. They have been around for centuries, and are growing more ferocious as the twenty-first century begins. The world we live in today is the product of the cumulative reactions to the dragons by the men and women in all of history. Surrounded by rapid and pervasive change in the late twentieth century, those of us alive today have had an especially large role in making the world what it is. However, the twenty-first century is a crossroad in time, a turning point in our social, political and technological direction. The political systems, social philosophies, and organized religions that we have tried so far have worked okay, but we know something else in needed.

================================

Living amid rapid change, those of us alive today have an unparalleled opportunity to make our world be exactly what we want it to be.

================================

A brief review of human history shows that new technologies, longer life spans, and increased wealth are not been enough to provide the happiness, satisfaction and peace we want:

• ***First Several Millennia.*** Mankind struggled to survive. Life was short. There was no escape from hunger or sickness. We searched everywhere for life's purpose. Monarchs ruled with absolute authority. We explored wildernesses and crossed the oceans. We sought peace in religion, but maimed and killed each other with crude weapons when religious beliefs differed. Change was slow. The human quest for a more fulfilling life led to a cultural *renaissance* and a religious *reformation*. By 1799, after thousands of years on earth, mankind still traveled from one place to another by foot, on the backs of animals, or by sail. We had never set foot on many portions of the earth. Doctors thought disease could be cured by bleeding it from the body. The knowledge acquired throughout history could be stored in a library with a relatively small number of books.

• ***Nineteenth Century (1800-1899).*** The pace of change accelerated. The French and American revolutions gave birth to high expectations and democratic ideals that fractured centuries-old political establishments. Even as we celebrated new freedoms, we exploited slaves in pursuit of wealth and comfort. In the United States, supposedly a showplace of freedom, brother fought brother and father killed son in the name of freedom, the freedom to own slaves versus the slaves' freedom. We eradicated Indian cultures, and confiscated their land and their treasures. We invented new gadgets that made life easier and produced more food in less time. A technological revolution, unequaled in history, began. New economic empires were built on crude oil, steel and railroads. In 1899, after a just 100 years of change, we traveled by "horseless carriages," steam ships, and railroads. We drew detailed maps of the earth, but still had not explored the far corners of the globe thoroughly. Our knowledge had expanded so much that no single library could hold it. Doctors found drugs that relieved many of our physical pains and cured some of our debilitating sicknesses.

• ***Early Twentieth Century (1900-1935).*** Nineteen hundred years after the birth and death of Jesus, we knew there was a better way to live but most of us did not practice it in our daily lives. Change spread across the globe. The industrial revolution moved electricity from the laboratory into our homes. We communicated by radio and telephone, and mass produced automobiles at a low price that everyone could afford. But the industrial age still did not give us the joy, happiness and peace we expected. Rampant greed, worker exploitation, child labor and other capitalistic abuses erased the benefits of prosperity and new amenities. Two men offered a manifesto, an viable alternative to the abuses of capitalism. They proposed an economic system where workers would contribute according to their ability, and benefit according to their need without greed or competition. The concept drew many followers who felt powerless to change their lives while they toiled in horrible working conditions. World War I was fought and won by an alliance of democracies. As the war neared its end, the Russian people overthrew the

Czar and implemented the "Workers' Manifesto." The world wondered if two very different economic views, capitalism and communism, could co-exist peacefully. The early twentieth century ended as we recovered from a "war to end all wars" and the most severe economic depression in history. In 1935, just thirty-five years into the new century, we traveled by automobile, airplane and electrified railroad. We had explored the far reaches of the globe. Knowledge had grown so much that a college degree was essential for success in technical and business careers. Doctors had developed serums to prevent diseases that in the past had wiped out entire populations. And we wanted more.

• ***Mid-Twentieth Century (1935-1970).*** The world changed faster than ever. Life expectancy exceeded sixty years, but something important was still missing. World War II began before the wounds of World War I healed. After six years of atrocities in the name of racial purity, the combined forces of capitalism and communism conquered the fascist foes who instigated the war. The war spawned incredible new technologies including jet engines, radar and atomic bombs. But its most devastating legacy was a deep mistrust between west and east. A wall in Berlin symbolized the intensified conflict between capitalism and communism. We built bomb shelters in our homes as protection from nuclear destruction in the next war. The post-war United States stood alone as the most powerful country on earth, leader of the western alliance. Its affluence grew as the world bought American products. Technology appeared omnipotent as we watched on TV when men walked on the moon. Baby boomers grew up in material abundance believing we lived in the land of the free, with liberty and justice for all. Then, amid riots and burning cities, we heard a black man say "I have a dream." His passion and clarity forced us see the gross disparity between the image of the "land of the free" and the reality of discrimination and racism. He was shot and killed. In the 1960s, young people resisted blind patriotism and objected to fighting a war whose purpose was vague at best. Soldiers killed college students who protested that war. By 1970, another thirty-five years into the twentieth century, we traveled the globe in jets and shot communications satellites into space. Doctors transplanted hearts and other organs from one body to another, and knowledge had expanded so fast that computers were needed to process it. Yet, amid unparalleled prosperity and fascinating new technologies, we lived in constant fear of instant global destruction.

• ***Late Twentieth Century (1970-2000).*** The pace of change became a frenzy. Communism and capitalism cultures cautiously moved together, each aware of its shortcomings and the futility of confrontation. American presidents spent billions on defensive weapons that were more than we needed and more than we could afford. Fortunately, communism went bankrupt trying to keep pace. It had forgotten that the Workers' Manifesto was for the good of the people. The wall in Berlin was torn down. In the United Sates, confidence in government staggered as elected officials lost the trust of the people. Special-interest groups replaced the common good. Capitalism had forgotten that freedom depended on free will of the people. Technology liberated us from mundane chores. Computers invaded our workplaces, homes, appliances, cars and toys. Computers were upgraded every two years, even before we learned to use the old ones. The Internet let us communicate with anyone, on any subject, at any time, for free. But material prosperity and technology did not equate to joyous, satisfying lives. Life expectancy neared eighty years. Doctors said to live longer and better we should lead simpler lives, eat healthy, and exercise like we did hundreds of years ago. We had seen that peace and happiness do not come from wealth, technology or long life. For many, attendance at places of worship became more a social event than a refreshing of the spirit. Even still, we sensed there was a new spiritual awakening just over the horizon, and we began to consider alternative points of view. *Who am I? Why am I here?* and *Where am I going?* were common questions. But even in a world of abundance, we had not found simple, satisfying answers to these questions.

• ***Early Twenty-First Century.*** The pace of change in the first decade of the twenty-first century has been breathtaking. But change is not the only chaos in our lives. Terrorists destroyed the World Trade Centers, two of the tallest buildings in the world and to many a symbol of man's achievements. Just after Christmas, we watched on television as a tsunami drown over one hundred thousand people in and around Indonesia. Two of strongest hurricanes in history struck the Gulf Coast within a week of each other, destroying New Orleans. Despite spending several hundred billion dollars on first-responder capabilities since the terrorist attacks, nobody responded effectively to that disaster. Trust in government has reached new lows as the war in Iraq and the war against terrorism drag on with no end in sight. It seems obvious that we need something different to find the peace and happiness that we continue to seek.

The lessons of history have given us a clear choice: we can destroy our world and ourselves *or* we can work together to build a world that works for everyone. We have the awesome power to do either. What will history record as the major events of the twenty-first century? The changes in that century will eclipse the combined changes that have occurred in the last twenty centuries of human endeavor. You and I are writing that new history today. Maybe we should try something new to get better results than in we have seen in the past.

==========================

As human beings, we are not yet what we want to be. But let's be thankful that we are no longer what we were.

==========================

The twenty-first century has the potential to be like no previous period in history in terms of sharing, trust and cooperation among mankind. You may say that I am a dreamer. I am! I enjoy being a dreamer. It is more exciting, more rewarding, and brings more happiness than hearing that the world is sick, worrying if we will destroy ourselves and our world, and feeling powerless to change it. Saying we are powerless is our powerlessness.

There is a growing team of dreamers today. Join the team. The team does not compete, at least not in the conventional sense. Each member is a leader for their special cause, in their own way, living a bigger-than-me dream. Teammates respect each other's beliefs, support each other's dreams, and admire the differences. You will recognize a teammate because he or she will tell you what they believe in, and what they stand for passionately and clearly. My dream is:

To create a trusting environment where families grow and prosper, starting with my own family.

You may not be inspired by my dream or the dreams of our other teammates. You may not even agree with some of the dreams. That is okay. Instead of fighting them, however, admire the courage of a teammate who declares his or her beliefs openly. Find teammates who have dreams that are like yours, and work with them to achieve your shared dream, a vision for a better world.

You may ask: "What happens when a teammate's dream opposes mine. For example, I'm pro-life and they're pro-choice (or vice-versa)." Such issues are so charged that most people either ignore them, or cannot see any way there could be a third alternative. The third alternative, a joint dream, can be found only by working together. Listen closely to each other. Discover what each party really wants, the higher good they are searching for. From my uncommitted view, pro-choicers and pro-lifers seem to want the same thing: respect for human life. Maybe that can be the basis for joining together to support a third alternative. Teammates listen to each other, *especially* when they see things differently. Differences are a golden opportunity to build new possibilities that neither of us can see by ourselves. We will achieve our collective dreams in the twenty-first century by actively working with some teammates, and providing encouragement and support to others.

My dream grows from a belief that changes in our world will begin and grow in renewed family values. How can we have peace on earth until we have peace in our families? Whatever has been our family's history, we are its future. We must perpetuate qualities that work, like unconditional love, honesty and giving. To the extent that our family may lack one of these qualities, we can start a new tradition.

No matter how damaging the actions of past generations or our own past actions may have been, those actions can stop now. We can end generations of violence, anger, divorce, ignorance, competition, addiction and crime today. We determine the future of our families by planting the seeds for new values. We can forgive family members, understand that they did the best they could, and build loving relationships. These changes are not a quick fix, rather they are a new way of living. Be patient if change occurs slowly. Their initial reaction may be apathy, ridicule, rejection or even hostility. But the actions we take and changes we make will define the future. Positive change begins with a dream, a possibility for tomorrow. The dream becomes reality when we share it with others and take action.

Whatever has been your family's history, your dreams are its future. Change in our world will begin and grow with people like you and me.

As the twenty-first century begins, a subtle shift from a *ME*-focus to an *US*-focus is occurring. It is a shift in how we think about people and things, how we conduct ourselves in relationships, and the things we choose to do. That shift will be more significant than Gutenberg's printing press, more global than the Internet, and more important to world peace than demolishing the Berlin Wall. As we look at our environment, our cities, our governments, our families and our schools, there is disappointment with the selfishness, anger, waste, poverty, hunger and crime that we find.

Many people think that we cannot fix our world, that we are stuck with what we have. To change the world, we must eliminate that erroneous belief first. History is crowded with wonderful precedents for huge paradigm shifts. Beliefs that the world was flat, that heavier-than-air machines could never fly, that travel to the moon was impossible, and that common people would not use computers have been replaced with the reality we know today. In each case, the sweeping change only required a few courageous men and women who steadfastly challenged old beliefs. And one by one, those old beliefs were replaced by the new realities.

We need skills in the twenty-first century unlike the competitiveness, aggressiveness and ambition used to succeed in the industrial and information ages.

The challenges our world faces today should not be minimized. They are complex. On the other hand, if each of us does our small part, collectively we will eliminate every one the problems. By taking personal responsibility, each of us will see that we are in exactly the perfect place and time *to make all the difference in the world* in the area that we feel is the most important. And that would be the biggest change of all for our families, our careers, or our world!

Light the first candle and use it to light many other candles. The brightness of the first candle is not reduced by lighting other candles. Having a dream is lighting the first candle. Sharing your dream with clarity and passion fills the world with candles. I can only light my candle, and share it with you. You can choose to light your candle and share it with others.

To change the world, I need only change myself and be ***who I am. Who I am*** *will serve as a living example for family and friends. They may choose to grow and be examples in our towns and cities. Our towns and cities will be examples throughout our country. Our country will be the example that leads the world to change. It all starts by changing ourselves to be the dream of* ***who we are****.*

Working together to tame the dragons of change will build a better world for us, for our children, and for their children. It will be a world where cooperation, service and contribution replace competition, selfishness and possessiveness. A world that is open, honest and trusting rather than defensive, adversarial and afraid. A world that is loving, accepting and gentle rather than harsh, judgmental and cruel. Such a world is possible when a critical mass of people believe that it is possible and act from that belief. Happiness and success can be found in transforming the dragons of change into helpful playmates in the playgrounds of future changes.

Acknowledgments

An author's first book is a miracle. It requires a large investment of time, imagination and perseverance by the author; and help, lots and lots of help, from many others. I certainly had my share of the latter. The vignettes you have read in this book are golden nuggets that help me enjoy each day. But I could not create them alone. Most of them came from people who shared intimate moments with me. In some cases, several people gave me part of a nugget. I picked the pieces I liked, put them together, and tested the concept in my world. The result is a set of nuggets about joyous living in the twenty-first century that work for me. This book shares those nuggets with you.

I owe the nuggets to very special people. Thank you from the bottom of my heart to:

• My wife Mary Ellen, who is unquestionably my best friend and biggest teacher. I have been blessed that her set of nuggets for joyous living is different than mine. After almost forty years of marriage, it is not surprising that some of my nuggets have become hers, and many of hers are now mine. Yet we remain unique individuals who celebrate our differences. I especially appreciate the hours she sacrificed from our time together to allow me to write this book. If this book is fun to read, thank Mary Ellen.

• My beautiful, caring and insightful daughters, April and Tracy: how much a teacher learns from his students! They probably were not consciously been trying to teach me, but they have consistently shown me what works in relationships and what does not.

• Martha Borst for abruptly awakening my heart. Having earned a PhD in engineering, I had no idea there was so much *I didn't know that I didn't know*. But she enabled me to see what is possible for our world, possibilities more exciting and powerful than any I had imagined. Martha's comments on early drafts of this book, typical of the controller personality that she and I share, were critical, cogent and helpful.

• My two mothers and fathers (biological and adopted), from whom I received my initial set of values. Many of them are effective and still with me, and those that did not work so well in a changing world have been discarded.

• My cousin, Bill Stieglitz, whose written comments and verbal feedback during our weekly lunches challenged me to clarify the message.

• Gordon King, who casually recommended during a golf game that I contact PublishAmerica to publish this book. It worked! Prior to his suggestion, I had unsuccessfully contacted over 50 agents and several publishers to get this book published.

• Other authors who freely share their ideas with us. The leaders on a long list who inspired me include: Richard Bach, Deepak Chopra, Stephen Covey, James Redfield, Anthony Robbins, and Neale Donald Walsch. After struggling so hard and long to write this book, I appreciate the fantastic gift they give us by sharing deep insights in a way that so many people can understand.

By naming anyone, I risk leaving out someone who made an important contribution to this book. To those left-out someones: thank you too.

One event stands out as a turning point in my life and warrants a special acknowledgment. At the time it seemed like my worst failure, but it actually was the seed from which my happiness and success have sprouted. Specifically, the pain of my daughter's drug addiction and the day in a Chicago courtroom caused me to stop and examine my beliefs and strategies: "Wait a minute. This isn't what I want for my family and me. What am I doing that causes this?" That seemingly sad day was the beginning of recovery for the Stieglitz family. Thank you, Tracy. Perhaps your life has had days that seemed *bad* at the time, but really were the corners where you changed direction and found joy and success.

Thank you again to everyone who contributed to this book not only for making this book possible, but more importantly for helping me find success and happiness in my life.

Printed in the United States
86192LV00003B/116/A

9 781424 122226